NARVIK AND THE ALLIES

The Polish Brigade at Narvik 1940

Evan McGilvray

Helion & Company

Helion & Company Limited
26 Willow Road
Solihull
West Midlands
B91 1UE
England
Tel. 0121 705 3393
Fax 0121 711 4075
Email: info@helion.co.uk
Website: www.helion.co.uk
Twitter: @helionbooks
Visit our blog at http://blog.helion.co.uk/

Published by Helion & Company 2017
Designed and typeset by Mary Woolley, Battlefield Design (www.battlefield-design.co.uk)
Cover designed by Paul Hewitt, Battlefield Design (www.battlefield-design.co.uk)
Printed by Lightning Source Limited, Milton Keynes, Buckinghamshire

ISBN 978-1-911512-28-8

British Library Cataloguing-in-Publication Data. A catalogue record for this book is available from the British Library.

For details of other military history titles published by Helion & Company Limited, contact the above address, or visit our website: http://www.helion.co.uk We always welcome receiving book proposals from prospective authors.

This work is about the co-operation between the Allies in Norway between April and June 1940 by initially considering the military-politics of the period August 1939 until the German invasion of Norway in April 1940. Much of the work examines the role of the Independent Podhalian Rifle Brigade and its interaction and dependency on the Allies as the Polish troops found themselves under French command. Other aspects of the Norwegian Campaign are also explored, including inter-service co-operation amongst the Allies, how the Western Allies were still uncertain who their enemy really was and how successful Narvik actually was and what it meant for the UK during the summer of 1940.

Evan McGilvray was born in August 1961 in Winchester, Hampshire. He is a graduate of the School of Slavonic and East European Studies, University of London (UCL). Following this he undertook post-graduate studies at the University of Bradford and the University of Leeds, where he researched the politics of the Polish Army from 1918 to date. He also taught at the two universities. Evan is quite happy to challenge the myths that Poles have created around the Polish Army and the role of Poland during the Second World War. He also has an interest in other militaries and their role in society – quite simply civil-military relations – Poland being one of the most interesting European examples.

Evan has written four previous titles for Helion – *The Black Devils' March – A Doomed Odyssey. The 1st Polish Armoured Division 1939-45* (2004), *A Military Government in Exile. The Polish Government in Exile 1939-45, a Study of Discontent* (2010), *Man of Steel and Honour: General Stanislaw Maczek: Soldier of Poland, Commander of the 1st Polish Armoured Division in North-West Europe 1944-45* (2012) and *Days of Adversity: The Warsaw Uprising 1944* (2015). To relax he has learnt to ignore the rest of the world, and notes, "Despite what Poles think, I am not a Scot, only in name!"

Contents

List of Illustrations

Introduction and Acknowledgements

This work was originally suggested to me by Duncan Rogers at Helion & Company. Originally it was to be based on the actions of the Podhalian Independent Rifle Brigade, but as I researched the project I realised that there was far more to the story than the Podhalians. It became obvious to me that the entire Norwegian campaign was not only the first time that the Allies (France, Norway, Poland and the UK) co-operated, but it was an inter-service venture with the three main branches of the Allied armed forces working together. It was also the only example of the German armed forces joining together in their endeavours.

The Norwegian Campaign was also a time for the Allies to grow up and realise what the war was about and so the venture falls into two definite halves: that of the lame duck Chamberlain and that after 10 May 1940 of Churchill. Once Churchill took over, the Allied war effort was conducted with more vim and reality. There was no question of trying to perhaps strike a deal with the Germans – with whom the Allies were at war – at the expense of the Soviet Union, which was not an enemy of the Allies: only Poland was officially at war with the Soviet Union. The Norwegian Campaign took place at the time of the German invasion of Western Europe, which saw France defeated and the British driven from the European mainland by German armed forces. Once treed in the UK, the British began to take the war far more seriously under the inspired leadership of Winston Churchill. The Poles however were always on the fringes of the Allied effort after 1940, despite their gallantry in both Norway and France.

In writing this work I received a great deal of help from Dr Andrzej Suchcitz and Jadwiga Kowalska at the Sikorski Institute (PISM) in Kensington, as well as great help and co-operation from the staff at the Special Collections, John Rylands Library, University of Manchester. I would also like to thank my old school friend, Ian Bellingham MBE, an award Ian received for his work in Afghanistan and elsewhere, whilst serving in the Royal Navy between 1977 and 2000. Ian was good enough to give me information regarding the anchoring of ships and the terms to be used regarding this.

To you all, thank you!

1

Autumn 1938 – Autumn 1939: The End of Talking

On 3 September 1939 the United Kingdom (UK) and France went to war against Germany. The cause of the war, *casus belli*, was the German and Slovak invasions of Poland two days earlier; 1 September 1939. However, this was not a convincing argument for going to war, as German aggression had gone unheeded since Adolf Hitler and the Nazi party took power in Germany in 1933. Furthermore Italy and Japan had both proceeded on programs of invasion and annexation of their neighbours and those not so close. The Italian annexation of Abyssinia (modern Ethiopia) had been seen almost as a progressive move and bringing civilization to the 'savages'. Poland was not immune in this stance towards pursuing an aggressive line in its foreign policy, and during late autumn 1938 had participated in a cowardly attack on Czechoslovakia, at a time when civilised people were trying to avoid war. As the British and French governments tried to prevent yet another European war, Poland, Hungary and Germany all annexed Czech territory.

However, as always, there is more to this action than immediately meets the reader's eye. Poland was sandwiched geographically between its two worse enemies: Germany and the Soviet Union. As these two countries had descended into dictatorships; each as ruthless as each other, Poland had to maintain correct relations with both Hitler's Germany and the Soviet Union under Joseph Stalin. This was to prove to be a tricky diplomatic course for successive Polish governments, especially after 1933 when Hitler's dictatorship in Germany meant that Poland's largest neighbours were totalitarian states, as Stalin had achieved absolute power in the Soviet Union during 1929. Even though Beevor concedes that Poland had been cautious in its foreign policy, especially that concerning the Soviet Union and Germany, he is quite right to observe that the Polish invasion of Czechoslovakia was a huge mistake.[1] It certainly lost possible allies as the Permanent Undersecretary at the British Foreign Ministry, commonly known as the Foreign Office or FO, Sir Alexander Cadogan, at the time of Polish aggression against Czechoslovakia, described Colonel Józef Beck, the Polish Foreign Minister, as a 'brute'.[2] The Polish historian, Deszczyński, considers that the Polish annexation of the Czech territory of Teschen, was merely an attempt to boost the popularity of Marshal Edward Śmigły-Rydz, the failed military ruler of Poland.[3]

It should be seen that problems for Poland began in 1918, when the modern state of Poland was resurrected after being subject to annexation and imperial rule by the three east-central empires of Austria, Germany and Russia from 1795. Polish independence in 1918 and the confirmation of

1 Antony Beevor, *The Second World War* (London: Weidenfeld & Nicholson, 2012), p. 15.

2 David Dilks (ed.) *The Diaries of Sir Alexander Cadogan, 1938-1945* (London: Cassell, 1971), diary entry, 1 October 1938, p. 111. Hereafter referred to as *Cadogan Diaries*.

3 Marek Piotr Deszczyński, *Ostatnio Egzamin Wojsko Polskie Wobec Czechosłowchiego, 1938-1939*, (Warsaw, Neriton, 2003), p. 424.

her western borders in 1919, meant that large numbers of ethnic Germans were left stranded in a country, which was largely undeveloped and remained so throughout the inter-war period. Many Germans left Poland and went to Germany. After 1933 the gripes of Germans living in Poland, or of the German minority still living in Poland, were to be greatly exaggerated by Nazi propaganda.

However, the greatest source of German resentment against Poland was the new Polish frontiers, which left a divided Germany, owing to an ill-thought out idea of giving Poland access to the Baltic Sea. Polish access to the Baltic coast was basically a strip of Polish territory, the so-called 'Polish corridor', which streaked northwards to the coast and severed East Prussia from the rest of Germany. It was a poor and foolish mistake made by the Western powers, as they recreated Europe in 1919. A further mistake was the creation of the Free City of Danzig (today Gdańsk). Danzig was notionally independent of both Germany and Poland; the desired effect was to grant Poland an established port to trade through. This did not happen, as German interests seemed to dominate the Free City; eventually Poland was forced to develop the fishing village of Gdynia into a functioning port. These were the main German gripes against an independent Poland.

The Soviet government, under Lenin until his death in 1924 and later under Stalin, also hated independent Poland. The relationship was definitely soured for a generation after the 1919–1920 Polish-Soviet War, which actually saw Poland defeat the Soviet Army, or Red Army, at the Battle of Warsaw in August 1920. This war had come about as the Polish Army, in the guise of helping Ukraine gain independence, swept eastward and actually reached the Ukrainian capital; Kiev, during May 1920. The Soviets, who had been distracted by civil war and revolution within Russia, recognised the danger that the Polish Army posed to Soviet or Bolshevik aims; the spread of the International Revolution, counterattacked and drove the Polish Army all the way back to Warsaw. Despite all of the Polish national mythology about the skills of the Polish officers and how they defeated the 'heathen Bolsheviks' and therefore earned the right to rule Poland, Polish officers actually performed extremely poorly against the Soviet counteroffensive. Indeed, most actually fled and left their troops in the lurch, as the Red Army advanced westward. French officers, from the French Military Mission, present in Poland, restored order within the Polish Army and had to remind Polish officers of their duties.[4]

Curiously, Stalin was also in Poland during August 1920. He was a political officer with the Red Army and whilst he was there, Stalin committed a huge mistake, as he distrusted a professional military officer's decision to request reinforcements and so countermanded it. Stalin's decision denied the Red Army the necessary strength to win the Battle of Warsaw, and so denied the Bolsheviks their world revolution.[5] In effect, Stalin's distrust of just about everybody he had ever met prevented the further spread of communism into Europe for at least a generation. Even so, the Poles may have won the war against Soviet Russia, but they were duped at the peace treaty signed in 1921 at Riga. McCauley observes that the Soviet government ceded more territory in the east, than the Polish government really wanted.

The Soviet theory was that the more non-Poles that Polish authorities had to rule over would make Poland unstable.[6] By the 1930s the Soviet view was becoming more realistic, as the Ukrainian resistance movement (OUN) in Polish occupied Ukraine, launched a guerrilla war against the Polish government and Polish landlords. This led to a so-called 'pacification' of eastern Galicia by

4 Evan McGilvray, *A Military Government in Exile. The Polish Government-in-Exile 1939-1945, a study of discontent*, (Solihull: Helion & Company, 2010), pp. 23-5.

5 Ibid. p. 21.

6 Martin McCauley, *The Soviet Union, 1917-1991*, (London: Longman, 1994, 2nd Edition), p. 30. The Polish 1931 Census revealed that only 69% of Polish citizens living in inter-war Poland were actually of Polish nationality. 15% of Polish citizens were of Ukrainian nationality predominately living in East Galicia, the area ceded by Soviet Russia.

the Polish Army, which was badly handled and saw the Polish Army go on the rampage in that area.[7] It could be argued that Polish heavy handiness, during the inter-war period of Polish rule in western Ukraine, sowed the seeds of hatred between Poles and Ukrainians, which saw Ukrainians help the Germans massacre Poles, especially Jews during the Second World War. To round off the Soviet concept of the Treaty of Riga, and how both imperial Russia and the Soviets perceived peace treaties, Borzęcki notes that the Treaty of Riga was a break, as with all treaties with 'bourgeois countries', until the balance of power shifts back to further Soviet or Russian interests.[8] It is interesting to note that General Władysław Anders, the famous Commander of Polish Second Corps, more popularly known as 'Anders' Army', during November 1945, as he railed against what he saw as a flawed peace in Europe and Western complacency, which had seen Poland annexed by the Soviet Union, made the observation that the Soviet government had adopted similar tactics to imperial Russia and had in fact improved on them. Anders noted that Stalin had expanded Soviet frontiers further than the former Russian Empire had ever enjoyed and still threatened peace in Europe. However, all of this was done under the guise of 'liberating' countries rather than invading them.[9] Of course the Western allies were not interested in what Anders had to say, the Second World War was over as far as they were concerned and in reality Poland had lost.

To return to the inter-war period, the one thing that the Russians and Germans shared was a hatred of Poland. As already discussed, both had lost their Polish territories as a result of the outcome of the First World War and both viewed the revived Polish state with disgust and contempt. Another thing rarely considered is the 1922 Treaty of Rapallo, which was the basis of mutual beneficial economic co-operation between Germany and the Soviet Union. It also allowed for the German Army, known as the *Reichwehr*, between 1919 and 1933 to side step the restrictions of the Versailles Treaty, which brought peace between the Allies and Germany after the First World War, but many considered to have been unnecessarily harsh.[10] Indeed German rearmament began earlier than most would want to consider, but after 1933 it was more open in Germany and of course far reaching. The fact that the Polish Republic had defeated Soviet Russia and its attempt to spread the International Revolution, served to increase this hatred. Once Stalin confirmed his authority in the Soviet Union by 1929, Poland had plenty to fear from the east. Within the Soviet Union, Poles, as with most minorities living there, were persecuted, while the Polish state was considered to be an outpost of Western imperialism.

Indeed the West did view Poland as a bulwark against the spread of Bolshevikism; the Polish victory at Warsaw merely confirmed these credentials. Poland was certainly a thorn in the side of the Soviet Union and its ambitions, and so was hated by the Soviet government. However, after 1933 and the takeover of Germany by Hitler and the Nazi Party, Polish enemies increased and so Poland had enemies of both its eastern and western frontiers and so had to adapt to this unhappy situation. The best way was to try to maintain correct relations with both Germany and the Soviet Union, but at the same time, try to prevent the two states coming together in some form of formal common interest against those of Poland. The Republic could survive if Germany and the Soviet Union were hostile towards each other, or merely uninterested in each other. The nightmare situation for Poland was if Germany and the Soviet Union were ever to become allies. The respective ideologies of the

7 Hans Roos, *A History of Modern Poland: From the Formation of the State in the First World War to the Present Day*, (London: Eyre & Spottiswoode, 1966), p. 136. See also Hugh Seton-Watson, *Eastern Europe Between the Wars, 1918-1941* (New York: Harper & Row, 1967, 3rd Edition), pp. 335-36.

8 Jerzy Borzęcki, *Pokój Ryski Roku 1921 i Kształtowanie Się Międzywojennej Europy Wschodniej* (Warsaw: Polski Instytut Spraw Międzynarodowych, 2012), pp. 388-89.

9 Polish Institute and Sikorski Museum (PISM) (Kensington, London, UK), KGA, General Anders' Collection, KGA/5a, General Anders' Memorandum of the Present Military Situation, November 1945.

10 Ian Kershaw, *Fateful Choices: The Decisions that Changed the World, 1940-1941* (London: Allen Lane, 2007), p. 57.

two countries seemed to preclude this but their mutual hatred of Poland overarched this, while the Russian/Soviet attitude towards peace treaties was not foreseen at the time and given the events in Ukraine during 2014, one wonders if Western governments have yet understood this lesson.

Poland had tried to create a central European bloc against German expansion, a so-called 'Third Europe'. However, like all Polish schemes during the inter-war period, it proved to be delusional while Polish Foreign Policy tended to dismay both the British and French governments.[11] The attitude of the Soviet Union rather precluded too much co-operation between Poland and the Soviet government, and so the Polish government was rather pushed into the arms of Germany. It should be considered that Poland and Germany prior to 1939 had much in common, especially the anti-communist stance of both countries. By 1939 however, Western diplomats began to recognise that Polish Foreign Policy was shifting away from being a creature of Nazi Germany, and was reaching out to other sources for support.

On 25 March 1939, Sir George Ogilvie-Forbes, British Chargé d'Affairs in Berlin, reported to the British Foreign Secretary, Viscount (often referred to as Lord) Halifax, that the Polish government had 'flatly turned down' proposals made by the German government to the Polish Ambassador in Berlin, that Poland should join the Anti-Comintern Pact. The Polish military was anxious that the Polish government should exercise the greatest caution vis-a-vis Germany.[12]

The Anti-Comintern Pact was Germany's reply to the threat of the International Revolution. In 1936, Japan had joined it, followed by Italy in 1937. Clearly the Axis powers of the Second World War were joining up, and Poland so nearly became part of that infamous confederation. It was noted that the Poles were 'rather thick with the Japs' and there was a suggestion that perhaps the British government used the Polish-Japanese friendship, as a lever to try to prise apart the Anti-Comintern Pact. It was also reported that the Japanese Foreign Minister told the Polish Ambassador to Tokyo, that the Japanese government was 'all for a quiet life'.[13] Hitler thwarted in his plans for Poland, led to his undisguised hatred for that land and its people. He began a campaign, in which he alleged, that the Germany minority living in Poland were persecuted and needed defending from Polish aggression. It should be noted that the British government had little, if any, faith in Beck, however he was astute enough to recognise that Hitler's overtures had only been an attempt to reduce Poland to that of being a German satellite or vassal state, there was no genuine interest in Poland beyond that which would serve the German Reich or empire.

Indeed Clifford Norton, Head of Chancellery at the British Embassy in Warsaw, reported a conversation, which he had had with Beck during July 1939. It should be considered that Beck and Norton were quite friendly and Beck was willing to confide in Norton. Beck told Norton that he had been aware, as early as 4 January 1939, that Hitler's attitude towards Poland had changed and that the German and Polish governments had reached a parting of the ways. Norton learnt from Beck that whilst the Polish Foreign Minister was visiting Hitler at the Berchtesgaden on 4 January 1939, Hitler made a mistake in conversation. In previous meetings, while conversing with Beck about Polish-German relations, Hitler had always said 'Ich möchte' or 'I would like' but on 4 January 1939 he said 'Es muss sein' or it must be. Hitler tried to retrieve in vain the situation, as he had seen Beck's facial muscles tighten and realised that he had made a slip. Beck was thinking 'Was ist das, das ich höre?'[14]

Beck also told Biddle, the American Ambassador to Warsaw, of his visit to Germany. Beck

11 Beevor, op. cit. p. 15.

12 *Documents on British Foreign Policy (DBFP) Third Series, Vol. 3 IV 1939* (EL Woodward, Rohan Butler (eds.) London, HMSO, 1951, No. 520), p. 504, Sir G. Ogilvie-Forbes (Berlin) to Viscount Halifax, 25 March 1939.

13 *DBFP 5*, No. 224, Letter from Mr. Norton (Warsaw) to Sir O. Sargent, 3 July 1939, pp. 248-9.

14 Ibid., No. 223, Letter from Mr. Norton (Warsaw) to Sir A. Cadogan, 3 January 1939. pp. 246-8.

informed Biddle that Hitler was certainly behaving somewhat differently towards him than in previous meetings; Hitler would normally look Beck in the eye when in discussion, on this occasion he continuously looked up at the ceiling while delivering a lengthy monologue, going on for hours, as was Hitler's want. Beck sensed that this was not the man that he had known previously. Beck also suspected that von Rippentrop was not briefing Hitler in full, as Hitler was a monoglot and only knew German. He was therefore at the mercy of translators, who were controlled by von Rippentrop. Overall Beck left Germany with the realisation that from there on Poland would have to be more cautious in its dealings with Germany.[15]

Indeed, its more than likely, it was his solo interview with von Rippentrop, which put Beck on the alert because, as Bloch relates during the January 5–6 meetings between Beck, Hitler and von Rippentrop, Hitler did at least try to flatter Beck and assured him of his desire for a strong anti-Communist Poland, as well as giving his sympathy for Polish expansionist ambitions into Ukraine. However, Hitler at the same time did press his demands dating from October 1938, concerning Danzig and access across the Polish Corridor. Beck said that he would consider Hitler's demands. However, the next day the head of German diplomacy acted like a bull in a china shop and relentlessly tried to grind Beck down with hours of demands again relating to Danzig and the Polish Corridor. Even German diplomats, who were quite used to their boss's lack of sensitivity and perspective, were amazed at von Rippentrop's tactics used against Beck. However the more von Rippentrop demanded, the more Beck resisted. As Bloch notes the German had met his match, when it came to 'pride and obstinacy.' All that von Rippentrop got from Beck was an invitation to visit Warsaw later that month, to commemorate the fifth anniversary of the Polish-German Pact of 1934.[16] Von Rippentrop returned from his Warsaw visit empty handed, after this Hitler upped the ante against Poland, and made it clear that Poland was to be excluded from any share of the spoils from the destruction of the Czech state. Furthermore with Slovakia being turned into German puppet-state, the Polish southern frontiers were under threat from Germany, even if indirectly. Hitler had hoped that the destruction of Czechoslovakia would cause the Polish government to become more co-operative with Germany.[17]

There are slightly differing accounts of the January 1939 meeting, including when it happened, as the Polish Ambassador to Berlin, Józef Lipski, considers that it happened a day later and that von Ribbentrop was the aggressor rather than Hitler, but Beck maintained the version given to Norton, as is witnessed in Beck's 'Final Report', published post-war and in the case of Beck posthumously.[18] On 5 January 1939, Beck informed von Rippentrop that he feared that Polish-German relations were coming to an end.[19] Whatever the date was and it seems to be a matter between Beck's memory and when things were reported, Domarus noted the terseness of an official German communiqué, which reported the visit of Beck to Hitler and von Ribbentrop. The brevity of the note was confirmation of Hitler's irritation of Beck not falling with his ideas regarding Poland and Germany's potential annexation or '*Anschluss*' of Danzig.[20]

15 *Poland and the Coming of the Second World War. The Diplomatic Papers of A.J. Drexel Biddle Jr. United States Ambassador to Poland, 1937-1939* (eds.) Philip V. Cannistraro, Edward D. Wynot, Jr. Theodore P. Kovaleff, Columbus, Ohio State University, 1976, p. 44.

16 Michael Bloch, *Ribbentrop* (London: Bantam Press, 1994), pp. 213-4.

17 Ian Kershaw, *Hitler, 1936-1945: Nemesis* (London: Penguin, 2001), p. 166-7.

18 See: *Papers and Memoirs of Józef Lipski, Ambassador of Poland. Diplomat in Berlin, 1933-1939*, (ed.) Wacław Jędrzejewicz, New York, Columbia Press, 1968, p. 482. Colonel Joseph Beck, *Dernier Rapport: Politique Polonaise, 1926-1939*, Brussels, Histoire et Société D'Aujourd'Hui, n.d. p.182-3. Lipski's version is maintained in Roman Debicki, *Foreign Policy of Poland, 1919-1939. From the Rebirth of the Polish Republic to World War II* (London, Pall Mall, 1963) p. 130.

19 *Lipski Papers*, p. 482.

20 Max Domarus, *Hitler: Speeches and Proclamations, 1932-1945. The Chronicle of a Dictatorship. Volume III, 1939-*

A later British report concerning the situation in east-central Europe noted that much of Beck's Foreign Policy since 1934, had been that of removing Poland from the sphere of the Western powers and becoming close to Germany. This pro-German policy was unpopular in Poland, where there was a considerable anti-German sentiment, while many Poles were quite pro-French. However since the beginning of 1939, there had been a major alteration in Polish Foreign Policy and the FO recognised the fact that Beck was trying to improve Polish relations with the West, the Soviet Union and with Romania. Clearly Beck had recognised that his previous policy had been, to say the least, foolhardy, especially the participation in the dismembering of Czechoslovakia, as well as giving up the Polish seat at the League of Nations.

The British report observed that the Polish authorities had finally recognised that further agreements with Germany gave no guarantee against German aggression. Furthermore, internally Poland was beginning to experience security problems with the German minority, numbering about 800,000, resident in Poland. At the time of the report, it was considered that the German minority were unorganised and quite insignificant compared with the Ukrainian minority of five million living in south-east Poland. The Ukrainians as already discussed, were badly treated by the Polish Army, while events in Czechoslovakia merely served to encourage Ukrainian nationalists to try further to break free from Polish rule. Even so the report considered that Poland was wide open for German intrigue and internal disruption.[21]

This report was reasonably accurate but did underestimate the ability of the German minority and that of the German government to use this minority to undermine Polish sovereignty. When the report was written, as already mentioned, the British government had little faith in Beck and was happier to negotiate with Marshal Śmigły-Rydz, the military dictator of Poland, or with the Polish president, Ignacy Mościcki. It was left to the discretion of Sir Howard Kennard, the British Ambassador to Warsaw, in how to proceed.[22] Mościcki actually had no power and was a fig leaf of respectability, as the reality of Poland was that the Polish Army ruled via Beck and Śmigły-Rydz. As General Edmund Ironside noted, whilst he was present in Warsaw during July 1939 leading the British Military there, Beck and Śmigły-Rydz ran the country, while the President and the Prime Minister of Poland were expected to keep their mouths shut.[23]

After the German annexation of the remainder of Czechoslovakia during March 1939 and the increasing German hostile rhetoric against Poland, the British government felt unable to tolerate any further German aggression in Europe. Both the British Prime Minister, Neville Chamberlain and Lord Halifax questioned whether the German annexation of the rump Czechoslovak state was the end of an old adventure, or the beginning of a new one. Both argued that the German actions went totally against the spirit of the Munich Agreement, which bound all the signatories to the agreement, Germany included, to a peaceful settlement.[24] During March 1939 von Ribbentrop, as he had done during January 1939, continued to try to bully Beck and the Polish government into accepting German demands relating once more to Danzig, the Polish Corridor and links to East

1940 (Wauconda, IL. USA: Bolchazy-Carducci, 1997), p. 1415. A check on the internet for the 'Thursday' mentioned in the German note would suggest that Beck is wrong and everything and that he met with Hitler and von Rippentrop on 5 January 1939 and the next day in Munich alone with von Rippentrop.

21 *DBFP 5*, Annex II, *Appreciation of the Situation in Central and Eastern European Countries*, 29 March 1939, pp. 616-7.

22 Ibid., No. 563, Viscount Halifax (FO) to Sir H. Kennard (Warsaw), 29 March 1939, p. 543.

23 The National Archives (TNA) Kew, London, UK, PREM 1 (Prime Ministers' Office) PREM 1/331A, Roseway to Rucker, August 1939.

24 *Miscellaneous Notes No.9 (1939) Documents Concerning German-Polish Relations and the Outbreak of Hostilities Between Great Britain and Germany on September 3, 1939*, London, HMSO, 1939, Cmd. 6106. 'Deterioration in the European situation resulting from German action against Czecho-Slovakia on March 15, 1939, p. xii.

Prussia. This was against Hitler's expressed wishes, as he feared that von Ribbentrop's veiled threats of military action might push Poland into the arms of the UK.[25] However, Hitler was quite capable of shooting himself in the foot; Germany's annexation of the rump of Czechoslovakia pushed the British towards Poland, as even Chamberlain had had enough of German aggression.

On 31 March 1939, Chamberlain announced an Anglo-French guarantee and support of Polish independence. The British government guaranteed Polish independence against German aggression, however, the British guarantee did not go as far as to guarantee Polish frontiers, as they stood at the time, and failed to make any provision in the case of an attack by the Soviet Union on Poland. In March 1939 this probably did not seem very important and the case of a Soviet attack not realistically considered by the British government; what was important was that the British government had made a major departure from its usual circle of diplomacy and had given a quite serious undertaking to an unimportant and unknown Slavic state. An undertaking which in no way could have served British interests; a fact often overlooked by Poles, as they continue to scream treachery, rather than look at the misguided actions of the illegal Polish military regime between 1926 and 1939.

Once Poland received confirmation of the British guarantee of Polish independence, Beck began to take an unrealistic approach towards it. Beck failed to realise that Britain was not a military power and never had been, it was a naval power and would be of little assistance to Poland if attacked by Germany. The reality of the British pledge was that the British government was putting Germany on notice, that it would no longer tolerate its aggression and annexations of its neighbours. In fact, the German government was 'completely surprised at the British guarantee to Poland.'[26] Even so the most unrealistic people were Polish officials, who having become secure in the conditions of a military dictatorship, rarely encountered any measure of questioning of the reality of the situation in Poland. After March 1939 statements made by Polish officials, especially those in the Polish military, began to make British officials nervous. Beck told Eden, the future British wartime Foreign Secretary, that Poland was a 'nation of soldiers' and was convinced that 35 million Poles could not be wiped out and that the nation was determined 'to protect its existence at all costs.' Beck also considered that reports, made available to Polish authorities, proved that the efficiency of the German Army was greatly exaggerated.[27] Beck's claim of 35 million Poles ready to defend Poland was clearly rubbish, because as we have seen there were 80,000 Germans and five million Ukrainians, who were at best apathetic towards the Polish state and its continued existence.

Sir Howard Kennard had a different view of Polish preparations for war and totally refuted Beck's claims concerning Poland's ability to fight Germany, and produced reports from his Military Attaché, Lieutenant Sword and from Group Captain Vachell, British Air Attaché to both Warsaw and Berlin. Sword told Kennard that there had been no marked alteration in the capacity of the Polish Army for war. There had been acceleration in arms production since 15 March 1939, including anti-aircraft equipment. However, according to Sword, the Polish rearmament program still needed another year to complete its program. An aspect of Polish defence policy which concerned Sword, was the fact that there were strained relations between the Polish General Staff and the Polish Air Force Commander, General Rayski, who had departed 'on long leave,' a Polish euphemism for 'sacked.' Vachell told Kennard that at present the Polish Air Force (PAF) was of limited value for war and needed another year before it might be satisfactory. Overall according to Vachell the Poles tended 'to gloss over' the shortcomings and weaknesses of its air force, while beyond doubt Polish

25 Bloch, op. cit. pp. 217-220.
26 *DBFP Vol. 5*, No. 8, Sir G. Ogilvie-Forbes (Berlin) to Viscount Halifax, 5 April 1939, p. 28.
27 Ibid., Letter from Mr Eden to Viscount Halifax, 5 April 1939, pp. 36-7.

aircraft were inferior to those of Germany.[28] In another report, Vachell, while casting more doubt on the efficiency of the PAF, also predicted the outbreak of fighting within a few months.[29] The concerns of British diplomats and service staff were justified and a few comments should be made to consider Polish defence policy after 1935.

1935 was a pivotal year for Poland, as it was the year that Józef Piłsudski, so-called liberator of Poland and dictator after 1926, following a military coup in Warsaw in May of that year, died. After Piłsudski's death, the Polish military began to take a more rational look at plans for the defence of Poland. Between 1926 and 1935 Piłsudski alone had made all of the choices within the Polish Army. He had micromanaged it and had allowed it to become backward and obsolete, largely dependent on horsed cavalry. There had been no attempt to modernise the Polish Army, while many of its senior officers were more interested in political intrigue rather than military doctrine, or in advances made elsewhere in military technology and thought. In many ways by 1939, the Polish Army was an irrelevance. Indeed, after the September 1939 Campaign, one of the senior Polish generals to manage to escape to the West, General Kazimierz Sosnkowski, said that the Polish Army was like something from the 17th Century.[30] A little harsh perhaps but one gets the picture.

Concerning Polish defence policy, Piłsudski had always declared that of the two traditional Polish enemies, the greatest threat came from the east; from Russia or the Soviet Union. Little of this nature was seen after 1926, as in contrast with defensive plans prepared during the tiny era of democracy in Poland between 1921 and 1926, which saw plans prepared to defend both the Polish eastern and western frontiers; after 1926 nothing of this sort was prepared or rehearsed by the Polish military. Quite simply defensive plans fell into neglect, as the Polish Army largely became a political arena for second rate officers and even worse politicians.

After Piłsudski's death, as already mentioned, new breath was breathed into the Polish military but even so it was that of an asthmatic and of limited scope and duration. However, the Polish government did manage to recognise shortfalls in its military doctrine and, as a consequence, established a military industrial complex, but its geographic positioning suggested that the Polish government and military only considered that Poland would be attacked by the Soviet Union. Incredibly it was not until October 1938 that the Polish authorities began to take a more realistic approach to how to defend themselves from an attack by the Soviet Union. For once the Polish High Command ordered exercises based on reality and not wishful thinking. The exercises Plan 'W' (*Wschód* [East]) revealed a lack of sufficient ammunition for Polish armed forces. Plan 'W' was not completed until 20 March 1939. Plan 'Z' (*Zachód* [West]) a preparation for war with Germany, did not begin until 4 March 1939. This plan was defensive in nature and allowed the enemy every military advantage possible. A further problem for Poland was that it was an extremely poor country and despite spending 50% of its GDP on defence between 1935 and 1939, Germany easily outspent it. Germany spent 30 times more on the Wehrmacht alone, during the same period.[31] Despite the Polish authorities trying to cover up their military, political and diplomatic weaknesses, the Western powers including the UK, were well aware of Polish deficiencies and bluster.

As the spring and summer of 1939 progressed, it was becoming increasingly obvious that Germany was seeking war and was going to use the Free City of Danzig as an accelerant, in order to try to provoke Poland into doing something foolish. This might then have allowed the Germans

28 Ibid., No 12 + Enclosure 1, Sir H. Kennard (Warsaw) to Viscount Halifax, sent 5 April 1939 (Warsaw) received (FO) 10 April 1939, pp. 38-42.

29 Ibid., No. 33, Sir H. Kennard (Warsaw) to Viscount Halifax, sent Warsaw, 8 April 1939, received FO, 14 April 1939, pp. 68-70.

30 PISM, B.I.86/A, General Sosnkowski: Memories of September 1939.

31 McGilvray, op. cit. pp. 35-6.

to claim that they had been provoked into going to war against Poland, and perhaps avoid the British guarantee of Polish independence being invoked. During this time, France and the UK were sounding out the Soviet Union, and its attitude towards Poland and Germany, and if it might be possible to avoid a European war. However Kennard advised Sir Alexander Cadogan that caution should be used in any negotiations with the Soviet government, as they were causing anxiety in eastern Europe, especially in Poland. The whole concept of diplomacy with the Soviet government played into the hands of both Hitler and the Italian dictator, Benito Mussolini, who were both totally opposed to communism, especially that of the Soviet Union.[32] Therefore western approaches towards the Soviet Union had to be of a low level and conducted with care. This of course made the intention difficult, as it might not be clear to a possible enemy that the purpose of negotiations was to seek alliances, in order to defend oneself against future aggression. Equally such talks might also be the reason for an enemy to attack in their own interests, such as a preventative war. Kennard told Halifax that almost all of the Polish press had stressed that Polish Foreign Policy, despite the Anglo-Polish agreement, should continue to be neutral.[33]

Internationally the Poles were getting a bad press, as the German government repeatedly claimed that the German minority was being routinely abused in Poland. Kennard reported back to Halifax that the German minority was not being ill-treated in Poland and that the Polish minority in Danzig was not a threat to Germany or German interests. Indeed according to many Poles, the German minority were a problem and causing anxiety in Poland.[34] Kennard was an excellent source of information for the FO regarding Poland, he reported factually and nothing else. Despite having previously told Halifax it would seem that the German minority was the problem in Poland, he did inform Cadogan that in his opinion the Poles continued to disregard too lightly the German threat. At the same time he did warn Cadogan that Poland needed financing, in order to rearm in the face of the German menace; if the West failed to provide such funding, the Poles, uncharacteristically, might be forced to go and ask the Soviet government for a loan, but that would only be as a last resort.[35]

The question of Danzig from May 1939 seemed to get worse, as Germany made ever increasing demands for it to be returned to Germany, while frequently claiming Polish duplicity connected with the Free City. Kennard told Cadogan that he had already cautioned Beck against falling into a German trap and casting Poland in a bad light, in the eyes of world opinion. The danger was that opinion was already against Poland, who then had to be careful in how it responded to (ill-founded) charges that the German minority were being harshly treated in Poland.[36] Kennard had previously pointed out to Halifax that Beck may be the Polish Foreign Minister and a military officer, but he was probably the most 'pacific' of the Polish leadership. The British Ambassador went further in his briefing and asserted that the Polish military was able to utterly and totally interfere with the work of Beck and that of the Polish Foreign Ministry.[37] This suggested that there was some form of schism within the Polish military junta, as logically only Śmigły-Rydz had the power and

32 *DBFP 5* No. 213, Letter from Sir H. Kennard (Warsaw) to Sir A. Cadogan, 18 April 1939, pp. 236-7.

33 Ibid., No. 33, Sir H. Kennard (Warsaw) to Viscount Halifax, sent 8 April 1939; received 14 April 1939, pp. 100-104.

34 Ibid., No, 290, Sir Howard Kennard (Warsaw) to Viscount Halifax, sent 26 April 1939; received 27 April 1939, pp. 339-40. Elderly Polish acquaintances and relatives living in the Łódź area during the inter-war period have told the author that the German minority living in that area were generally wealthier than local Poles and enjoyed a good life. The German minority in this area was quite substantial.

35 *DBFP 5*, No. 340, Letter from Sir H. Kennard (Warsaw) to Sir A. Cadogan, 2 May 1939, pp. 397-8.

36 Ibid., No. 543, Letter from Sir H. Kennard (Warsaw) to Sir A. Cadogan, 17 May 1939, pp. 587-8.

37 Ibid., No. 290, Sir H. Kennard (Warsaw) to Viscount Halifax, 27 April 1939, pp. 339-40; No. 685, Sir H. Kennard (Warsaw) to Viscount Halifax, 1 June 1939, p. 739.

the corporate support to interfere with such a high profile and powerful figure, as Beck indeed was. However it did present a serious problem for Polish diplomacy if the work of Beck, who was considered by Kennard to be a reasonably safe pair of hands, could be sabotaged by less responsible Polish military officers, at a time of a growing international crisis which centred on Poland and its continued existence, or otherwise.

During early June 1939, the Polish government petitioned the British government for financial and economic assistance. Kennard supported the Poles in their quest and in a letter to Cadogan warned that if the Polish mission to London failed, the Axis powers would 'have cause for unholy glee.' He had already said that Polish soldiers were cheap or rather their lives would be, if the British government did not grant Poland economic aid.[38] Halifax was quick to inform Kennard that the Poles were not going to get any money.[39] Clearly this was a slap in the face for the Poles, while their enemies could interpret the British move that despite having a British guarantee of Polish independence, the reality was, it meant very little, if anything. The German government mistakenly thought that Britain would not go to war over Poland.

After the British refusal to refinance Poland, German intensions over Danzig became even more intense. Mr Shepherd, the British diplomatic representative at Danzig, reported back to the FO on a visit to see Dr Viktor Böttcher (Head of the Foreign Department of the Danzig Senate). Böttcher told Shepherd that Danzig was indisputably German and that it was unthinkable that East Prussia should be separated from the city. He told Shepherd bluntly that if the problem could not be solved peacefully, it would be solved using other means. How and when this might happen depended on Hitler. What Böttcher made very clear, was that he considered that if the British had not interfered into Polish matters, the entire Polish question would have been solved already.[40]

Shepherd also reported more problems concerning Böttcher, who also told Shepherd that the British stance over Poland was denying Germans 'elbow room on the continent.'[41] This was the truth and what the British plan was. The British government had made it quite clear to the German government that the UK would not accept any further annexations by Germany of foreign territories. Quite simply in the collective mind of the British government, Germany had been given more than enough elbow room on the Continent, as Europe was referred to at that time.

At this time the Polish government was beginning to feel uneasy about the British guarantee. The British and French governments sought a practical and, one could argue, a simple method of neutralising German aggression towards Poland and so began to make overtures towards the Soviet government. The Polish government, as ever mistrustful of anything which concerned Russia, informed the British government that they did not want to be included in any arrangement made between the Western powers and the Soviet Union. The Poles said that they would much rather deal directly with the Soviet government.[42] This suggests that the Polish government did not completely trust the French or British governments to deal adequately with Polish interests, in negotiations with the Soviet government. Given the post-war settlement of east-central Europe, which saw the entire region handed over to the Soviet Union, thus allowing for the re-birth of the Russian Empire, the Polish government during the summer of 1939 no doubt had a point.

However throughout the summer of 1939, the main problem in German-Polish relations remained the question of Danzig. Kennard told Halifax that he had learnt from Roland Sword, his

38 Ibid., No. 680, Sir H. Kennard (Warsaw) to Sir A. Cadogan, 31 May 1939, pp. 734-5.
39 Ibid., No. 692, Viscount Halifax to Sir H. Kennard, 1 June 1939, pp. 747-8.
40 *Documents of British Foreign Policy* (*DBFP*) *Vol.7*, London, HMSO, 1954, No. 1, Mr Shepherd (Danzig) to Viscount Halifax, 8 June 1939, p. 1.
41 Ibid., Mr Shepherd (Danzig) to Viscount Shepherd, sent 8 June 1939, received 13 June 1939, p. 1.
42 Ibid., No. 22, Minute by Mr. Strang, (FO) 10 June 1939, pp. 24-5.

Military Attaché in Warsaw, that the Germans, according to the Polish General Staff, had drafted an additional 6,000 SA troopers into Danzig. This meant that at the time of this report, there were 18,000 SA troopers stationed in the Free City. The SA in Danzig was armed with rifles but with no other type of weaponry. The Danzig police had in total 550 machineguns, of which 300 were light machineguns but had no artillery. German military garrisons in East Prussia gave no indication of what German intentions might be, as German troops were not being concentrated anywhere out of the ordinary; there were no mobilization orders and regular leave was still being granted to German troops.[43] Quite simply Danzig was being infiltrated by para-military forces coming from Germany, which tended to be more rightwing or quite simply Nazi in outlook than the Wehrmacht was at that time, while of course the appearance of Wehrmacht troops in Danzig would prove beyond doubt German interference in the city.

Nevertheless the clandestine German build up in Danzig continued without a break. Shepherd confirmed a visit by 6,000 SA men from East Prussia to Danzig, who came with arms and ammunition. It was also reported that local and visiting SA men said that the 'Danzig problem' would be solved during August (1939). This served to increase tensions in the area, which had begun to show signs of tensions easing somewhat. There was also a rumour of a *Freikorps* of 8,000 men, based on the Sudeten model, was to be established and was to be composed predominately of Germans, who were to receive good salaries. Furthermore, a small detail but interesting all the same, 1,200 iron beds were said to have been ordered locally.[44] This all pointed towards a German annexation by stealth and infiltration of Danzig, especially as the *Freikorps*, as with the SA, were nothing but thugs and bully boys. Russian actions in Ukraine during 2014 bear an uncanny similarity, but the world continues to refuse to see this.

Tensions between Poles and the German minority in Poland increased. Kennard reported on the closure of German institutions and told Halifax that he intended to 'convey a hint that action of this nature may be interpreted as being unduly provocative unless there are serious grounds' (for this action).[45] Minister Mirosław Arciszewski explained the Polish action and did indeed agree that some of the Polish measures might have seemed extreme but argued that the German minority was 'getting out of hand.' In the frontier area of Teschen, local Germans had torn up the frontier posts on a road belonging to Poland, thus trying to include it into German territory. The Polish authorities had immediately replaced the posts and had even arrested the German frontier guards responsible for patrolling the road. Arciszewski noted that if the Polish authorities had not acted promptly, the road would have been lost to Germany.[46] This was just one of a number of small measures permitted by Germany to try to anger the Poles and push them towards war. It should be noted that the German minority in Poland were more than willing to aid Berlin in provocation against Poland.

It was not only the use of minor acts with which the German government tried to provoke Poland into acting rashly. The German propaganda minister, Joseph Goebbels, visited Danzig during June 1939. His speeches were anti-Polish and with a definite aim of stirring up further trouble between Poles and Germans in Danzig.[47] The Polish ambassador to the UK, Count Edward Raczyński met with Cadogan on 10 June 1939. During this meeting Raczyński asserted that, in his opinion, Hitler was not after a European war, but instead was seeking to encircle Poland further with the

43 Ibid., No. 62, Sir H. Kennard (Warsaw) to Viscount Halifax, received 17 June 1939, sent Warsaw, 15 June 1939, p. 80.
44 Ibid., No. 70, Mr Shepherd (Danzig) to Viscount Halifax, 17 June 1939, p. 87.
45 Ibid., no. 79, Sir H. Kennard (Warsaw) to Viscount Halifax, 20 June 1939, pp. 94-5.
46 Ibid., No. 90, Sir H. Kennard (Warsaw) to Viscount Halifax, received 21 June 1939, sent 19 June 1939, pp. 105-6.
47 Ibid., No. 93, Shepherd (Danzig) to Viscount Halifax, received 22 June 1939, sent 19 June 1939, p. 108.

incorporation of Slovakia into the Reich. Furthermore, Hitler needed to produce some measure of success before the September 1939 Nuremberg Rally.[48] The annual Nuremberg rallies were a stage show of the triumph of Nazism and a display of how Germany and life there had improved under Nazi rule. However, as early as November 1938, the FO was aware that Germany was on the verge of bankruptcy and needed a war in order to loot Europe and Asia in a drive towards India; it was considered that Germany was indeed after the British Empire and thought that the UK would be unable to defend its possessions.[49]

By September 1939 Germany was at war with France and the UK. Raczyński was quite astute in his observations, as Hitler did need to show success at Nuremberg; he did include Slovakia into the Reich and he did encircle Poland using Slovakia. However, Hitler did miscalculate, as following the German and Slovak invasion of Poland on 1 September 1939, France and the UK actually did go to war against Germany and were not intimidated by his armed forces. Hitler's concept that he might be able to overwhelm the Allies with force, or make them accept a negotiated settlement did close in 1940.[50] The French were defeated in Europe and forced to accept such a settlement, while the British, forced out off the European mainland, were at least able to defy Germany from across the seas, which acted as a defensive moat and enjoying continued support from its empire and commonwealth as well as exiled forces, notably Polish. The French were not wholly defeated, as for much of the war half of France remained unoccupied, while parts of the French Empire still rallied to the exiled French authority based in London under General de Gaulle. All the same, in 1939 it was not the war that Hitler sought, or the time for war in the calculations of Hitler.

The situation concerning Danzig and Poland continued to deteriorate with German encouragement. Furthermore the Nazi leadership including Hitler, Goebbels and Dr Ley (Leader of the German Labour Front) started to be anti-British in their rhetoric. There were more German visits to Danzig, including 1,000 SS men from East Prussia, as well as a number of high ranking SS officers came in from Germany itself. Heinrich Himmler, the SS leader, was also present in Danzig even if *incognito*. As Shepherd remarked, overall the situation was worsening and it was noted that ammunition and gas masks were being stored by Germans in Danzig. Kennard had already told Halifax, that it was feared that arms had been smuggled in from East Prussia for the *Freikorps* in Danzig.[51] The fact that Himmler was in Danzig secretly rather illustrated the clandestine and illegal action of all of Germany's action in Danzig, throughout the summer of 1939.

The Allied situation concerning Poland and Danzig was frustrated when the French government expressed apprehension about rumours, which were gaining 'considerable ground,' that the British and French would not implement their guarantee in the event of hostilities breaking out over Danzig. Some people within Polish military circles advocated that it was essential that Poland should go to war with Germany, before the German Army reached its full efficiency. It was considered that the German Army had a shortage of officers and Non Commissioned Officers (NCO). Those expressing such thoughts considered that it would be better if Poland struck whilst the iron was still hot, rather than waiting for six months; a period estimated by some Polish military officials to be that of when Germany would have optimised its military strength, while the UK and France may have changed their minds over helping Poland in the face of German aggression against Poland.[52]

48 Ibid., No. 117, Viscount Halifax to Sir H. Kennard (Warsaw), 21 June 1939, p. 132.
49 Andrew Roberts, *'The Holy Fox'. The Life of Lord Halifax* (London: Phoenix Giant, 1997), p. 129.
50 Kershaw, *Fateful Choices*, p. 394.
51 *DBFP 7*, No. 155, Shepherd (Danzig) to Viscount Halifax, 29 June 1939, pp. 177-9; No. 154, Sir H. Kennard (Warsaw) to Viscount Halifax, received 30 June 1939, sent 27 June 1939, pp. 176-7.
52 Ibid., No. 163, Letter from Sir H. Kennard (Warsaw) to Sir A. Cadogan, 28 June 1939, pp. 185-6.

If the Polish government had heeded such ideas it would have been madness. The Germans were much better prepared for war than the Poles were, but many Poles overestimated their own abilities, while underestimating those of Germany. However Clifford Norton, Head of the Chancellery at the British Embassy in Warsaw, in a letter to Sir Alexander Cadogan made some personal observations of the character of Beck (who Norton knew well), as well as his perception of the abilities of the Polish President, Marshal Śmigły-Rydz and of Beck himself. The trio, according to Norton, were not given to rash decisions and provoked into minor follies. Therefore when 'the man in the street' or Polish military officers opined that maybe an attack on Germany by Polish armed forces would be a good thing, it carried 'no weight with them at all'. According to Norton, even though Danzig was being re-militarised by Germany, in affect Polish interests had not been damaged and that the 'famous strangle hold' on Poland was only really a menace. In his opinion, Norton considered that by 1940 or 1941, it would be obvious that the 'peace loving powers' would be stronger and could force the measures taken during 1939 by Germany over Danzig to be withdrawn. He did concede that Beck probably would not agree with this opinion, as repeated German provocation was continuously stirring up Polish public opinion against any concessions with Germany.[53] It is very possible that Norton was engaging in some very wishful thinking but he was privy to the private side of Beck's character and perhaps hoped that war could be prevented, but he was also aware that Beck, especially, was not one to act rashly and react to public opinion, or that of some in the Polish military, who advocated attacking Germany rather than waiting for a German attack. The German government no doubt, were hoping that German provocation would eventually lead to a Polish attack against Germany and render the British guarantee of Polish independence null and void.

Towards the end of June 1939, Halifax shared with Kennard a summary, which he had received from the French Ambassador to Berlin. The French report, dated 27 June 1939, summed up a senior official from the Reich Chancery view of Hitler's intentions towards Danzig. The report was quite disturbing, as it revealed that the Germans were building an army in Danzig, with the use of troops entering the Free City as tourists and therefore not violating statutes that regulated the city. An anticipated two-day visit by Hitler beginning on 20 July 1939, was to announce the theoretical return of Danzig to the German people. According to the French report, the only authorisation, which might be required from the Polish government, would be in respect of a small German naval guard of honour.

Hitler's proposed visit was to be followed up with visits by Goering, the Luftwaffe chief and the German naval cruiser, *Konigsberg*. This was to signal the formal placing of the city under the protection of the German Reich. The German government anticipated that the Western democracies would take no action, and that Poland would be forced to accept this *fait accompli* and begin negotiations with Germany. Hitler planned to leave the problems of the 'Polish Corridor' and of Silesia in western Poland, where a substantial German minority lived, until later, as he realised that trying to solve everything at once might well start a war. It was also reported by the French that a number of SS troops were already in Danzig and had Polish military uniforms with them, which might enable them to act as *agents provocateurs*. The French Ambassador in Rome reported that Italian official circles had already taken the line that the question of Danzig was already as good as settled. Germany was to take over Danzig without causing a war.[54]

53 *Documents of British Foreign Policy (DBFP) Vol. 5*, London, HMSO, 1952, No. 223, Letter from Mr. Norton (Warsaw) to Sir A. Cadogan, 3 July 1939, pp. 246-8.

54 *DBFP 7*, No. 170, Viscount Halifax to Sir H. Kennard (Warsaw) 29 June 1939, pp. 192-3. It should be noted that during this period a substantial number of Germans especially those who had their roots in what was historically Poland, could speak excellent Polish thus being able to cause further internal turmoil in Poland by committing anti-

The German government was relentless in its anti-Polish program. Kennard made Sir Orme Sargent at the FO aware, that the German Ambassador to Poland had alleged, that members of the German minority had been sacked from their jobs in factories in the Teschen and Bielsko areas of Silesia. In Upper Silesia, it was claimed that the unemployment rate amongst the German minority was 70%, at a time when the unemployment rate was 16%.[55] Halifax, in turn, urged Kennard to see Beck and ask him about the situation in Poland and how would the Polish government deal with Hitler if he continued with his rhetoric, alongside the proposed Danzig *fait accompli*. Halifax was concerned that the Poles should continue to proceed with caution in these matters, so that they could not be accused of being the aggressors in any future confrontation between Poland and Germany.[56] This was a very serious problem for the Poles, as many people wanted to avoid war and might have been quite willing to sacrifice Poland, as Czechoslovakia had been the previous year at Munich. If somehow Poland could be made to look like the aggressor, in connection with either Danzig or the German minority in Poland, Western states could have sidestepped their commitment to preserving Polish independence.

The Polish General Staff admitted to have been disturbed and embarrassed by the re-militarising process in Danzig. However, they were not alarmed by it and had advised the Polish government not to act immediately to it.[57] As we have already seen, Norton was quite aware of what was going on in Poland and how the Polish leadership would react to events there. Halifax told Norton that General Sir Edmund Ironside was to be sent to Poland, to discuss the military situation there with the Polish General Staff. There were also to be talks with Śmigły-Rydz.[58]

It was about time that the British military authorities came out to Poland to see the situation for themselves and not try to decipher what the diplomats were saying. Lieutenant-Colonel Sword, the British Military Attaché in Warsaw, whilst on leave in London, met Ironside who told Sword that it seemed that his mission to Warsaw was to guarantee that the Poles would not start a war through a corporal blowing up a bridge.[59] Clearly some of the British military-political elites had a very dim view of their Polish counterparts and their abilities. All the same, the Polish government was delighted that such a senior British figure was going out to Warsaw and the Polish Ambassador to the UK, Count Raczyński had already said that Ironside's visit would make the best possible impression in Warsaw.[60]

Indeed Ironside's visit did make a great impression on the Polish population; both Śmigły-Rydz and Beck were extremely pleased that the British government had sent such a senior and distinguished military figure. Ironside was cheered in the streets of Warsaw and the Polish President was allowed into Warsaw to have lunch with Ironside. Norton believed that Polish confidence, in the determination of both the UK and French governments to wholeheartedly support Poland in the event of a German attack, was the safeguard against the possibility of the Polish government being 'rattled' by public opinion, into rash actions being taken against Germany or German interests. Furthermore, Ironside's visit had taken some of the sting out of the impasse in the financial negotiations between Warsaw and London.[61]

German acts whilst in the guise of Poles.

55 Ibid., No. 178, Letter from Sir H. Kennard to Sir O. Sargent, 29 June 1939, pp. 204-6.

56 Ibid., No. 184, Viscount Halifax to Sir H. Kennard (Warsaw) 30 June 1939, p. 211.

57 Ibid., No. 241, Mr. Norton (Warsaw) to Viscount Halifax, received 7 July 1939, sent 5 July 1939, p. 262.

58 Ibid., No. 250, Viscount Halifax to Mr. Norton (Warsaw) 6 July 1939, pp. 274-5.

59 Edward Roland Sword, *The Diary of a Military Attaché in Warsaw, 1938-1939*, Elizabeth Turnbull & Andrzej Suchcitz (eds.) (London, Polish Cultural Foundation, 2001), diary entry 14 July 1939, p. 47.

60 *DBFP 7*, No. 290, Viscount Halifax to Mr. Norton (Warsaw) 11 July 1939, p. 323.

61 Ibid., No. 361, Mr. Norton (Warsaw) to Viscount Halifax, 20 July 1939, p. 400.

At a stroke it can be seen by any intelligent or astute observer that the Anglo-Franco guarantees were more of a public warning to Germany. There was little material commitment; no British ships had been sent to the Baltic, not even to visit, while the French Army had not been sent to practise war games perhaps with the Polish Army. Furthermore, the British government was not willing to waste money underwriting Polish rearmament. It would have been money down the drain and the British government knew it. Basically the British government was trying to buy time as war was inevitable, but it should not be started by any unnecessary premature Polish action against Germany.

The next day, 21 July 1939, Norton made an observation, which perhaps many people were trying to ignore. Norton reported Soviet fears concerning Hitler's intentions of breaking up, if not destroying European Russia, as Hitler had clearly outlined in his infamous work *Mein Kampf*. Stalin, unlike many Western leaders, had actually read this work and had underlined the passages dealing with Germany's need to acquire land, at the expense of Russia. Therefore Stalin understood what was going on in Hitler's mind, and needed to buy time to try to prevent Germany being able to do this.[62] The Soviet government considered that this program was still going ahead, despite German denials. Norton told Halifax that the Soviet government wanted Germany as far away from Soviet frontiers as possible. Therefore, a German attack on Poland would be proof to the Soviet government of Hitler's intentions. According to Norton, the Polish government's policy towards the Soviet Union was one of cautious but detached rapprochement.[63] Therefore, it should be considered that Poland and the Soviet Union had much in common regarding defensive measures against Germany. But the Poles could not trust the Soviet government, which in reality was just Stalin and they were right not to trust him or his government. Equally the Polish government read too much into the British guarantee. Indeed Beck admitted that he accepted it 'in the time that it takes to smoke one cigarette.'[64] The curse of dictatorships: no discussions and a worthless guarantee went through unchecked and unqualified.

In view of the fears of the Soviet government concerning possible German aggression against the Soviet Union, the British government tried to persuade the Polish and Soviet governments to come together, in the face of a potential common enemy. Halifax cabled Kennard with the observation, that from a military point of view every effort should be made to persuade Poland and Romania to agree to the use by Soviet armed forces of their territories. Halifax wrote that without early and effective help from the Soviet Union, neither Poland nor Romania would be able to withstand a German attack by land or air for more than a short time. Halifax noted that a supply of arms or war materials was not enough and that there was a great need for Soviet forces to collaborate effectively on Polish and Romanian soil. He claimed that in time of war, Poland and Romania would have their backs to the wall and would be grateful for support from any quarters. Halifax's conclusion was that an agreement with the Soviet government was essential, in order to prevent a war in Europe from breaking out, or to secure, if war did come.[65]

Halifax was probably correct in his assessment but for two things: the Polish government would have never agreed to granting Soviet armed forces the right to enter Polish territory; there was just too much history between the two countries. Secondly, the Soviet government and the German government were already in negotiations for a non-aggression treaty, as well as planning an attack on Poland and its division between Germany and the Soviet Union, as a spoil of war. The Soviet

62 Kershaw, *Fateful Choices*, p. 258.
63 *DBFP 7*, No. 394, Mr. Norton (Warsaw) to Viscount Halifax, 21 July 1939, pp. 439-41.
64 Ibid., No. 397, Letter from Mr. Norton (Warsaw) to Sir L. Oliphant, 21 July 1939, pp. 446-8.
65 *Documents of British Foreign Policy (DBFP)* Vol. 8, (London: HMSO, 1955) No. 38, Viscount Halifax to Sir H. Kennard (Warsaw), 17 August 1939, p. 39.

government doubted whether the French or British would be able to protect Poland, and they certainly had no faith in the abilities of the Polish Army. Therefore, the Soviet government bought time by allying itself with Germany. On the surface, this seemed to be the most logical thing to do: from the point of view of the Soviet government it made perfect sense. Kershaw also makes the observation that the Red Army in 1939 would have been of little or no value, as no military preparations had been made by it for intervention in the West, as the Red Army was still trying to recover from Stalin's murderous purges made against the Soviet officer corps during 1937. Kershaw also notes that both Chamberlain and Halifax hated Communism and totally distrusted Stalin, so it was unlikely that eventually alliance would have been made.[66]

Halifax's ideas concerning the use of Soviet forces on Polish soil were put to the Polish General Staff, via the French Military Attaché to Warsaw. General Wacław Stachiewicz (the author of the Polish defence plans) expressed grave doubts about Soviet motivation and could see no benefit in allowing the Red Army to operate in Poland against German armed forces.[67] Kennard and the French Ambassador to Warsaw, Leon Noël, with their military attachés, tried every argument to allow the Red Army into Poland, but to no avail. The Polish government stoutly refused to have anything to do with Soviet soldiers being granted access to Polish territory. The Poles considered that the presence of the Red Army in Poland, would actually mean the destruction of Polish independence, rather than its preservation. Kennard considered that the Polish argument was one of mainly medium range and did not interfere with the British longer-term argument, that the Soviets were essential to winning a war against Germany.[68]

As we have already seen, the Soviet and German governments were already negotiating away Poland; Polish fears were not only realised in September 1939 but also after 1943, once the Red Army went over to the offensive in their war against Germany and her allies and began to 'liberate' east-central Europe, in the Soviet westward advance towards Berlin. The 'liberated' areas were annexed, occupied and became part of the Soviet empire. It was not until the early 1990s before Soviet troops actually left east-central Europe. However in August 1939, the Soviet-German agreement came as a complete surprise to the Polish government.[69] Even so the overall Polish reaction to the agreement was not one of panic but that of calm, as possibly the Polish government could have never ever expected any help from the Soviet Union, while bitter experience had conditioned Poles to expect such dubious behaviour from the Russians.[70]

In Germany, in a speech to Chief Commanders and Commanding Generals, Hitler made his vision for the future very clear, as he announced that Poland was to be depopulated and then resettled with Germans very much in a pioneer spirit. Hitler remained more cautious in his rhetoric towards the Soviet Union, but was willing to wait for the death of Stalin before he turned his ire towards the Soviets. Hitler had the same notion for the Soviet Union, as he had for Poland, as he was preparing to attack that country. Hitler in this speech denounced most of the world and no longer cared what it thought, as he considered 'the world only believes in success.'[71]

This source, which was censored slightly to protect the identity of its supplier, certainly put the world on notice of Hitler's intentions, but no doubt many still considered and hoped that he was bluffing and that there would be no war. Hitler had certainly underestimated the will of the British

66 Kershaw, *Fateful Choices*, p.18.
67 *DBFP 8*, No.60, letter to Sir H. Kennard (Warsaw) to Viscount Halifax, 19 August 1939, p.39.
68 Ibid., No. 119, Letter from Sir H. Kennard (Warsaw) to Sir A. Cadogan, 21 August 1939, pp. 112-3.
69 Ibid., No. 124, Sir H. Kennard (Warsaw) to Viscount Halifax, 22 August 1939, pp. 116-7.
70 Ibid., No. 252, Sir H. Kennard (Warsaw) to Viscount Halifax, received 25 August 1939, sent 24 August 1939, pp. 204-5.
71 Ibid., Enclosure in No. 314, *Contents of the Speech by the Führer to the Chief Commanders and Commanding Generals on the Obersalzberg, August 22 1939*, pp. 258-9.

government at least. After the signing of the Molotov-Ribbentrop Agreement, the British and Polish governments responded by signing a further agreement: the Anglo-Polish Treaty of Mutual Assistance. This was wildly received in Poland.[72] Just hours before Germany invaded Poland, Beck told Kennard that if he was summoned to Berlin, he had no intentions of being treated like President Hacha.[73]

The unfortunate Hacha had been President of what was left of Czechoslovakia in March 1939 and was invited to Berlin, where he was kept waiting for hours by Hitler. Eventually he was summoned into the presence of the Nazi dictator and told bluntly that he either accepted a German annexation of his country, or the bombing of the Czech capital, Prague, would begin immediately. Hacha, an elderly and unfit man, of course fainted at the prospect of such horrors, no matter how it was viewed. Once he was revived, Hacha agreed to the German annexation of the remainder of Czechoslovakia.[74] Beck was quite right in his attitude, as all he had left was his dignity and that of his country and he made this very clear in a speech, made on 5 May 1939, responding to the demands of Hitler. Beck said that everybody deserved but that peace had a price, however there was one thing which was priceless and that was honour.[75] Indeed, it was for honour, which the Poles fought for during the Second World War and beyond, therefore Poland fought German aggression when Poland was invaded. Regarding Germany, Hitler was hell bent on taking Poland and colonising it anyway but it would have been easier if fighting was averted and the country occupied peacefully. Within hours Poland was invaded by both Germany and Slovakia.

The Second World War was to show just how flawed the British Guarantee to Poland actually was; it was a noble gesture but that was all. It was not a practical solution to dealing with tyranny on the European mainland. It is not clear when the Soviet government decided when to join the Nazis rather than the West, but Miner considers that a meeting between Ribbentrop and the Soviet Charge d'Affairs in Berlin, Georgii Astraknov on 2 August 1939, opened proceedings.[76] Once the protracted negotiations between Nazi Germany and the Soviet Union were concluded, in the dying hours of 23 August 1939, and a non-aggression treaty between the two countries signed – the oft-called Molotov-Ribbentrop Pact; Poland's fate was sealed. This was a big enough shock for the Chancelleries of Europe but they were still unaware of the secret protocols within the treaty, which allowed for the annexation of Romanian, Polish, Lithuanian, Latvian, Estonian and Finnish territories into Soviet and German spheres of influence. The Polish state was to have no future, as far as German and Soviet governments were concerned. Germany invaded Poland on 1 September 1939, which was how the UK entered the war on 3 September 1939, as it honoured its pledge to defend Polish independence against German aggression. On 17 September 1939, the Soviet Union invaded Poland and annexed eastern Poland – territory which Poland has never been able to retrieve.

However, in September 1939, many in the UK were unclear why they were at war once more with Germany. The Poles may have thought that the war was about them, but later events proved that to have been erroneous. Poland was just the final straw, as far as the British government had been concerned; somewhere Hitler's aggression had to be stood up to and Poland just happened to have been highlighted as his next victim. Poland was not a popular country nor was its people,

72 Ibid., No. 348, Sir H. Kennard (Warsaw) to Viscount Halifax, received 28 August 1939; sent 26 August 1939, p. 281.

73 Ibid., No. 608, Sir H. Kennard (Warsaw) to Viscount Halifax, 31 August 1939, pp. 450-1.

74 Bloch, op. cit. pp. 216-7.

75 *Józef Beck's Speech. 5 May 1939*, www.youtube.com/watch?v=IZps7xSHwcy accessed 11 September 2014.

76 Steven Merrit Miner, 'His Master's Voice: Viacheslav Mikhailovich Molotov as Stalin's Foreign Commissar' in *The Diplomats 1939-1979*, Gordon A. Craig; Francis L. Lowenheim (eds.) Princeton, Princeton University Press, 1994, p. 74.

which were often depicted in the West as backward looking anti-Semites. At times, it seemed that Germany and the Nazis were more popular than the enemy. The British poet, WH Auden, living in New York, noted that an American cinema audience, in a largely German speaking area of Manhattan during November 1939, watching a German language film giving a Nazi account of their conquest of Poland, screamed 'Kill them!' whenever Poles appeared on film.[77]

The British or the French were probably not so extreme but all the same there appeared to have been an air of unreality once war was declared. British politicians did not know how to proceed, or even perhaps how they had arrived at a state of war with Germany, over such an obscure country, to their minds, as Poland. The clues had been there since 1935, as German foreign policy became much more aggressive, while the Spanish Civil War (1936-39), which had recently ended, saw both Nazi Germany and Fascist Italy use Spain as a vast military training ground in preparation for future wars. Hitler in his speeches, as well as in his infamous political outline *Mein Kampf*, had made his love of conflict and the necessity in his view for a German empire to the east of Germany very clear. As we have already seen Stalin, at least, was aware of this, but he was part of the problem.

Western politicians lived in a state of denial regarding Hitler, Germany and the Nazis. The Western bogeyman was communism and the Soviet Union. It seemed that only Winston Churchill, back at the Admiralty as First Sea Lord, after lacking a decent political role for many years, had any idea of how to proceed once war was declared. Even so, Churchill exasperated the Chief of the Imperial General Staff (CIGS), General Ironside, as well as the Royal Navy, as he constantly changed his mind about things.[78] It should be noted that Ironside had more idea about what was happening in Germany and east-central Europe, than most within British senior military-political circles. During 1937, whilst visiting Germany, Ironside managed to get three German generals drunk on Scotch Whisky. The trio of drunken German Generals, Richtman, Reichenau and Koch, owing to the effects of Ironside's whisky, let their usual guard down and *in vino veritas* began to become indiscrete. General Reichenau wanted to drink to 'brotherhood with England,' but only for two years. This event happened on 25 September 1937.[79] The timing was uncanny. Furthermore at the beginning of 1938, Ironside commented that he considered that Poland could become another Spain, with a struggle between Fascism and Communism. The prediction being that Germany and the Soviet Union would fight on Polish territory.[80]

It seemed as if the British General Staff were at best bemused about the state of war, which now confronted them and needed to be dealt with. Ironside lamented the actions of his Minister of War, Leslie Hore-Belisa, who appeared to have no idea of what he was to do and what was expected of him. Furthermore, it was quite obvious that years of defence cuts had left the British Army unprepared for a major war in Europe. It was not totally clear who the enemy really was: Germany or the Soviet Union? The UK was officially at war with Germany over the German invasion of Poland, but the Soviet Union, as we have seen, also invaded Poland on 17 September 1939, and annexed eastern Poland. The Germans and the Soviets divided Poland up between themselves, as well as allowing for Soviet annexation of other territories in eastern Europe. During November 1939, the Soviet Union invaded Finland, which did stir up the Western democracies, as Finland was one of theirs, a Western democracy. Poland, the original cause of the war no longer existed, only as an underground state and as an exiled government and army in Paris; largely ignored by the British and French governments. Therefore, by the end of 1939, the Soviet Union appeared to be

77 Humphrey Carter, *W.H. Auden. A Biography* (London: George Allen & Unwin, 1981), p. 282.
78 Beevor, op. cit. p. 75.
79 Denis Kelly (eds.), *The Ironside Diaries*, Colonel Roderick Macleod (London: Constable, 1962), pp. 27-8, Diary entry 25 September 1937.
80 Ibid., p. 44, 7 January 1938.

more aggressive than Germany, as the West were not really aware of the horrors being meted out to Poles, especially Jews, by the Germans. Equally the Soviets were also deporting Poles to the Soviet interior as slave labour. The holocaust had not yet begun, while the Soviets were yet to murder most of the Polish officer corps and other Polish elites, held in Soviet captivity.

The Soviet Union was the state, which the Western democracies feared most. The Spanish Civil War reinforced this attitude. Even though the Spanish fascist leader, General Franco, was on the whole seen as nothing more than a gangster; his overthrow of a legitimate, if communist leaning government in Spain, to many in the West, was still preferable than a Communist victory in Spain. Who the enemy was remained unclear at the time of the Narvik campaign during 1940, but at its conclusion it was very clear who the enemy was. The confusion was cleared up, however it was not until the autumn of 1940, before the British really understood the nature of the war on which they had embarked the previous year.

2

The Destruction of Poland

After the signing of the Molotov-Ribbentrop Agreement, the British government never really expected to save Polish independence once war broke out, but hoped that an eventual Allied victory would restore independence once more to Poland. The ability of the Poles to resist the German onslaught had been wrong, as it had been considered that the Poles might have been able to last out for three to four months. The British also did not expect to escape unscathed from German aggression during the opening phases of the war; anticipating erroneously heavy air attacks on ill-defended cities, as well as an all-out assault on the Western Front.[1] The British assessment was wrong.

The original assessment made on 4 September 1939, was merely wishful thinking by politicians, who considered that once the Poles had been defeated after two to three months, on the Western Front, there was to be a period of stalemate. General Edmund Ironside (CIGS) saw the entire situation differently. He admitted that the concentration of 32 German divisions in Slovakia had come as a complete surprise to him, and that in his view the Poles would be defeated within a few weeks.[2] Another British senior officer, who actually had lived in Poland since 1919, General Adrian Carton de Wiart, also gave his opinion and reported that the situation in Poland was 'extremely serious' and that the UK and France needed to find a means of supplying Poland with aircraft, machineguns and ammunition. The War Cabinet seemed somewhat confused and pointed out that the only way to give substantial aid to Poland, was to wage war against Germany and that until such a time Poland could only be 'rehabilitated'. The War Cabinet did seem to understand that their lack of inactivity could be used by the German government, to convince the Poles that the British were about to desert them. As a result, some urged that a 'Statement of Reassurance' should be made to Poland but Chamberlain was still not convinced and wanted to remain cautious in his policy towards the 'war' against Germany.[3]

At a time of extreme German aggression in Poland, including the massacre of civilians, a cautious note of reassurance was of no use to the Poles, who were fighting for their very existence and of course the Allies were about to abandon them. That was military commonsense. However, there were British politicians and civil servants, who declined to see the situation realistically, as in a note from Maurice Hankey to Lord Halifax, in which Hankey noted that it was obvious that the Poles had no chance against Germany, there is marginalia, which reads 'defeatist'.[4] Lord Salisbury also wrote to Halifax, commenting on British inactivity in the war and considered that it seemed to him that the UK was waiting for Germany to crush all British 'friends' in Central Europe.[5] The timing

1 *British Foreign Policy in the Second World War. Volume 1*, (ed.) Sir Llewellyn Woodward, London, HMSO, 1970, p. 10. Hereafter known as *BFP1*.
2 TNA, CAB 65/2 (39) 4 September 1939.
3 TNA, CAB 65/8 (39) 8 September 1939.
4 TNA, FO 800/309 H/XV/260, Hankey to Halifax, 12 September 1939.
5 TNA, FO 800/317 H/XV/288, Salisbury to Halifax, 22 September 1939.

of Salisbury's message to Halifax is interesting, as it is dated five days after the Soviet invasion of eastern Poland. It should also be considered that Romania also had been guaranteed by the UK government earlier in 1939, but could do little to defend it against Germany, as Germany was more subtle than it had been with Poland and used influence and bullying rather than outright invasion. Furthermore, Greece had also been guaranteed by the UK and the events of 1941, when the UK and her allies came to Greece's aid, illustrated perhaps why the UK did very little to help Poland in 1939, as there was little that could be done. The Allies were of course driven from Greece.

In 1939, the British view was one of pragmatism and the reality Poland was of very little importance to the UK; it was where the inevitable war began, as was widely predicted. Men like Ironside had been to Poland during the summer of 1939 and had met with senior Polish officers, including the Polish Chiefs of Staff and he knew that Polish preparations for war were inadequate and therefore the British were not going to waste men, equipment or money trying to defend Poland. The attitude about a stalemate on the Western Front was in many ways accurate, regarding the period September 1939–April 1940, as nothing happened there. The Allies did not foresee the Soviet invasion and annexation of eastern Poland and were indeed caught out by it. The war was largely fought in the east, as both Germany and the Soviet Union committed horrors in Poland, while the Soviet Union also launched a foolhardy invasion of its neighbour to the west, Finland.

Even so the Poles, during the September 1939 Campaign, defended their country bravely and fought very well. Later once France was invaded, during May 1940, the French Army did not perform better than the Poles. The French Army, at the time, was considered to be the most formidable army in the world and with a well educated Officer Corps, but still France, with much of Western Europe and Scandinavia, was easily overrun by invading German forces. Therefore, the Polish Army in 1939 should be seen as having done rather well, given its disadvantages.

There had been a plan that the Polish Army should make a stand on the far side of the River Vistula, which was the first major obstacle that the invading Germans met with, as they moved from the north and west across the flat Polish terrain. However the weather had more or less condemned Poland to defeat, as near drought conditions in Poland for the previous two years had allowed German armour to rampage across Poland. Even though the Poles destroyed the bridges over the Vistula at Warsaw, the river was so low that German troops merely waded to the far shore.[6] Indeed, Captain Davies of the British Mission to Poland, commented in a report that 'the exceptional dryness of the ground and rivers had facilitated the German advance.'[7]

A major concern for the defence of Poland was the lack of air superiority, as the Polish Air Force (PAF) had been largely destroyed, once the Germans ruthlessly attacked Polish airfields and aircraft; more or less putting them out of the campaign within a few days. Even so the PAF, as Michael Alfred Peszke observes in his excellent essay, fought credibly against overwhelming odds, destroying 285 German aircraft and damaging a further 279 German aircraft during the September Campaign; the PAF on 1 September 1939 only had 433 combat aircraft, therefore quite a feat but hamstrung by economics.[8] It should be noted that even Neville Chamberlain was aware of air power and how, during the September Campaign, the ability of the Luftwaffe to gain and hold mastery of the air, meant that Polish land operations became paralyzed.[9] The French government

6 TNA, CAB 65/9 (39) 9 September 1939.

7 TNA, CAB 79/1 COS (39) 8th Meeting, 9 September 1939.

8 Michael Alfred Peszke, 'The Forgotten Campaign: Poland's Military Aviation in September, 1939' originally in *Polish Review*, 39 (1994) pp. 51-72, cited in *The Second World War: Volume 1 The German War 1939-1942*, Jeremy Black (ed.) (Aldershot, UK: Ashgate, 2007) pp. 1-22.

9 Neville Chamberlain to Winston S. Churchill (Chamberlain Papers) 16 September 1939 cited in Martin Gilbert, *The Churchill War Papers, Volume 1: At the Admiralty, September 1939-May 1940*, London, Heinemann, 1993, pp. 100-1. Henceforth cited as *Churchill 1*.

urged the British government to help the Poles in this matter. Captain Davies made an oral report to the British Chiefs of Staff, in which he emphasised the importance of the immediate dispatch of material assistance to Poland. He underlined the necessity for machineguns and aircraft; asserting that the receipt of such materials would greatly improve morale in Poland. This was an important point because, as we have seen previously, it was considered that the Germans might have tried to convince the Poles that the British had abandoned them. Therefore, it should have been important that certain war materials should have been despatched to Poland before the German government started to offer the Polish government peace terms.

Sir Alexander Cadogan was pessimistic about Poland's chances of defending itself against Germany, but he did reveal in his diary that the French were about to attack the Germans, at the Siegfried Line on the Western Front. Cadogan hoped that this might have some effect on the German Army in Poland.[10] This was a forlorn hope, as the Germans were better prepared than the French, while the Germans were also determined to destroy Poland and take its lands. The German government also knew that the Soviet Union would soon want its pound of flesh or rather half of Poland, as according to the secret protocol of the Molotov-Ribbentrop Agreement.

By 12 September 1939, the Germans were held about fifteen miles outside of Warsaw, as the weather had finally broken and the German invasion was being slowed by the poor Polish roads, which turn into quagmires once heavy rain falls. The British military-political elites were aware of how the weather was a factor in the Polish defence of their country; bad roads made it difficult for an army to advance along. Cadogan wished it to pour down in Poland but by 15 September 1939, he was moved to write 'Poland had been crumbled up.' Cadogan considered that, for the next four years, the Allies will know nothing but defeat before any significant victory would be gained by them. He also observed that German air power in Poland had been quite overwhelming.[11]

The British had made poor provision of aircraft to the Poles. No fighters were sent, but 20 Fairy Battle single engine light bombers had been made immediately available to the PAF.[12] Even though this aircraft had only entered service with the British Air Force (RAF) in 1937, it was already out of date. It was slow with a limited range and defended with a single machine gun. By the end of 1940, it was withdrawn by the RAF from active service and thereafter used for training purposes. However, the killer blow, as far as the defence of Poland was concerned, was the Soviet invasion of eastern Poland on 17 September 1939. In effect Poland had been dastardly stabbed in the back by a Slavic brother, but many Poles expected nothing less from the Russians. It was how things were between Poland and Russia, or the Soviet Union, as it was known in 1939.

Before the Soviet invasion there had been grounds for limited optimism, that perhaps Poland might be at least able to hold the Germans at Warsaw, which may have allowed the Allies an opportunity for a strong military response to the German invasion of Poland. Even though the Polish Army had been badly administered and led during the inter-war period, certain Polish officers came to the fore during the September 1939 Campaign. The Polish rank and file served their country, as loyal as ever. One of these officers, often overlooked in Western military historiography, was Colonel Stanisław Maczek, Commanding Officer of 10th Motorised Brigade, Polish Army. In 1939, this brigade was the only totally mechanised brigade in the Polish Army. Maczek, a totally professional officer, in contrast with many Polish military officers, whose careers owed more to political allegiances than ability, had since the 1920s advocated the mechanisation of the Polish Army. He was ignored. Maczek was not the only Polish officer, whose talents were ignored or marginalised, as Carton de Wiart noticed, when he observed that for political reasons General

10 *Cadogan Diaries*, 11 September 1939, pp. 215-6.
11 Ibid., 12-15 September 1939, pp. 216-7.
12 TNA, CAB 65/15 (39) 14 September 1939.

Władysław Sikorski was not even employed, when Poland was under attack. Carton de Wiart also considered that there was a 'lamentable delay' in using General Kazimierz Sosnkowski, who was one of Poland's most brilliant generals and the only Polish general to defeat the Germans, when he and his forces met the enemy near Lwów.[13]

Sikorski was to become Polish Prime Minister and Commander-in-Chief in exile from October 1939, until his premature death on 4 July 1943. Sosnkowski was also to become prominent in exiled circles, during the Second World War. After the war he immigrated to Canada, where he died in 1967. However Carton de Wiart does raise the question of politics within the inter-war Polish Army and how quite capable officers could see their careers ended, if the military junta ruling Poland after 1926 deemed them to be politically suspect. Between 1926 and 1935 it should be seen that Marshal Piłsudski, the so-called liberator of Poland, decided more or less alone on promotions within the Polish Army. After 1935, it was a matter of proving loyalty to *Sanacja*, the Polish military regime headed by Beck and Śmigły-Rydz. It would seem that the regime was willing to gamble with their country's fate, rather than appoint officers such as Sikorski to help defend Poland and perhaps defeat the invading Germans. However, as we have already seen, the Polish Army in 1939, was in a woeful state and even if Sosnkowski used a certain amount of hyperbole, when he suggested that the Polish Army was like something out of the 17th Century; it was certainly unlikely to have been able to defeat the Germans alone; let alone deal with the treacherous Soviet stab in the back.

However, how true wąs it that the Polish Army was as useless as the Allies considered it to be? As already noted, Sosnkowski did well and if we now look at Maczek's Brigade, one can see the potential of the Polish Army in 1939. Maczek and his men were given the task of defending southern Poland, as the enemy streamed out of Slovakia through mountain passes and into Poland. Maczek's Brigade, 10th Motorised Brigade, as part of Army 'Krakow,' supported by a battalion from the Border Defence Infantry, an artillery battery and volunteers of the Polish National Defence organisation, took on the invading Germans who were supported from the air. The Polish force was outnumbered 10:1. Maczek knew which forces lay before him, from intelligence gleaned from prisoners and captured documents and so he was aware that German 2nd Panzer Division, 4th Light Division and 1st Mountain Division were trying to trap his force in a pincer movement and hold them in southern Poland. Maczek and his force were never intimidated by the superior numbers or weaponry of the enemy and fought a brilliant campaign.

Even though Maczek and his men were fighting a running battle, they still made life extremely difficult for their enemy. The Poles blocked German advances and held the high ground as much as possible, in order to attack German positions at night, as well as keeping a running check on German numbers and presence of enemy motorised units. Within the first two days of the German invasion of Poland, Maczek and his men were disrupting enemy advances, including an armoured attack, during which the Poles destroyed 30 tanks out of an attacking force of 200 tanks and forced the Germans to withdraw.

Under the command of Maczek, it was proven that Poles could fight and fight effectively. Equally it was illustrated that the Germans were not invincible and that a well led and determined force, even though it was much smaller, had the potential of defeating them. Even so Polish casualty rates were very high while Maczek, as with other Polish commanders, could not help but note the disparity between Polish resources and of those available to the Germans. At one stage of the campaign, several modern Polish fighter-bombers (Łos [PZL.37]), which had escaped destruction on the first day of the invasion, were able to bomb German positions. Maczek regretted that the Poles did not have more of these aircraft at their disposal.

13 Lieutenant-General Sir Adrian Carton de Wiart, *Happy Odyssey* (London: Jonathan Cape, 1950), p. 156.

Maczek's tactics for defending his allotted area, actually had more to do with offensive rather than defence, with the use of audacious raids on German positions, which forced the enemy onto the defensive, locally at least. This tactic of hit and run was reminiscent of Maczek's early career during the Polish Wars of Independence, 1918–20. As a young officer Maczek had led small units of men, heavily armed with automatic weapons and hand grenades, and frequently attacked the enemy from an unforeseen direction, which caused alarm and dismay. Basically Maczek had introduced the commando raid into the Polish Army by 1920, but as already related, his work went ignored for nearly two decades and when it was all too late.

Despite all of Maczek's efforts and the bravery of his men, who were fighting night and day, they were on the whole retreating but making the enemy pay for every step that they took into southern Poland. Eventually just outside of Lwów, having made the enemy fight for every bridge and ford as they advanced, crossing rivers, south-eastward, 10th Motorised Brigade counterattacked the Germans and drove a German mountain division off the Zboiska Heights. But this was all in vain, as during the night of 16–17 September 1939, the Soviet Union invaded Poland. Maczek was actually in Lwów attending a meeting, when the news of the Soviet invasion was received. He immediately returned to his brigade and gave orders to cease fighting and move southwards towards the Polish-Hungarian frontier.[14]

Therefore, the question arises could the Poles have held the German advance, if the Soviet Union had not betrayed their brother Slavs, in their hour of need? The Allies, as we have already seen, were quite sure that the Germans would defeat the Poles, however it was the speed of the overall German advance which took the Allies by surprise. The French Army was due to launch a general offensive against Germany, fifteen days after declaring war. On 6 September 1939, there had been some limited action against Germany by the French Army, however during a meeting of the Supreme Allied Council in Abbeville on 12 September 1939, Poland's position was considered to have been 'catastrophic'. This meant the cancellation of the French offensive; the Polish government was not informed of this decision. 12 September 1939 marked the first day of the 'Phoney War,' or rather there was no further action until Germany attacked, on the so-called Western Front, in the spring of 1940.[15] The lack of Allied action in the West gave both Hitler and Stalin a free hand in eastern Europe and in the Baltic Republics, who, while the UK and France stood idly by, German and Soviet armed forces with their security services ravaged, robbed, murdered and enslaved across the newly stolen acquisitions.

Despite the destruction of Poland, not all was lost to the Polish people. The Polish government, prior to the Soviet invasion, had already cravenly fled to Romania, leaving their army still fighting against the Germans. As the collective authorship of *Guilty Men*, a condemnation of the events leading up to the outbreak of war in September 1939 and how the Chamberlain government dealt with events, noted that Marshal Smigly-Rydz [sic] was the first to flee to Romania, while noting that his name meant 'Lightning'.[16] This was basically what happened and was to haunt the exiled Poles for years, if not decades. The fleeing military junta, had hoped that they would receive a sympathetic reception from the Romanian government, but the German government had already taken measure to prevent this. On 14 September 1939, the Romanian government informed the Polish government, that if the Polish government and its military commanders crossed into

14 For Maczek's early career see: Evan McGilvray, *Man of Steel and Honour: General Stanisław Maczek, Soldier of Poland, Commander of the 1st Polish Armoured Division in North-West Europe, 1944-45* (Solihull: Helion & Company, 2012), Chapters 3 & 4. For the September Campaign, see Chapter 6.

15 T. Panecki, 'Polish Destiny: From Westerplatte to Narvik' in *Narvik 1940. Five Nations in the High North*, (ed.) Karl Rommetveit, Oslo, Institutt for forsvarsstudier (IFS) 1991, pp. 45-61.

16 'Cato' (Frank Owen, Michael Foot and P.D. Howard) *Guilty Men* (London: Victor Gollancz, 1940), p. 96.

Romania, they would be interned.[17] This dashed all hopes of Śmigły-Rydz and Co of being able to get to Paris and establish a Polish government in exile from there. The internment of the Polish government confirmed its failure, as they need not have gone into internment, but their arrogance knew no bounds and so the Romanian warning went unheeded. There were other routes to Paris but they chose the easiest and the most foolhardy: it seemed to sum up Polish governments since 1926. A moot question was would the French government have allowed the Śmigły-Rydz junta to carry on in exile in Paris. I rather doubt it.

The interment of the pre-war Polish government left a power vacuum, which the pre-war Polish opposition was all too happy to take advantage of. The French government also lent its support for Polish opposition figures, especially General Sikorski. There is some debate to the extent that the French government were involved, to ensure that Sikorski became Polish Prime Minister and Commander-in-Chief of Polish Armed Forces. Also did the French government have the foresight to ensure that this wish was realised? However, Sikorski was pro-French and was not tainted with the illegal Polish military junta. Furthermore, the Polish authorities had denied him public and military offices since 1926, as he was considered to have been politically unreliable for the regime. What is quite clear was that Sikorski, having been denied any role in the September Campaign, was leaving Poland for Romania and no doubt internment, when on 18 September 1939, the French Ambassador to Warsaw, Leon Noël, advised him to go directly to Paris.

It would seem that the French really had no plans for Sikorski beyond using him, as the most senior Polish officer to arrive in the West, as a figurehead around whom they could rally Polish exiles, especially military personnel and somebody with who the French government could work.[18] Earlier in the year *The Manchester Guardian* reported that Sikorski was part of a Polish delegation in Paris. He was described as a 'leading military expert' and an intimate friend of the late Marshal Foch, as outspoken and devotedly pro-French' It was also reported that, for a long time, Sikorski had been denied a passport by the Polish regime and only recently been granted one.[19] Foch of course was a French military hero, while the granting of a passport to Sikorski was evidence of the political bankruptcy of the Polish junta, as they had few friends in the West, but even so still refused to use Sikorski's abilities, even when Poland was facing its direst test.

The French support, not surprisingly, caused friction amongst Poles, especially when there was a rumour that the French authorities were ensuring that supporters of the Polish regime, were not permitted to find sanctuary in France. It should be recognised that the French government were right to be cautious in who they allowed into France, as the arrival of the likes of Beck and Śmigły-Rydz in France, who no doubt have been a distraction and probably would have caused a split within the embryonic exiled Polish establishment with intrigue. Both sides admittedly were quite capable of this, but as the pre-war Polish leadership had been interned, French resolve was never tested.

Sikorski was well aware of the situation concerning the former Polish leadership, as he had been briefed by a Polish officer, Lieutenant-Colonel Jan Kornaus, who had recently returned from Romania. Kornaus bluntly told Sikorski that Beck was a danger to Polish interests and should remain interned in Romania.[20] The Allies were also quite clear of the situation regarding Śmigły-Rydz and Beck, as Sir Howard Kennard, the British Ambassador to Poland, told Lord Halifax that 'the Polish collapse and hasty retreat into Romania have caused great resentment amongst

17 McGilvray, *A Military Government*, p. 39.

18 Anita J. Prażmowska, *Britain and Poland, 1939-1943: The Betrayed Ally* (Cambridge: Cambridge University Press, 1995), p. 11

19 *The Manchester Guardian*, 21 February 1939.

20 PISM, PRM 14B/40, '*Notatka Służkowa ppłk. J. Kornaus, Bucharest*', 9 March 1940.

representative Poles. The Marshal (Śmigły-Rydz) and Colonel Beck are especially criticized and it is freely stated that Polish people will not trust their future destiny to their former leaders.'[21]

Later the whereabouts of Beck and Śmigły-Rydz was one that Stalin put at different times to General Władysław Anders, as Anders with the British and Polish authorities negotiated the establishment of a Polish Army in the Soviet Union, following the German invasion of the Soviet Union during the summer of 1941. Anders, a Polish General, had been in Soviet captivity from 1939 and was released in August 1941. He had been ill-treated while in Soviet captivity and did not trust the Soviets; equally Stalin did not trust him. Stalin first asked Anders about Beck, and was told that, as far as Anders knew, Beck remained interned in Romania. Stalin disagreed and claimed that Beck was in Germany with his friends.[22] This was perhaps a cheap jibe at Beck's perceived pro-German past, but coming from Stalin, who had overseen the dismemberment of Poland, it was more than cheek. It was also how Stalin tested people; to see if they would cow before him. Anders was not one to bow before Stalin, while his ill-treatment at the hands of the Soviets made him all the more defiant. During March 1942, in talks with Stalin, Anders was asked by Stalin about Śmigły-Rydz. Anders told him that he was in Warsaw, but very ill with angina.[23] Whether this was news to Stalin or not we cannot tell, but it illustrates how both Beck and Śmigły-Rydz still had the potential of haunting negotiations between the Allies and the Poles. Equally Stalin may have only been trying to test Anders and see if he was truthful in his replies to him, rather than evading difficult issues.

Overall though it was quite clear that many Polish people wanted a clean and clear break with the past and did not want the exiled Polish establishment to be represented by members of the former military junta, as they could not be trusted. The French therefore had made the correct decision in supporting Sikorski, but it had more to do with luck rather than judgment. It should be noted that the British government were not so persuaded though, as it considered that it was only avenging Poles, who were trying to keep Beck from the West and that the British should not 'pander to the vengeful feeling of the present Polish government and keep Colonel Beck out of the United Kingdom.' It was considered by some that Beck in the end proved to have been a loyal ally to the UK.[24] Later, when Beck had escaped from Romania, the Polish exiled government, by now domiciled in London, panicked as he was a symbol of what they were not. By October 1940,with the Polish Army defeated for a second time and now Sikorski and his confederates having tasted the fruit of defeat and ejection from the European mainland, Polish troops now camping out in Scotland began to hanker for the glory days of the former regime. It was reported by the FO that the Polish troops regarded Beck as 'the symbol of the alliance with this country (UK), which enables their army still to exist and go on fighting for the good cause.'[25] Later during the same month, Frank Roberts (FO) noted that the Polish government did not want Beck at large and defiantly did not want him in either the UK or the USA. At best the Poles wanted him interned in British custody, on the island of Cyprus. The panic was not over until December 1940, when Beck was recaptured in possession of a British passport and Turkish diplomatic visas.[26] The wily Beck free, no doubt, could have caused damage to the Polish government-in-Exile, as he very probably could have persuaded

21 TNA, FO 371/2315C/14615/456, Kennard to Halifax, 22 September 1939.

22 PISM, KGA (General Anders' Collection) KGA/7g, Polish-Soviet Relations, Writings, 1941-1942. Anders to Sikorski, 9 October 1941.

23 PISM, KGA/7c, Polish-Soviet Relations, talks with the Soviets, 1941-1942, Anders talk with Stalin, 18 March 1942.

24 TNA, FO 371/24474/C4193/252/55, Activities of Colonel Beck in Romania, Strang to Kennard, 11 April 1940.

25 TNA, FO 371/24474/C8736/252/55, Possibility of Escape from Romania (Beck), Savery to Roberts, 1 October 1940.

26 Ibid., F.K. Roberts, 25 October 1940; 8 December 1940.

the ever political Polish military to support him. This meant that Sikorski had to start to chalk up some successes to try to overcome this threat. Regarding Stalin; one gets the impression that he was playing mind-games with Anders and found a worthy opponent.

The setting up of an exiled Polish government and the re-establishing of its armed forces in the West, was not as easy as the Poles might have thought it might be. The major hindrance to Polish plans was that they were now domiciled overseas; they were subject to interference from their hosts. Furthermore, the Allied High Commands had little regard for the Polish armed forces following their defeat, during the September Campaign. The Allied attitude stemmed from ignorance, as they had not appreciated the strength and rapidity of the German assault on Poland. They made even less of the Soviet invasion from the east, thus undermining any Polish successes, which were eventually being made against the German invasion. One of the few senior British officers, probably the only one, who had any meaningful knowledge of Poland, Lieutenant-General Adrian Carton de Wiart, left his home of nearly 20 years in Poland, during the opening phase of the German invasion of Poland and made for London. He went straight to the War Office to see General Ironside (CIGS), who met him with the remark 'Well! Your Poles haven't done much.' Carton de Wiart kept his council, but reflected later that the Allies had not understood the nature of the German assault on Poland. The German tactic of 'Blitzkrieg' or 'lightning war,' which called for rapid movement of land forces supported from the air, had been devastating in Poland, which was underarmed and unprepared.[27] Alan Moorehead, the war journalist, writing in 1944, considered that the Allies underestimated the power of the German dive bomber, noting that the Stuka (JU 87) was actually part of the German artillery in his estimation. Moorehead went further and asserted that Stukas more or less replaced artillery during the 1941 Greek Campaign.[28] The Allies attitude was that Germany had defeated an inferior force and that it would not happen to them: they were wrong.

Within a year much of Western Europe had been conquered by Germany using the same tactics. The UK was only spared owing to its geography, as being an island the Germans were prevented from sending armoured columns to swarm over British frontiers. Germany needed air and maritime supremacy, in order to conquer Britain. The British victory during the Battle of Britain, in the summer of 1940, denied Germany aerial supremacy over the UK and so prevented Britain from suffering the same fates as France, the Low Countries, Denmark and Norway, which had all been overrun by Germany, by the end of the summer of 1940. As we shall see British naval operations off the coast of Norway, ensured that Germany was unable to gain mastery of the seas surrounding the UK.

However, despite what could be seen as a debacle by the winter of 1939, regarding allied preparations for a war, which had been long coming, the Allies had not been totally negligent, as they had made some provisions for the event of the military defeat of Poland, owing to German aggression. Part of this provision concerned the fate of the Polish Navy. During Anglo-Polish Staff conversations, it was established that it was unlikely that the Polish Navy would remain in Polish waters once hostilities began. The question was whether it would make for the UK via Danish waters or head towards the Soviet Union.[29] By the outbreak of war, it was extremely unlikely that the Polish Navy would have been foolish enough to have headed for a Soviet port. On 8 September 1939. it was reported that three Polish Destroyers had escaped from the Baltic Sea and were en route to the North Sea, where they were to join the Destroyer Fleet of the Royal Navy.[30] Later, after an

27 Carton de Wiart, op. cit. pp. 160-1.

28 Alan Moorehead, *The Desert War. The Classical Trilogy on the North Africa Campaign, 1940-43* (London, Aurum Press, 2009), pp. 142, 149. Originally published, Hamish Hamilton, 1944.

29 TNA, CAB 66/1 Enclosure II, Anglo-Polish Conversations, 12 June 1939.

30 TNA, CAB 66/1, War Cabinet, Chiefs of Staff Committee, 8 September 1939; CAB 80/1 Weekly Resume (no.1)

interesting crossing from Poland, the Polish submarine, *Orzeł*, arrived in the Firth of Forth on 14 October 1939.[31] During September 1939, activities of the Soviet Fleet in the Gulf of Finland increased, following the escape of *Orzeł* from internment in Tallinn, Estonia.[32]

Once Sikorski had assumed power, as the leader of the exiled Poles in the West, naturally he wanted to revive the Polish armed forces in the West. He needed to do this to show to the world that Poland, as a geographic state, had been overrun by its enemies, but it was not defeated. He also had some legal basis to begin his work, as the former Polish regime, before fleeing into exile, had concluded two agreements with the French government. These provided for a Polish force, to the strength of a division, to be raised and established in the West, but this division was to be operationally subordinate to the French High Command. The British may have given some thought about what the Polish Navy might do once war begun, but did not conclude any agreements concerning the future of Polish service personnel heading westward and how to employ them usefully. This was probably because the British authorities were reluctant to see Poles serving alongside British servicemen.[33]

Much of the problem was a lack of understanding of each other: the Poles overestimated their own abilities, while the British underestimated Polish abilities. This was vividly illustrated by the treatment of Polish pilots, who considered that they were very experienced. This is not strictly true, as most of their aircraft were outdated and they actually had little, if any, combat experience. Furthermore, on the whole, they did not speak English well, assuming that they spoke any and were unused to radio transmitters in the cockpits of their aircraft. However the greatest problem or insult, as far as Polish officers were concerned, was that of their perceived status.

In Poland the military was more or less a caste and officers were considered to be officers and gentlemen, even if many came from peasant backgrounds, including Sikorski and Śmigły-Rydz but most had pretentions. The PAF was actually part of the Polish military, rather than being a separate service. The status of PAF officers was subliminally brought home to them once they arrived in the West and the British placed the Polish pilots with the Royal Air Force Volunteer Reserve (RAFVR). The problem was that the Poles were aware of the alleged social status of the RAF. The members of the regular air force, the RAF, were considered to be officers trying to be gentlemen. The part time RAF auxiliary force was considered to be full of privileged young men, some of whom actually owned their own aircraft, such was their wealth, but were considered to be gentlemen trying to be officers. Those in the RAFVR were considered to be those trying to be both. The Poles were outraged, owing to their hurt pride and sensitivities and no doubt their skin was somewhat thin by 1940; the Polish pilots had always considered themselves to be both officers *and* gentlemen. Being placed into the RAFVR suggested that they were judged to be neither.[34]

The British without a doubt did not have any intention of slighting the Polish pilots; they made a professional judgment and the Polish pilots were considered not adequately trained, but they were aware of how much Poles valued their prestige, as one report on the Poles and the Czechs considered that the Czechs were less obsessed with 'the issues of prestige' than the Poles were.[35] Even so the British were aware that being a member of PAF was not as prestigious in the eyes of the

of the Naval, Military and Air Situation from 12 noon 7 September 1939, minute 3, 8 September 1939.

31 TNA, CAB 66/2, WP (39) 44 also COS (39) 92, 19 October 1939.

32 TNA, CAB 80/3 COS (39) 43 JP, Weekly Resume of the Naval, Military and Air Situation from 1200 noon 14 September 1939 to 1200 noon, 21 September 1939.

33 McGilvray, *A Military Government*, p. 45.

34 Lynne Olson & Stanley Cloud, *For Your Freedom and Ours. The Kościuszko Squadron. Forgotten Heroes of World War II* (London: Arrow, 2004), p. 99.

35 TNA, CAB 85/19 AFO (40) 1st Meeting, Allied Forces (Official) Sub-Committee, 29 July 1940.

ordinary Pole, as being part of the Polish land forces.[36] However, by the latter stages of the Battle of Britain, Polish pilots now re-trained by the RAF and flying 'Hurricane' fighter planes acquitted themselves well and were to become the 'darlings' of the fighter pilots. Polish squadrons, 302 and 303 were reported as being 'heavily engaged' in the fighting during mid-September 1940. 303 Squadron was credited with shooting down over 70 enemy aircraft, while British commanders reported that the morale of Polish pilots was 'excellent' and their bravery 'much above the average'.[37] A year later, Air Chief Marshal Sir Hugh Dowding wrote a glowing report of the exploits of 303 Squadron. He confirmed that 303 Squadron in No. 11 Group, during the course of a single month, September 1940, as they became operational on 30 August 1940, shot down more German aircraft than any British units had during the same period. Dowding made the observation that the Poles and Czechs, who had fought 'very gallantly,' were used in small numbers in the Battle of Britain and would have probably been more effectively deployed in their own national units. However he did point to the fact that both the Polish and Czech pilots spoke little English, which was a problem.[38] It should be recognised that the Poles and Czechs were like a fresh pair of legs when they entered the Battle of Britain, as the British and Commonwealth pilots had been fighting since July 1940. The PAF was deployed late in the Battle of Britain, not only because Polish pilots needed to be trained to fly modern fighter planes, as well as try to address the language barrier, but also because the Poles distrusted the British. Many Poles feared that the RAF wanted to sacrifice Polish pilots; the RAF said that this was not the case and would only draw on them in an emergency. Sikorski was asked to deal with the matter.[39] It would seem that Sikorski must have done so and the emergency was reached, with the relentless German aerial attacks against the UK during the summer of 1940. Flattering reports of Polish pilots in the British press and on the wireless raised Polish morale.[40] Today the bravery of Polish pilots, during the Battle of Britain, had been largely forgotten by the British general public. Regarding the Polish Navy, which arrived in UK waters during the autumn of 1939, this was eventually regulated by the Anglo-Polish Agreement of 18 November 1939. The Polish Navy was defined as being a naval detachment attached to the Royal Navy and under the operational command of the British Admiralty (the Admiralty).[41] The two navies seemed to have had a harmonious relationship, with the Polish Navy playing its part in full at Narvik and later on during the war. Churchill had always considered that Polish Naval units (three Destroyers and two submarines), under British command, could be used off Petsamo and Murmansk, because as Churchill noted, Poland was at war with the Soviet Union and 'could legitimately sink Russian ships, without involving us in the charge of committing hostile acts against the Soviet.'[42]

Given the circumstances of defeat and exile, as well as the gulf between Poland and its allies, not only in terms of distance but also that of culture and understanding, it was not surprising that the Poles were treated somewhat distantly. They could not have expected anything else and it was for them to try and persuade their Western allies, that they were better than they considered them to be. This was a task for Sikorski. Furthermore, Sikorski not only had to prove to the world that Poland still existed, even if in the conditions of exile, he also had to show that Poland was still relevant to the war. The only way to prove this, was to raise a fighting force and return to the battlefield at the earliest opportunity.

36 TNA, PREM 3/351/1, Polish Forces Committee (PFC) 7th Meeting 1 July 1940.
37 TNA, CAB 66/12 WP (40) 384, 25 September 1940.
38 TNA, PREM 4/3/19, Battle of Britain, Despatch by Air Chief Marshal Sir Hugh C.T. Dowding, 2 August 1941.
39 TNA, CAB 92/110 PFC (Official) Committee 40, 10th Meeting, Appendix I (Polish Air Force), 26 July 1940.
40 TNA, CAB 66/12, WP (40) 377, 19 September 1940.
41 McGilvray, *A Military Government*, p. 27.
42 War Cabinet: Confidential Annex, CAB 65/11, 24 January 1940, *Churchill 1*, p. 685.

3

How to Proceed?

The demolition of Poland, by the end of October 1939, left the Allies in a quandary – how to proceed? The Soviet invasion of Poland, even if it could have been predicted, certainly upset the Allied applecart. As Sir Alexander Cadogan, Permanent Under Secretary at the FO and in charge of diplomacy, noted in his diary: there had to be a revision of British 'War Aims' following the Soviet invasion of Poland. The British government could no longer demand that aggressors leave Poland, unless the UK was willing to go to war with the Soviet Union. This the British government did not want to do.[1]

It appeared that a British declaration of war against the Soviet Union would not serve Poland well, as it was feared that it would make the situation of Poles, living in Soviet occupied Poland, even worse than it already was. Furthermore, war with the Soviet Union might have made the war against Germany even more difficult, as the Soviet Union might have been forced into even closer co-operation with Germany and possibly threaten British interests in the Middle East, owing to Soviet access from the Caucasus.[2] Quite simply, the British establishment was uncertain of how to proceed with the war, regarding the Soviet Union and its aggression against Poland.

A meeting of British Chiefs of Staff reached an erroneous conclusion early in the war, as it was asserted that there was little opportunity for Germany to receive substantial supplies from the Soviet Union.[3] Later, it was discovered that right up to the time of the German invasion of the Soviet Union, Germany had been receiving plentiful supplies of materials from the Soviet Union. By the end of September 1939, the British government decided that war against the Soviet Union was unnecessary and worse of all, war with the Soviet Union would threaten the security of India.[4]

By the end of September 1939, Hitler was trying to come to terms with the British and French governments. The gist of Hitler's terms was that Germany was to be given a free hand in central and eastern Europe and in return the British Empire was to be guaranteed by the German government.[5] However, the entire world knew that deals struck with Hitler, were not worth the paper on which they were written. This particular proposal was quite repugnant, but even so, as Cadogan knew, there had to be some form of reply and that should be that the German government should 'get rid of Hitler'. Cadogan considered that the French government would not agree with this sentiment, nor might some members of the British War Cabinet.[6]

Cadogan's view revealed the splits within the Allies and within the British War Cabinet regarding the war and who actually was the enemy: Germany or the Soviet Union? Hitler later tried to argue, that as both the UK and France had failed to save Poland, they might as well make

1 *Cadogan Diaries*, 23 September 1939, p. 219.
2 *BFP 1*, p. 12.
3 TNA, CAB 79/1 COS (39) 25th Meeting, 22 September 1939.
4 TNA, CAB 79/1 COS (39) 32nd Meeting, 29 September 1939.
5 *Cadogan Diaries*, 28 September 1939, p. 220.
6 Ibid., 7 October 1939, p. 221.

peace.[7] However, it would seem that enough members of the British War Cabinet had finally learnt their lessons about Hitler and did consider that his word was utterly worthless; the British Prime Minister, Neville Chamberlain certainly had every cause not to trust Hitler a single inch. On 12 October 1939, in a speech Chamberlain made, it was quite clear that British resolve was absolute and the war with Germany would continue. Hitler had misread the overall British attitude and their resolve to fight him and his tyranny. From then until the Fall of France during June 1940, Hitler made no more 'peace-feelers'.[8]

The exiled Polish leader, General Władysław Sikorski, now domiciled in Paris with his exiled government and military force, had to work out a way to keep Poland relevant to Allied war aims, as the Soviet invasion and annexation of eastern Poland had caused little comment amongst the Allies, who also failed to declare war against the Soviet Union, despite the obvious aggression against Poland and its people. This was at a time when the Soviet occupation forces were busy rounding up hundreds and thousands of Poles and deporting them as slave labourers, into the wastelands of the Soviet interior. However there was one British politician who was determined to have none of the shilly-shallying of some of his colleagues and others in the British establishment. He was of course Winston Churchill.

Churchill had had a chequered career by 1939 and was a backbencher, having previously enjoyed high office. By 1939 he had been out of office for a number of years. Indeed the decade of the 1930s when connected to Churchill, is known as the 'Wilderness Years,' owing to his lack of influence at that time. Churchill, once he turned his hand to politics, had seen his career rise dramatically. No doubt family connections helped but his energy and enthusiasm cannot be denied once applied to politics. Having enjoyed periods of high office, including being Home Secretary and Chancellor of the Exchequer, prior to the outbreak of war in 1914, Churchill was to suffer a major setback, owing to his support and backing for the ill-fated 1915 Dardanelles Landings. The Dardanelles was a major offensive on the Turkish mainland and should have knocked Turkey, a German ally, out of the war and relieved pressure on Russia, a British Ally. The plan was well conceived but poorly executed, as well as being denied the necessary resources to carry it out. The campaign ended in failure and Churchill, as a prime backer of the cause, served, what could be seen as an act of penance, the year 1916 in France on the Western Front. However he was soon back but during the 1930s he suffered further setbacks, as his brand of politics was deemed as inappropriate.

The 1930s was branded a 'dishonest low decade' by a poet and so it was. It was a decade of aggression by both Germany and the Soviet Union, who tightened up domestic dictatorships and spread terror, while Germany re-armed and then annexed various territories, in pursuit of a policy of returning Germans to Germany. It was rank hypocrisy and naked aggression, while the democracies pursued a course of disarmament; very commendable but naive in the face of German aggression, as well as that of Italy and Japan, as the world cranked up for war once more. Churchill, and a small brave band of followers, continually spoke out about what was happening in the world, as Italy and Japan invaded and annexed different parts of the world, while Italy and Germany prepared for war by using Spain and its civil war (1936–1939), as a large war game played in real time. The German air force certainly took full advantage, as their 'tourists' entered Spain and flew bombers against Spanish government forces and defenceless civilians.

Churchill challenged the policies of the UK government and, embarrassingly frequently, he commented on how Germany was rearming and breaking the Versailles Treaty at will. This attitude led to him being branded a warmonger, and the sad tale of the Dardanelles would be dredged up by

7 Ibid., note by Dilks, p. 223.
8 *BFP 1*, p. 13.

his enemies. However, it should be seen that Churchill was one of the few realists sitting in the British Parliament, and eventually he was proven to be correct, and by the late 1930s, it was obvious that the policies of pacifism and disarmament were irresponsible and only pandered towards dictators.[9] On 3 September 1939, the British Prime Minister, Neville Chamberlain, appointed Churchill First Lord at the Admiralty. It was the post which Churchill had held in 1914, when Britain went to war with Germany. This did not bother Churchill; he was back in government and a member of the British War Cabinet. He had power once more.

On the Western Front very little was happening and so the 'phoney war' set in, as the Allies and the Germans sat entrenched and tried to stare each other out. In the east it was all very different and the war was fought on the high seas. The lack of action was a period of frustration for Sikorski, as he tried to regroup and renew the Polish Army in exile. In the middle of November 1939, Sikorski made proposals for the formation and equipping of Polish forces in France. This was discussed by the British War Cabinet on 15 November 1939. The British Minister for War, Leslie Hore-Belisha told the Cabinet that he had received a letter from Sikorski, which contained proposals for the formation of an armoured division and up to seven infantry divisions. Sikorski hoped to recruit from the Polish population living in France.

Sikorski's motivation was that he was anxious to preserve the identity of the Polish armed forces and did not want them to be incorporated into French or British units. Furthermore, he wished to conclude a formal agreement on this point. In addition Sikorski wanted Polish representation on the Supreme War Council, but was not going to press this matter. Equally he was very anxious, however, to have a representative with the Anglo-French Permanent Military Representatives in London. Sikorski considered that there was great political value in re-establishing a Polish Army to fight alongside British and French forces, including keeping the identity of the Polish nation, as one of the original allies.

The British War Cabinet took a more realistic approach and dealt with what was known, rather than possibilities. It was already clear that the Canadian government were not enthusiastic about Polish recruitment in Canada. It was conceded by the Allies that the Polish naval units, which had escaped from their homeland and had joined the Royal Navy, were of high calibre. Therefore there was an assumption that Polish troops who arrived, would be of the same type. 80,000 Polish troops had arrived in France, but there was an insufficient number of officers and more importantly a dearth of NCOs. Furthermore, the French government decided not to arm the Polish units with the same equipment that the French army had, and instead issued the Poles with inferior equipment. At the time it was impossible for the British government to provide the equipment necessary for an armoured formation, but training for such an eventuality could start as soon as possible. These ideas were to be put before the French government, in order to co-ordinate future co-operation connected with the Poles.[10]

Of course Sikorski was quite deluded with his ideas of Polish status within the alliance. Within a day he was informed that his idea of close military co-operation was under consideration, but the idea of Poland having permanent representation on the Supreme Military Council was rejected. It had been noted that during the First World War, countries such as Belgium or Romania were not consulted, until a situation involved them.[11] Quite simply Poland was not going to get any preferential treatment and was not considered to be a major ally.

Even though, at the time, the British government was trying to prevent the Poles from publishing

9 *Guilty Men*, op. cit. is perhaps the best contemporary source for this episode and the anger was still raw.
10 TNA, CAB 65/2, War Cabinet 84 (39) 15 November 1939.
11 TNA, CAB 65/2, War Cabinet 85 (39) 16 November 1939.

accounts of German atrocities in Poland, there were grounds for optimism in the Polish camp.[12] The British government was strongly in favour of Sikorski's plans for recruitment, even if the Canadian government was not encouraging and there was still a need to co-ordinate the entire plan with the French government. The biggest problem was who was going to pay for what?[13] The British government also relented slightly about military discussions and asked that the Polish government nominate a suitable Polish military officer, to be invited to Anglo-French military discussions in London, whenever Polish input was required.[14]

At the beginning of 1940 the French government suggested a way, in which Polish armed forces might be actively used in the war, but not directly against Germany, but instead against the Soviet Union, Germany's major ally. An opportunity had arisen during November 1939, as the Soviet Union invaded Finland expecting an easy victory, but this hope was terribly misplaced, as well led and well directed Finnish troops, few in number but well equipped, stalled the Red Army and made it fight hard and pay dearly for every foot of Finnish territory they acquired. The Soviet invasion of Finland presented the Allies a chance to have a swipe at Germany, through an attack against its ally but there were reservations amongst the allies about taking this course.

The overall aim of Soviet aggression was not entirely clear to some of the British authorities, while some wondered whether war with the Soviet Union was in British interests. The British Chiefs of Staff (COS), earlier in the war, had correctly concluded that the Soviet government's overarching aim was the spread of the 'World Revolution,' as well as regaining its former imperial territories (of which both Finland and large swathes Poland had been). The COS also considered that the Soviet Union wished to improve its strategic position and to establish fresh centres of propaganda.[15] These were accurate and useful observations. Another British report considered not only the question of the Soviet World Revolution, but also that the Soviet government would prefer a weak Germany as a neighbour and certainly did not want to see German penetration into the Balkans and to the Black Sea.[16]

Basically the British Service Chiefs predicted that in time the German-Soviet alliance would fold, especially given Hitler's gangster attitude towards agreements; Stalin was no better. Furthermore, the Soviet government had never stopped trying to complete the World Revolution and after 1943 was able to recover parts of the former Russian empire and beyond. A position held until 1989 and once more from 2014 Russia seems determined to recover the former Soviet empire, as the West looks the other way. In 1939 the British people may not have been particularly outraged by the Soviet invasion of Poland, but the Soviet attack on Finland did, as they recognised the fact that a democratic Western state had been outraged. This led to a demand for some form of Allied intervention against the Soviet Union, in the case of Finland. Halifax minuted that there were few people left in the UK who were willing to continue making excuses for the Soviet Union.[17]

The British government had been aware, since the end of 1939 that not all was well in the Soviet-German relationship. In an undated Confidential Annexe relating to a conversation between Edward Beneš, the Czech leader in exile and Ivan Maisky, the Soviet Ambassador to London, Beneš reported the conversation to Halifax. Maisky made several observations in his talk with the Czech leader. He told Beneš that at the time of the signing of the Nazi-Soviet Agreement, German intervention was limited to occupying Danzig and Western Poland. Therefore the speed and scope

12 Ibid.
13 TNA, CAB 65/2, War Cabinet 90 (39) 21 November 1939.
14 TNA, CAB 65/2, War Cabinet 94 (39) 25 November 1939.
15 TNA, CAB 80/3 66 (JP) 6 October 1939.
16 TNA, CAB 66/2, COS (39) 69, 9 October 1939.
17 TNA, CAB 65/5 War Cabinet 5 (40) 7th Conclusion, Minute 9, 6 January 1940.

of the German advance into Poland, was considered by the Soviet government to be a threat to Soviet security. This led to the Soviet occupation of eastern Poland. An interesting observation was made at the time, as the Soviet government considered using their influence to 'secure the establishment in Poland of a new Polish government protected from German domination.' Simply the Soviet government sought to establish a puppet Polish government as Sikorski feared might happen. However, the most important thing that Halifax learnt from this meeting, was that the Nazi-Soviet pact was one of convenience and had lost all significance, as Germany had taken more of Poland than had been originally agreed to.[18]

The information received from Beneš must have been reassuring for British officials, as just after the Soviet invasion of Poland, the UK government feared going to war with the Soviet Union. It had been estimated that in the case of war between the UK and the Soviet Union, the enemy submarine threat would be increased by over 200 vessels, once the Soviet Navy joined their German allies at sea, while the Soviet Air Force might well have been used to reinforce the Luftwaffe.[19] This estimation might well explain why the British government was reluctant to take any action, which might have angered the Soviet government. Even so the UK government still had to appease its own people regarding Soviet aggression against Finland.

To return to the French Ambassador's plan for possible Allied action against the Soviets in Finland, this called for the co-operation of Polish naval forces with the Finnish forces just off Petsamo. However Halifax urged caution, as it was a fact that Polish naval units were operating under orders from the Admiralty and were using British naval bases. Therefore the despatch of Polish naval units to Petsamo, might be well construed by the Soviet government as a British intervention, rather than a sovereign Polish action.[20] This was of course exactly what it was and may have well provoked an unnecessary war with the Soviet Union. The French wanted any such Polish action, that may happen against Petsamo, to be in the form of a raid; destroying the quay and port buildings, in an attempt to deny the Soviets their use. Overall though, the French plan was deemed as unlikely to happen and was merely an idea to be considered.[21] Given that the British government was aware of how the Soviet government viewed their treaty with Germany, the British had to tread very carefully, very carefully indeed, but surely at the back of their minds was what if it was all a trick. A further consideration was the capricious nature of Stalin. His diplomats may have had their ideas but they could all be swept away if Stalin deemed a different approach. However, the reality was that in Europe it seemed that Soviet aggression was going unchecked, but the Soviet attack on Finland could not be ignored indefinitely.

Soviet aggression in Scandinavia, during the winter of 1939–40, caused the Allies more anxiety than the Germans on the Western Front. However, as the Winter War in Finland dragged on, according to a secret transmission found in the Polish archives, which was sent in the middle of the night by the French Military Attaché in Helsinki, the Allies did consider intervention and were exploring the type of warfare which they might meet with and the calibre of soldier needed to fight, in such a theatre of operations.[22]

From the early days of the war Norway had been a concern to the Allies, owing to its ice free port of Narvik and its use to transport iron ore from it to Germany. Notes in *The Ironside Diary* discuss the importance of Narvik and the iron ore coming out from Sweden. In northern Sweden,

18 TNA, CAB 65/3 War Cabinet (39) 28th Conclusion, Minute 8, Confidential Annexe, Secretary of State for Foreign Affairs Gave the War Cabinet Substance of a Conversation between Benes and Maisky, re: Soviet Invasion of Poland, undated.

19 TNA, CAB 66/1, COS (39) 35, 18 September 1939.

20 TNA, CAB 65/5 War Cabinet 5 (40) Minute 4, 6 January 1940.

21 TNA, CAB 79/3 COS (40) 15th Meeting, 25 January 1940.

22 PISM, A.IV.11/58, *Sztab Głowny Armii – sekcja szyfrow i korespodencji telegraficznej*, 14 February 1940.

it was considered that in the Gällivare area, there was a large hill almost entirely made up of iron ore. This was Germany's main source of the mineral. During the summer months, the ore was exported to Germany via the port of Lulea at the northern end of the Gulf of Bothnia. During the winter, Narvik was used, as Lulea was frozen in. It was estimated, that Germany needed nine million tons of high grade iron ore for the first twelve months of the war. Churchill brought this to the attention of the British War Cabinet, as early as 19 September 1939. On 29 November 1939, Churchill was all for laying sea mines just off Norwegian waters, in an attempt to prevent Germany using Narvik.[23] Indeed on 11 December, the British War Council was sounding out the American President Franklin Roosevelt, regarding the possibility of the British mining Norwegian territorial waters and was able to report that Roosevelt was more than happy to allow this to go ahead. The British War Cabinet hoped that events might become, so that both Norway and Sweden were forced into a war with the Soviet Union, which would then give the British an opportunity to land in Scandinavia, without having to go to war with the Soviet Union. The overall advantage in this situation would lay with the ability to wage naval warfare in Scandinavian waters against nominally the Soviet Union, but the true target of course would be Germany and maritime fleets. [24] On the same day Churchill sent a personal minute to Admirals Pound and Phillips and to Sir Archibald Carter, in which he outlined the importance of the Baltic, as Churchill considered the possibility of being at war with the Soviet Union but allied to Sweden, Norway and Finland, while intriguingly also allied to Italy. Churchill noted that bases in the Baltic would provide air cover for the UK, but overall Churchill doubted such a situation becoming a reality.[25] It should be noted that at this stage of the war Italy had not shown its hand; in the First World War even though many considered that Italy would have joined Germany and Austria; in 1915 Italy became an ally of the UK and France. However, Scandinavia and the question of Germany being able to receive supplies of iron ore from Sweden began to obsess Churchill, as on 20 December 1939, he berated Admiral Godfrey for not being able to supple a daily report on the ice conditions at Lulea, which Churchill referred to as being a 'significant port'.[26] Churchill was trying to work with an early assessement made by the COS, who did not consider that Germany would attack Norway, unless the Allies landed there.

Much deliberation was also given to a Soviet invasion of Norway, beginning with an attack on Finland, followed by aggression against both Sweden and Norway. At the end of October 1939, the British Chiefs of Staff considered that owing to the geography and winter conditions found in Scandinavia, it was unlikely that the Soviets would invade Norway and Sweden from Finland with any 'measure of success' during the winter months.[27] Ironside was against having any British presence at all in Scandinavia; either as Military Mission or even a small force, as he considered that such commitments led to a larger one in the long run, in order to reinforce the original presence: today this would be called 'Mission Creep'. Ironside claimed that he had no forces to spare for Scandinavia and that to hold Narvik alone would require at least a Division, while a full scale military expeditionary force would be needed in order to prevent iron ore being supplied to the enemy at Narvik.[28] Admiral of the Fleet, Sir Dudley Pound, seemed to reinforce Ironside's points, as Pound made it very clear that Norway with its long coast may benefit from naval assistance, but it was impossible for Sweden, as it had a somewhat limited shoreline.[29] Quite simply supply and

23 *Ironside Diaries*, pp. 181-182.
24 Cabinet Paper 65/2, 11 December 1939, cited in *Churchill 1*, p. 492.
25 Admiralty Papers, 199/1928 First Lord's Personal Minute, Winston S. Churchill to Admiral Pound, Admiral Phillips and Sir Archibald Carter, 11 December 1939. Cited in *Churchill 1*, pp. 496-7.
26 Winston Churchill to Admiral Godfrey (Churchill Papers, 19/3) 20 December 1939, cited in *Churchill 1*, p. 545.
27 TNA, CAB 79/1 COS (39) 64th Meeting, 31 October 1939.
28 TNA, CAB 79/2 COS (39) 81st Meeting, 16 November 1939.
29 TNA, CAB 79/2 COS (39) 85th Meeting, 21 November 1939.

maintenance of an Allied force in Scandinavia would be very difficult, if it went ahead. This may have been wishful thinking for wanting to do nothing, as from the first day of British involvement in the war, the Chiefs of Staff ruled out any German attack on Norway, except as a reprisal measure, while the Allies thought that they might be able to 'exercise great economic command over Norway,' whatever that was supposed to mean. Overall the UK did not consider that Germany had the ability to attack, conquer and occupy Norway.[30] This may have been true in September 1939, because as James Holland suggests, Germany just about defeated Poland in 1939.[31] It took Soviet treachery to totally undo Poland, while in Norway there were significant well placed traitors who were to betray their country and their compatriots and allow the Germans to land, notably at Narvik, unhindered.

The situation in Scandinavia radically altered on 30 November 1939, when the Soviet Union invaded Finland.[32] By mid December 1939, the British Chiefs of Staff began to fear attacks on Narvik by both Germany and the Soviet Union. The British Service Chiefs worried that any attempt by the Allies to try to disrupt the supply of iron ore to Germany, would cause a German invasion of Scandinavia, while an invasion by the Soviet Union of the same area was also feared by the Allies. This led to the consideration for the necessity of an Anglo-Franco force to be ready to go to Narvik and possibly to northern Sweden, in case of an attack by the Soviet Union and/or Germany.[33] Just prior to Christmas 1939, a secret report was received by the British, which suggested that the Soviets were preparing a seaborne expedition from Murmansk, on the north Russian coast to Narvik. It was considered by the COS, that the Soviet Union was unlikely to undertake such an adventure but the British Chiefs of Staff realised that, in order to prevent such possible landings, there needed to be some joined up thinking and co-operation with the Scandinavians, or as it was termed 'obtain the prior concurrence of the Scandinavian states.'[34] It should be noted that the Norwegians, as early as September 1939, had feared an attack from Murmansk via Finland.[35]

As winter progressed into 1940 Scandinavia began to obsess the British authorities. It was not only the Soviet invasion of Finland, or the fear of a Soviet invasion of northern Scandinavia which focussed their minds. It was the realisation that soon the ice on the Gulf of Bothnia would soon melt and thus allow the Germans to dominate the Baltic Sea and its neighbouring waters. Ironside also feared that the Germans were planning to seize and occupy the Gällivare area. Even so the British were fairly confident that the Germans and Soviets did not trust each other and, as we have seen, Maisky more or less confirmed this to Beneš. As a consequence, the British government was cautious in its dealings with the Soviet Union, as it may become an ally in time and so any ill-considered act, which might lead to war between the UK and the Soviet Union, was to be avoided if possible. Ironside was further frustrated when he was told, by the Swedish Military Attaché in London, that he had learnt from his French counterpart that the Allies planned to land at Narvik. As Ironside remarked it was impossible to keep anything secret, when so many people were privy to the planning.[36]

If the Swedes knew of the coming Allied offensive, then of course the Germans knew of it. The commentary accompanying Ironside's diary makes it quite clear that the Allies had indeed

30 TNA, CAB 80, Chiefs of Staff Sub-Committee, CAB 80/1 COS (39) 5 (JP) 3 September 1939.
31 James Holland, *The Battle of Britain. Five Months that changed history, May-October 1940* (London, Corgi Books, 2011), p. 417.
32 *Ironside Diaries*, pp. 181-2.
33 TNA, CAB 79/2 COS (39) 109th Meeting, 18 December 1939; CAB 79/2 COS (39) 110th Meeting, 19 December 1939; CAB 79/2 COS (39) 111th Meeting, 21 December 1939.
34 TNA, CAB 79/2 COS (39) 112th Meeting, 22 December 1939.
35 TNA, CAB 80/3, Weekly Resume no. 4 of the Naval, Military and Air Situation (1200 noon 21st September – 1200 noon 28th September 1939), 28 September 1939.
36 *Ironside Diaries*, 20 February 1940, p.221.

assembled a force and ships to go to Norway. A Commander, General Mackesy, had been appointed to lead the entire Expeditionary Force and all that was needed was a decision from the British War Cabinet to go. The Cabinet was still divided, about 50:50; the latest diplomatic news had begun to make an impact, but not enough of one.

There were also signs that the Germans were planning to invade Scandinavia. As if to confirm this, reports of constant movement of troops towards ports in northern Germany were received, while night after night the RAF saw and reported long columns of lorries, with their lights blazing, moving in the same direction. The RAF asked for permission to bomb these columns but Chamberlain denied them, as he claimed he did not want to be responsible for the first bombs being dropped on land targets. Clearly he had already forgotten what the Germans had done in Poland. As early as 11 September 1939, Sir Howard Kennard reported to the FO, that for three days the Germans had repeatedly and deliberately bombed open Polish towns, which lacked any military targets. Kennard requested that the RAF should bomb German factories and other such targets, in an attempt to aid the Poles.[37]

In Stockholm the ever security conscious French diplomatic staff spoke openly of the coming Allied expedition to Scandinavia. Therefore giving the Germans the perfect excuse to strike first, whilst losing the Allies the element of surprise. Ironside pressed the Cabinet for a decision and finally it was agreed that some force might be used to allow British troops to enter Norway.[38] An overdue decision had finally been reached, after the most ridiculous indecision by British civilian politicians but at least the stupidity of French diplomats ensured that an agreement was reached, but all the same the Germans knew that the Allies were coming to Scandinavia. For the military and naval officers, who were expected to lead the expedition, it must have been an extremely frustrating experience, allowing yesterday's naive fools to decide on the lives and deaths of their men.

On 1 April 1940, the British War Cabinet approved plans from the Chiefs of Staff, which demanded that if after the laying of mines by the Royal Navy in Norwegian territorial waters, the Germans either invaded Scandinavia or were clearly about to do so, the British would then send a force to Narvik to secure the port and the railway as far as the Swedish frontier and so prepare the way to seize the iron ore region at Gällivare. Furthermore, British forces would be sent to Stavanger, Bergen and Trondheim, in an attempt to deny ports and airfields in those areas to the Germans. However no attempt would be made at landing British forces in Norway, without Norwegian co-operation.

The Germans also had plans for Scandinavia. Initially German naval chiefs wanted to seize Norwegian submarine bases, as early as October 1939 and then again during December 1939, they put forward plans to seize Norway and use its long rugged coastline with numerous inlets to attack British shipping from, as well as, block trade routes to the UK. The German naval chiefs briefed Hitler of their plans. The question of the Germans protecting their iron ore supply from Gällivare and the supply route from Narvik to the Baltic coast, had not yet arisen in German quarters, at the time. Prior to the German invasion, Churchill was always suspicious of how the Norwegians might behave; he did not trust them as the Norwegian government did nothing, even after the Germans had sunk three ships in Norwegian territorial waters.[39] At the time it would seem that perhaps the Norwegians were being naive and just hoped that the German menace might go away if they did nothing except for supply iron ore; the big fear of the Scandinavians was that of a Soviet invasion and occupation. Throughout much of Western Europe before the German invasions of

37 TNA, CAB 80/2 COS (39) 26, 'German Observation of International Law' Sir H. Kennard (Krzemieniec) 11 September 1939.
38 *Ironside Diaries*, p. 221.
39 War Cabinet: Confidential Annex (Cabinet papers 65/11) 10 January 1940, cited in *Churchill 1*, pp. 624-6.

Western Europe, the bogeyman was the Soviet Union. This anxiety of many Scandinavians had been noted by the British since the outbreak of war, as countries such as Denmark, Norway, and Sweden feared the disruption of their internal economies, if there was a long war between Germany and the UK, the principal customers of these countries, but was wholly afraid of a Soviet attack and occupation. Therefore the best outcome if peace could not come, might well be a German occupation, rather than a Bolshevik occupation.[40] The British War Cabinet was still thinking along the lines of interception at sea of German vessels carrying iron ore, with an intention of somehow trying to get the Scandinavians, especially the Swedes involved in a war with the Soviet Union.[41] It is quite clear therefore, that the British government at least lacked the confidence to initiate land warfare in Scandinavia, unless the Swedes and Norwegians were embroiled first in such an action: an invasion would have been handy as an excuse to land British troops in defence of Norway and Sweden, but as we have seen a Soviet invasion was the invasion of choice, as far as the British were concerned. The German invasion of 9 April 1940, was not convenient for British thinking, even if it was inevitable. By mid-January 1940, concerns about Narvik was put aside by the British authorities, as it became obvious that there was a threat to the Low Countries. This revelation had come about as a result of a German airplane being forced down, just outside the Belgian frontier. A German officer, Major Helmut Reinberger, was found to have plans, for a German invasion of Belgium to begin on 17 January 1940, on him. This invasion was postponed until Spring, owing to bad weather. Churchill observed to Lord Halifax, that it could be said, that it was good that the British had not to date violated Norwegian territorial waters, as the Germans might have been able to claim that by invading Holland and Belgium; they were only following the British example of ignoring territorial integrity; this was an argument that Churchill did not really agree with.[42]

Once the Soviet Union attacked Finland and rumours reached the German authorities that the British intended to aid the Finns, possibly via Narvik, alarm bells began to ring in Berlin. The German government had to consider that if these rumours were true, then there was a definite threat to Germany's supply of Swedish iron ore. In January 1940, Hitler set his Staff the problem of deciding how far an invasion and occupation was feasible, in relation to Germany's overall war strategy. The German General Staff was sceptical and did not believe that the war would be settled by an offensive in northern Europe. They maintained that such a move should follow a German attack to the West and not precede one. At the same time, the British War Cabinet, in a move instigated by Churchill, was also beginning to consider 'a daring scheme in Northern Scandinavia, which they (the Cabinet) think might bring Germany to her knees.'[43] John Colville, the author of these words, considered Churchill's plan to be folly and all too reminiscent of Churchill's plan for the 1915 Allied invasion of Turkey, which had been a disaster and for which Churchill was often unfairly blamed.[44] The next day Colville reported in his diary, that after a 'hectic morning,' the Cabinet discussed Scandinavia and had more or less agreed to adopt the concept of stopping the supply of iron ore from Narvik to Germany. Churchill according to Colville hoped that this would lead to a German invasion of Norway, which would allow the British to seize the iron ore fields by force. However, a need remained to consult with the CoS to consider just how such action might

40 *Great Britain. Foreign Office Weekly Political Intelligence Summaries, Volume 1, October 1939-June 1940, Nos. 1-38* (London: Kraus, 1983), (Hereafter *FO Summaries 1*) Weekly Political Intelligence Summary No.1 (Covering the Period from the Outbreak of War to October 3, 1939) pp. 8-9.

41 *Churchill 1*, pp. 624-6.

42 Winston S. Churchill to Lord Halifax, (Foreign Office Papers, 800/328) 15 January 1940, cited in *Churchill 1*, pp. 642-3.

43 John Colville: diary, (Colville Papers, 1 January 1940, cited in *Churchill 1*, p. 592.

44 Ibid. For a military-political judgement of the Gallipoli offensive, see Evan McGilvray, *Hamilton & Gallipoli* (Barnsley: Pen & Sword, 2015.

be undertaken and its consequences.[45] An immediate consequence was pointed out by Ironside (CIGS), who observed that the British had no ski-troops immediately available and that the Swedes faced with a British attack, might defend their country in the same manner, as the Finns had been doing very successfully in January 1940 against the Red Army.[46] In other words ski-troops fighting on their own ground defending their own country; a powerful motivation as the British were to find out, when they successfully defended the UK from German invasion, as the result of the aerial battles, commonly known as the Battle of Britain, during the summer of 1940. British and Commonwealth pilots flew and fought over the UK, defeating the Luftwaffe and causing the German invasion of the UK to be postponed and then abandoned, as Germany invaded the Soviet Union during June 1941.

However the Germans were aware that the Allies, following the boarding of the German tanker, *Altmark*, in Norwegian waters and releasing 299 British merchant seamen, captured by the Germans in earlier actions, did not regard neutrality as being sacred if it got in the way of British war plans. Persistent rumours that the Allies intended to land in Norway, caused the Germans to fear that the Allies might seize Scandinavia before them. This led to the German decision to occupy Norway themselves and so frustrate Allied plans. The Germans were clear that a successful invasion and occupation of Norway would ensure their supply of iron ore, whether via the Baltic during the summer or down the Norwegian coast during the winter. Furthermore, the German Navy and the Luftwaffe, in their words, were given 'a wider start line against Britain.' A German move into Norway also prevented Germany being outflanked and attacked by the Allies from Scandinavia. Even so the German General Staff still refused to see an attack on Norway as being nothing other than being a minor operation and so, with the exception for the deployment of mountain divisions, did not allot particularly strong forces to the operation. Furthermore, they did not make any preparations for meeting any Allied landings in Norway. Equally the British did not expect to meet German forces in Norway either once they landed. Curiously both expeditions sailed at the same time to Norway; neither side expecting to meet each other once they landed in Norway.[47]

Ironside's frustration with having to deal with civilian politicians is quite obvious and he cannot help but compare it with how he assumed Hitler might be chairing his Cabinet meetings (such as they were). Ironside assumed that the enemy's Cabinet meetings moved along far more briskly than the ponderings of the British War Cabinet, where just about everything was referred to a committee before a final decision could be made. He noted that Chamberlain was 'hopelessly unmilitary' and that Churchill, if kept in check, showed promise.[48] Ironside may have been right about Chamberlain but later CIGS were to complain about how Churchill ran the War Cabinet. Ironside was not the only man to be frustrated with events during the late winter of 1940, as Churchill himself was quite distressed with events prior to the German invasion of Norway, as German ore ships were able to move through Norwegian waters carrying iron ore back to Germany. It was clear to him that Norwegian neutrality was a fig leaf and that the Norwegian authorities favoured Germany. The *Altmark* incident to Churchill and many others was evidence of this partiality, even if Churchill toned down his remarks by observing that Germany was bullying Norway, he still advocated that a stronger line should be taken with Norway and once more suggested mining a section of Norwegian territorial waters, which would cause German shipping to take to the high seas and run the gauntlet of the Royal Navy, which would be waiting for them.[49] Regarding the

45 John Colville Diary (Colville Papers) 2 January 1940, cited in *Churchill 1*, p. 595.
46 War Cabinet Confidential Annex, (Cabinet Paper, 65/11) 2 January 1940 cited in *Churchill 1*, pp. 597-8.
47 Ibid., pp. 245-6.
48 Ibid., 7 April 1940, pp. 247.
49 War Cabinet Paper, 66/5, 14 February 1940, cited in *Churchill 1*, pp. 760-2.

eventual boarding of *Altmark* on 17 February 1940, by members of the crew of HMS *Cossack,* who then rescued 299 British prisoners illegally detained on her, it should be recognised that the entire situation was extremely delicate. The British did not seek to violate Norwegian neutrality, but at the same time were quite willing to take whatever measures necessary to secure the release of British seamen being unlawfully detained, which included firing on Norwegian vessels in the case of self-defence but using no more force than was needed. The British government was determined, as far as possible, not to be seen as the aggressor in Scandinavia.[50] A confidential annexe contained in a Cabinet Paper, just after the *Altmark* incident, notes that Churchill more or less desired a German invasion of Scandinavia, as it would be largely to the advantage of the British, as it would give a pretext to allow British troops to be landed in the area. The *Altmark* incident also galvanised the War Cabinet out of its usual naive lethargy, as it was realised that Churchill was a realist and that the Norwegians, far from being neutral, were actually playing fast and loose with their neutrality and clearly siding with Germany and so the decision was finally taken to mine Norwegian territorial waters.[51] However, as Prime Minister Chamberlain reported to the War Cabinet, public opinion in the USA was continuously looking for '...a stick to beat us (the UK) with.' Even if many Americans had accepted the *Altmark* incident as being on the whole a humanitarian act, it was unlikely that they would accept the mining of neutral waters.[52] To keep on the good side of international public opinion and in order to avoid being branded an aggressor, the British War Cabinet had to proceed with caution in its handling of Scandinavia, until such a time either the Soviet Union or Germany invaded either Norway or Sweden, if not both.

On 8 April 1940, Ironside recorded that the British had sewn mines off Narvik and had broadcast it to the world. On 5 April 1940, Ironside had written in his diary that no doubt the world would condemn the British for a 'brutal' violation of Norwegian neutrality, once they were told of the laying of sea mines by the Royal Navy. However, on 8 April 1940, British aerial reconnaissance showed a German fleet, with what looked like a troop ship with it, moving out of the Baltic Sea. A report came in from Copenhagen, which said that the Germans had started to occupy Narvik. Ironside noted that the British had HMS *Renown* and HMS *Birmingham* with twelve Destroyers just south of Narvik, while the Main Fleet was heading towards the Norwegian coast. Ironside considered that if the Germans were really off Narvik then they ought to be caught between the two British naval fleets. For good measure three Cruisers, armed with 8-inch guns were ordered out of their base at Rosyth in Scotland and head for the Norwegian coast. At this point Ironside was not clear as to what the Germans were up to and even considered that the transport ship might turn out to be a pocket-battleship trying to get to the open seas, in order to raid British shipping and supplies.[53] However despite the international clamour surrounding the British sewing mines in Norwegian waters, it should be remembered that Germany, as early as 7 November 1939, had done the same in Swedish waters. Later during the same month, the Germans extended their mining of Swedish waters, while the Danes engaged in questionable mining of waters, which could have had only one possibility: preventing British submarines from entering the Baltic Sea.[54] However these minings did not create too much sensation in 1939 and are not recalled today. One can only wonder why not.

50 Selected papers and correspondence cited in *Churchill 1*, pp. 772-6.
51 War Cabinet: Confidential Annex, Cabinet Paper 65/11, 18 February 1940, cited in *Churchill 1*, pp. 777-8; War Cabinet: Confidential Annex, Cabinet Paper 65/11, 19 February 1940, cited in *Churchill 1*, pp. 779-80.
52 War Cabinet: Minutes (Cabinet Papers, 65/5) 29 February 1940, cited in *Churchill 1* pp. 824-7.
53 Ibid., *Churchill* 1, 8 April 1940, pp. 247-8.
54 *FO Summaries1*, Weekly Political Intelligence Summary No. 7, 14 November 1939, p.7; Weekly Political Intelligence Summary No.9, 28 November 1939 pp.7-8.

The commentary accompanying Ironside's diary fills in the blanks, which he left. Indeed on the morning of 7 April 1940, German warships had been sighted moving north off the Jutland coast; later it seemed that a substantial fleet was moving up the North Sea. During the night 7–8 April 1940, the British Home Fleet and Second Cruiser Squadron sailed, in order to intercept the enemy fleet. First Cruiser Squadron, Royal Navy, which was preparing to embark British troops for Bergen and Stavanger, were ordered to stop doing that and join in the chase. Ships earmarked to escort troopships for Narvik and Trondheim were also ordered to join the rest of the Fleet, in pursuit of the enemy. It was feared that the Germans were trying to sneak out into the Atlantic Ocean, in order to attack British shipping; in fact it was the German invasion force for Narvik.

Between 0430 and 0500 hours, 8 April 1940, the British lay minefields off the port at Narvik. During that afternoon, the Norwegian authorities in Oslo were drafting protests against the British action ready for transmission to London, however this was interrupted when the British Admiralty told the Norwegian Legation, in London, that German warships had been sighted and seemed bound for Narvik. Furthermore, Denmark had just been overrun.

That night, despite Norwegian resistance, German troops landed near Oslo and at Kristiansand, Stavanger, Bergen, Trondheim and Narvik. At Narvik, what appeared to have been empty German ore ships arriving during the previous week, turned out to be supply ships bringing in both supplies and ammunition for the German assault force. Within 48 hours, all of the main Norwegian ports were in German hands.[55] The trickery at Narvik was quite reminiscent of German behaviour at Danzig during the summer of 1939.

Prior to the German attack on Norway, the Allies had investigated the probable consequences of a successful German invasion and conquest of Scandinavia. It made troubling reading. The British Ministry for Food observed that if Denmark was overrun by Germany, Danish food products would become unavailable to the UK; it would pose a serious problem. The problem was that 20% of butter, bacon and eggs eaten in the UK came from Denmark. If this supply was to be halted, then these articles would have to come from Canada, Australia or New Zealand.[56] In a way, this was perhaps a small point but such a realisation caused the British government to ensure that the use of British agriculture was optimised, in order to ensure a sufficient, if rationed supply of food, was made available to the British public. This then allowed British shipping to concentrate on importing war materials, rather than on the transporting of basic foodstuffs across the seas. The possibility of the denial of Scandinavian food sources was something that helped to concentrate the minds of the British War Cabinet. The experience of the First World War had taught the lesson that wars can be won or lost at sea, especially if enemy submarines were able to sink enough ships bringing supplies to the UK.

On 13 March 1940, the 'Winter War' finished with a Soviet victory over the Finns, who had sued for peace. An armistice was agreed and Finland lost territory. The British once more began to ponder the consequences of the Soviet victory and its impact on Scandinavia, as a whole. Halifax told Chamberlain that, in his opinion, once Finland had reached peace terms with the Soviet Union, which were to be detrimental to Finnish interests, Sweden will possibly fall more and more under the influence of Germany.

Halifax wrote to Chamberlain 'we have already seen in recent negotiations; the extent to which fear of Germany has eaten into the Swedish mind. After the capitulation of Finland, Germany will try to create in Sweden a similar fear of Russia and by a judicious mixture of threats and offers of protection, may well be able before long to exert very effective pressure on her. If so, we ought not, I

55 Ibid., pp. 248-9.
56 TNA, PREM 1/419, Invasion of Norway, Ministry of Food, 24 February 1940.

think, to preclude that Sweden might well be compelled to stop supplying us with iron ore.' Halifax expressed a fear that the UK might have to import iron ore from Spain.[57]

Having to rely on Spain as a source for iron ore was a risky strategy for the UK, as Spain had only recently emerged from a three year bloody and bitter civil war, which had seen fascist rebels under General Francisco Franco emerge as the victors. Franco and his forces had received covert military aid from both Germany and Italy and were therefore more likely to be sympathetic and grateful towards these two countries. Furthermore, it was still difficult to predict which way Franco might jump regarding wartime alliances. He certainly owed Germany and Italy allegiance but eventually he opted for neutrality, albeit sympathetic towards Germany and Italy. However apart from an iron ore supply, there was another headache regarding Spain, as the British colony of Gibraltar lay under the Spanish mainland's southern coast. Gibraltar was vital to British operations in and around the Mediterranean, as it stood as a vital sentinel in the western Mediterranean; the narrow Gibraltar Straits ensured that everything passing by Gibraltar was more than likely to be seen by the British and intercepted if necessary. However, Gibraltar was for much of the war under threat of invasion, either by the Spanish or by Germans coming out from Spanish territory, but events elsewhere were about to alter priorities, as on *Westertag*, 9 April 1940, and the German invasion of Norway, the 'phony war' in the West was over and the Allies could finally see what was before them. It was not necessarily to their advantage.

57 Ibid., Halifax to Chamberlain, 16 March 1940.

4

Operation *Weserübung*

The German invasions of Denmark and Norway (Operation *Weserübung*) were considered to be the German riposte to British and French intentions to invade the same countries. From notes in General Halder's war diary, it can be seen that the Germans knew that something was afoot, as on 8 April 1940, Halder records that radio silence from England (UK) was an indication that the British Fleet was putting to sea.[1] The main difference was just how well executed the original German plan had been. British Service Chiefs had been looking at the possibilities of warfare in Scandinavia since the beginning of the war but seemed quite lukewarm in how to approach the entire enterprise, unless either the Soviet Union or Germany invaded Sweden or Norway first. For the Allies it was always going to be a game of catch up. The Germans had a different approach.

For some German planners the case of Norway was not illogical but a sound investment for the prosecution of the war against the British, especially it's shipping. Grand Admiral Raeder, C-in-C German Navy and Admiral Doenitz, since October 1939, had been considering plans for the invasion and occupation of Norway. In a memo to Hitler; Raeder considered that German naval bases should be made available to the north of Germany, by applying pressure in unity with the Soviet Union on Norway and thus obtaining bases in Norway. Raeder was influenced by what he considered to have been the limitations of the German Navy during the First World War, which had not obtained Norwegian bases and so were limited in how they could operate against the Royal Navy during that war. Raeder considered that Germany should obtain bases north of the relatively narrow strip of water between the Orkney Islands and the southern tip of Norway. The possession of such ports would have allowed German submarines and commerce raiders to operate against Allied shipping in that area. In a further note to Hitler, Raeder recommended that he should read a study made by Admiral Wolfgang Wegener published in 1928. In this work Wegener had asserted that it had been a mistake that Germany had not occupied Norway in World War One.[2]

Wegener's work was very similar to the thesis that Donitz was putting in front of Hitler. The thrust of their arguments was that Germany must occupy at least two bases north of the Shetland-Norway Straits. These bases must be ice-free all the year round, as well as having adequate railway links. Doenitz made his recommendations: Narvik in the far north and Trondheim. Initially Hitler had little interest in the advice of his two admirals, as it seemed that his only awareness of Norway was a half remembered notion of the need for an uninterrupted supply of iron ore from Sweden, transported to Germany via Norway. Hitler was preoccupied with his plans for the invasion of France but fate was about to take a hand, in the form of the Norwegian arch-traitor Vidkund Quisling.[3]

1 Charles Burdick & Hans-Adolf Jacobsen (eds.), *The Halder War Diary 1939-1942* (London: Greenhill Books, 1988), p. 114. Hereafter referred to as *Halder*.

2 Ewart Brookes, *Prologue to a War. The Navy's Part in the Narvik Campaign* (London: White Lion, 1977), pp.16-7.

3 Ibid., p. 17.

Quisling was a Norwegian politician and had been Defence Minister between 1931 and 1933, but by 1939 he was on the periphery of Norwegian politics as leader of *Nasjonal Samling*, the Norwegian Nazi Party. In the opinion of Quisling, there would be little opposition to German landings in Norway, furthermore, he would be able to execute a coup d'état as German forces landed in Norway. Hitler remained unconvinced of the need for an offensive in Norway until he learnt from Quisling that the British were contemplating mining Norwegian waters or perhaps taking some of form of unspecified action that would disrupt the supply of Swedish iron ore via Norway to Germany. It was only then that the German dictator became interested in his admirals' plans for an invasion of Norway.[4]

The German plans had been thorough; very thorough and involved the abuse of Norwegian hospitality and kindness a generation earlier. No doubt the Nazis merely saw the Norwegian decency as weakness. This aspect of the German invasion of Norway dates back to the pre-Nazi era when Germany faced great economic hardship after its defeat in 1918 and it was seen that German children growing up in the 1920s were suffering as a result of hunger and poverty. In response to the plight of German children, Norwegians were convinced by influential members of Norwegian society to foster German children until such a time when conditions improved in Germany. Norwegians opened up their homes to these children; fed them, clothed them and generally treated them as their own children, even down to teaching them how to ski and of course the children became fluent in Norwegian. These were the very children, who as adults, the Nazi state sought and they returned to Norway on 9 April 1940, as invaders.[5] Of course this was a gross betrayal of Norwegian charity and hospitality but the Nazi state seemed to have rooted out decency in society between 1933 and 1939, with its relentless messages of hatred especially amongst its youth. Within Norway itself Conservative political circles blamed the ruling Labour administration for its pacifist policies, which had deprived Norwegian defences of the resources that they needed to defend the country.[6] It had been a period of wishful thinking and not understanding that, in some cultures, decency is seen as weakness and ripe for exploitation.

German preparations for the invasion of Norway were exacting, not only were the ex-child recipients of Norwegian hospitality sought, but their commander Karl Dietl was an accomplished ski-jumper and had been responsible for the organisation of the 1936 Winter Olympics. His nickname was '*The Bull*,' owing to his bad temper and brutal ruthlessness. However a non-military detail of the invasion, yet a stroke of genius, was the showing of a film shortly before Germany invaded Norway. On 5 April 1940, the German Minister to Oslo showed a propaganda film, *Baptism of Fire*, concerning the invasion of Poland to leading Norwegians. The German diplomat insisted that the film was about peace but the images of Poland being attacked from the air and land suggested otherwise. The German intention was to intimidate those Norwegians present at the viewing, as the Germans knew of the coming invasion in four days time, while the Norwegian audience having recently seen the film would naturally worry about what might happen to their country and people if Norway resisted German aggression or co-operated with the Allies.[7] It was indeed a stroke of genius.

There were further preparations made by the Germans, as troops and supplies had been hidden in German merchant ships berthed in Norwegian ports. Furthermore, there was an element of

4 Ibid., p. 18.

5 Herman K. Lehmkuhl, *Hitler Attacks Norway* (London: The Royal Norwegian Government Information Service, 1943), pp. 8-9.

6 *FO Summaries 1*, Weekly Political Intelligence Summary No. 11 12 December 1939, pp. 7-8.

7 Lord Strabolgi (RN) J.M. Kenworthy, *Narvik and After. A Study of the Scandinavian Campaign* (London: Hutchinson, 1940), pp. 21-30.

treachery abroad in Norway as Norwegian Nazis worked closely with the Germans; not only Quisling but also more importantly, the commander of the Narvik Garrison, Colonel Sundlo.[8] As we shall see Narvik was surrendered to the Germans by the Norwegian garrison there, without a shot being fired. Interestingly Strabolgi asserted that Oslo was also captured, owing to the work of Norwegian traitors.[9] However overall, aside from the treachery which undermined Norwegian defensive measures, it was also clear that Norway really could not defend itself from either the Allies and certainly not from a German attack. British intelligence reports indicated that once Quisling had served the German purpose in the betrayal of his country, he was quickly dropped by them and relapsed 'into his accustomed insignificance.'[10] Quisling was an all round loser and finally paid with his life once Norway was liberated and he was tried for treachery, sentenced to death and executed by the Norwegian authorities.

The *Altmark* incident revealed several things about Norwegian neutrality. The most obvious was that the Norwegians were very afraid of Germany and more or less allowed German shipping to violate Norwegian neutrality at will. However, the interception of *Altmark* by HMS *Cossack,* which led to the finding and release of the British seamen being illegally detained on the German vessel, also reveals that the Norwegians could not or would not do anything about the illegal presence of HMS *Cossack* in Norwegian waters. This is to say nothing of how many Norwegian port officials and elements of the Norwegian Navy had turned a blind eye to the German detention of the British sailors, as *Altmark* had been 'searched' several times.[11]

The *Altmark* incident enraged Hitler, who told Raeder that Norway was unable to 'maintain its neutrality.' This led to the *Weserübung* planning being resurrected and given the highest priority.[12] No doubt Hitler was concerned about the possibility of a British invasion of Norway, which might well have put Swedish iron ore out of the reach of Germany, hence the need of which, he had previously considered to have been unimportant, becoming an unwanted priority to Germany. And of course it had been demonstrated to Hitler that the British were not afraid to act illegally if pushed to do so and therefore, the supplies of precious iron ore might be disrupted by the British using legal means or others. It was rapidly becoming irrelevant, while a figure such as Churchill governing the Royal Navy ensured that the British were willing to take risks to protect their interests and unsettle the Germans. Just prior to the German invasion of Denmark and Norway, the FO reported that shipments of Swedish iron ore to Germany was down by 879,000 tons for the first two months of the war, compared with peace time. It was reported that sailings from Narvik to Germany were significantly lower, which may have been the result of the *Altmark* incident, which had proved the contempt that Germany held for Norwegian neutrality. However the FO conceded that sailing was beginning to increase once more.[13]

The eventual successful German invasion of Denmark and Norway was partially due to British wishful thinking and some faulty intelligence work. Strabolgi even considered that British intelligence had been caught napping. There were two major concerns regarding the Baltic area and Scandinavia. The first was the gross misreading of Soviet attitudes in the Baltic republics, as the British considered that the Soviet Union was not interfering in the affairs of the Baltic states, but were indeed just controlling their strategic 'strong points' and had thus far kept to agreements

8 Lehmkuhl, op. cit. p. 19.
9 Strabolgi, op. cit. pp. 46-7.
10 *FO Summaries 1*, Weekly Political Intelligence Summary No.28, 16 April 1940, pp. 6-8.
11 Winston S. Churchill, *The Second World War. Volume 1, The Gathering Storm* (London: Cassell & Co, 1948), pp. 443-6.
12 Nick Hewitt (Imperial War Museum) 'Norway 1940: How Churchill and the Navy Saved Britain' BCMH 2010 Spring Conference, Lady Margaret Hall, Oxford, *Britain and Scandinavia in the Second World War.*
13 *FO Summaries 1*, Weekly Political Intelligence Summary No. 25, 19 March 1940, pp.7-8.

between the three republics and the Soviet Union. However the major problem was the perennial issue of civilians versus the military, or in this case the navy. The British Admiralty had, since 1936, known of Wegener's ideas for the German capture of Norway but British politicians had steadily ignored this piece of intelligence.[14] However, as we have seen, Hitler was not that interested in the plans of his naval commanders until 1940. Finally, after a small Cold War of fudge and intrigue, Germany revealed its hand invading Denmark and Norway on 9 April 1940. The German invasion did not go as well as might have been expected; Denmark was captured within hours but despite German planning and deceit, coupled with the treachery of Norwegian Nazis; the Norwegian campaign dragged on for two months and it was only outside events that prevented it from carrying on further.

The invasion date had only been recently agreed between Hitler and Raeder on 26 March, as the latest possible date for the invasion of Scandinavia.[15] As we have seen, the Germans had laid some very careful and detailed plans but they still almost managed to lose the element of surprise. First blood in the Scandinavian campaign went to the Poles, as the Polish submarine, *Orzeł*; one of 20 Allied submarines patrolling the Skagerrak on 8 April 1940, torpedoed the German transport ship, *Rio de Janerio*, off Lillesand. Survivors from the German ship were picked up by a Norwegian destroyer and by fishing boats. Those Germans rescued in German military uniform claimed that they were on their way to Norway to save it from Allied aggression. This entire incident, despite being reported in the evening press throughout Norway and picked up by the international press, seems to have bypassed the British government, who remained ignorant of the events of 8 April. This was a consequence of not all news being spread during the 'phony war,' the period of inactivity on the Western Front, being taken at face value.[16] The incident passed off well for Germany, no doubt to a combination of Norwegian naivety and at least some sympathy for Germany from the treacherous element found in the Norwegian population.

The British were certainly caught on the hop, as Denmark was invaded, captured and occupied within a few hours; the German forces, which arrived in Norway, were quite staggering. On 9 April 1940, the COS noted the strength of the German force arriving in Norway and the Norwegian response to it. At Oslo, four large German warships entered the Oslo Fjord and were fired on by Norwegian shore defences. At Stavanger, a single enemy warship approached the town at 0325 hours, 9 April. Five enemy warships approached Bergen at the same time. The British Consul at Bergen reported that the port there was occupied by Germans by 0600. At Trondheim, two enemy warships had appeared, while not a single vessel had arrived at Narvik. It was reported that HMS *Renown* had fought a short yet unspecified action off Narvik that same morning. The British Service Chiefs began to plot their response to the German invasion.

An inter-service and inter-Allied response was clearly very necessary. The Royal Navy was to position a fleet off Bergen by 1000 hours, 9 April, while HMS *Renown* and her destroyers were to remain off Narvik. The British Army began its preparations with the first echelon of Force 'Avonmouth' ready to sail to Norway by midday, 9 April. The remainder of this force was being prepared to sail from Clydeside, in approximately four days time. A battalion ready to sail to Trondheim was already aboard a liner, while four battalions detailed for Stavanger and Bergen were not in a position to sail as yet. Much of the problem lay with the crossing of the North Sea and its hostile weather. The RAF had two squadrons of bombers stationed within bombing range of Bergen and possibly Trondheim.

14 Strabolgi, op. cit. pp. 62-4, p. 115.
15 Klaus A. Maier et al, *Germany and the Second World War, Volume 2, Germany's Initial Conquests in Europe* (Oxford, Clarendon Press, 1991), hereafter referred to as *Germany 2*.p. 206.
16 Brookes, op. cit. p. 28; PISM, A.IV.11/54, 20 April 1940.

The Allies objectives on the first day of the Norwegian Campaign were to stop the Germans from consolidating their positions at Bergen and Trondheim, to destroy German shipping or ports that they were trying to use and to prevent the arrival of German reinforcements. The second major objective was to get to Narvik, as soon as possible. The Royal Navy was ordered to send submarines to Oslo and Stavanger, where they were to attack German warships and transports. The British surface fleet was to steam to Bergen and to Trondheim, if enough ships were available for the latter destination but the primary objective was Bergen, where British warships were to destroy German naval ships and transports, as well as preventing reinforcements arriving.

The RAF operating from Lossiemouth and Kinloss in Scotland using two squadrons of light bombers, were to attack German warships and transports at Bergen and if possible at Trondheim. It was underlined that the RAF was to liaise with the Royal Navy, in order to avoid accidently clashing in 'blue on blue' situations or firing upon each other. The military plan was for the leading battalion of 24th Infantry Brigade to proceed to Narvik and was to leave at once. Other forces from 24th Infantry Brigade and five battalions of infantry earmarked for Operation 'Stratford' were to be ready to land at Trondheim and Bergen, as soon as possible. The British government considered that, for political reasons, it was important that the Norwegian government appealed for help. Furthermore, it was urgent that the Norwegians were informed of the proposed British naval action and to co-operate closely with it, at both Bergen and Trondheim. The Norwegians were also requested to cut the Bergen-Oslo railway line.[17] The British might have been caught out by the timing and size of the German landings in Norway but they clearly had plans in place ready to come to the aid of that country.

British intelligence concerning the German invasion seems to have been quite sketchy but from German sources more detail can be found. Thirty-one U-boats had been assigned to Trondheim and Narvik and were at sea by 11 March. By 3 April, the first seven merchant ships of the so-called 'export group' *Ausfuhrstaffel* – the codeword assigned to the transport of equipment and stores to Norway, were at sea. This group was accompanied by the first eight tankers for the invading German force. On and after 6 April, ships of the Sea Transport Group *Seetransportstaffen,* which included 26 ships available for the transport of troops, as well as their equipment and supplies, followed *Ausfuhrstaffel.*

The German C-in-C of the Fleet heading towards Norway, Vice Admiral Lütjens, set sail from Schillig Reede in the Jade Estuary at 0515 hours, 7 April 1940. With him came the warships assigned for Narvik and Trondheim. These included the Heavy Cruiser *Admiral Hipper*, the battleships *Scharnhorst* and *Gneisenau,* accompanied by 14 Destroyers. With this fleet were German land forces ready to land in Norway – 2,000 troops were earmarked for Narvik and 1,700 for Trondheim. Despite bad weather, which might have masked the progress of the German fleet, it was sighted by a RAF reconnaissance patrol and later 35 bombers from Bomber Command attacked the German ships, but to no avail.

The C-in-C of the (British) Home Fleet, Admiral of the Fleet Sir Charles Forbes, only learnt of the German Fleet heading for Norway on the afternoon of 7 April; his ships did not put to sea until 2115 hours the same day. By the time the British warships had reached the waters off the Norwegian coast; the German ships had already passed by. However, heavy seas had caused the German destroyers to unintentionally scatter. At 0900 hours, 8 April, the German Destroyer, *Bernd von Arnim* sighted the British Destroyer, HMS *Glowworm,* which was sailing on an opposite course. HMS *Glowworm* belonged to the escort group of the Battle Cruiser HMS *Renown,* stationed off the Vest Fjord to cover the British mining of Norwegian waters, as part of Operation

17 TNA, CAB 79/3, COS (40) 70th Meeting, 9 April 1940.

'Wilfred.' HMS *Glowworm* had become separated from its main group, as it was searching for a crewmember who had fallen overboard. On sighting *Bernd von Arnim*, the British ship abandoned the search for the unfortunate seaman and began to pursue the German vessel. Owing to heavy seas, *Bernd von Arnim* could not shake off HMS *Glowworm*. Lütjens sent *Admiral Hipper* to intervene; HMS *Glowworm* was sunk as *Admiral Hipper* and HMS *Glowworm* rammed each other after engaging in a firefight.[18]

After the engagement with HMS *Glowworm*, *Admiral Hipper* with four destroyers left the main group and as it was still too early to put into Trondheim, set off on a westerly course. At 1530 hours, they were discovered by an RAF Flying Boat. The British incorrectly reported that they had seen a Battle Cruiser, two Cruisers and two Destroyers. In order to intercept the German force, Forbes altered his course at first to the north and then to the north-west but away from the Norwegian coast. HMS *Renown* was assigned to intercept any German force trying to enter Vest Fjord. For this purpose, the (British) Admiralty placed all the destroyers involved in the mining operations off Norway under the command of HMS *Renown*. However, this meant that on the morning of 9 April, HMS *Renown* and her Destroyers were about 50 nautical miles west of the Lofoten Islands, while the Vest Fjord went unprotected. Furthermore, the first Cruiser squadron with Allied troops aboard and waiting at Rosyth to sail and eventually land at Stavanger, was ordered to disembark the troops and join the Home Fleet at sea. Another force consisting of a Light Cruiser and six Destroyers assembled complete with land forces and ready to go to Norway was also ordered to disembark the troops, who were earmarked to land in Trondheim and Narvik, and set out to sea to join forces with the Home Fleet. This meant that the likelihood of British ground forces being landed in Norway had receded for the foreseeable future. During the evening of 8 April, Forbes broke off the search in the north-west and decided to intercept a strong German force reported on a northerly course in the Skagerrak. Forbes detached a Battle Cruiser and a Light Cruiser with Destroyers to support HMS *Renown*. At 2100 hours, Forbes set out on a southerly course and continued along it until morning. Early 9 April, Forbes and his force was still 80 nautical miles south-west of Bergen.

In contrast on 8 April at 2100 hours, the C-in-C of the German Fleet had reached the mouth of the Vest Fjord. From there he sent his Destroyers on to Narvik, while setting a north-westerly course with two battleships. However early morning 9 April, Lütjens and his Battleships encountered HMS *Renown*. At 0507 hours, HMS *Renown* opened fire on the German ships. After 18 minutes, the British hit *Gneisenau*; further hits by the Royal Navy wrecked the electrics of the German ship. Lütjens broke off from the engagement, as he thought that he was fighting two ships. This was due to the gun flashes from HMS *Renown*, which had confused the Germans. At 0528 hours, Lütjens set a north-easterly course but could not shake off the pursuing British until 0730 hours. Halder records this action as including both *Gneisenau* and *Scharnhorst*, west of the Lofoten Islands.[19]

On 9 April, German Destroyers commanded by Commander Bonte entered Ofot Fjord. At 0440 hours, two German Destroyers landed troops near Ramnes and Hamnes, with the intention of occupying Norwegian coastal artillery batteries, but instead discovered that they did not exist. Three Destroyers were detached to land troops in the Herjangs Fjord, while Bonte sailed for Narvik with three other ships. Shortly after 0600 hours, the leading Destroyer was stopped by a Norwegian Coastguard ship *Eidsvold*. The Germans tried to negotiate with the Captain of *Eidsvold* but the Norwegian was made of stern stuff and he attacked the German Destroyer. The Germans retaliated with several torpedoes, which hit *Eidsvold* breaking it up and sinking it. *Eidsvold's* sister ship *Norge* also fired on a German Destroyer, which was trying to tie up at the pier at Herjangs Fjord, but *Norge*

18 *Germany 2*, p. 208. See also http://www.youtube.com/watch?v=6aks1mcfQNA, 1 March 2009. Accessed 1 March 2016.

19 *Halder*, 9 April 1940, p. 114.

was also sunk by torpedoes. The German operation against Norway was being undertaken with little difficulty. The Norwegians taken by surprise, or in the case of Narvik betrayed, surrendered both Narvik and Elvegaarsoen to German land forces. Only a small group of about 250 Norwegian troops managed to withdraw to the east.[20]

Admiral Hipper on 8 April was steaming up and down the Norwegian coast with her escort of four destroyers. On 9 April at 0030 hours, this group set course for Trondheim and by 0400 hours had entered the fjord there. The German ships sailing at 25 knots had already passed searchlight stations, when the Norwegian battery at Hynes opened fire on the German craft. *Admiral Hipper* returned fire with both her rear turrets. The German shells threw up clouds of dust and smoke, which obscured the Norwegian view and ensured that they ceased firing. The Germans landed troops from their Destroyers to occupy the Norwegian artillery positions, while *Admiral Hipper* and one of her Destroyers anchored at the harbour at 0525 hours. The populace in the city did not resist the landing Germans, but not all of the artillery positions were captured by the Germans. Furthermore, the nearby airfield at Værnes remained in Norwegian hands.

The German force sent to Bergen was impressive and included the Light Cruisers *Köln* and *Königsberg*, the gunnery training ship *Bremse*, two torpedo boats, five motor torpedo boats and a single supply ship. There were also 1,900 troops ready to land. At 0200 hours 9 April, the German ships entered Kors Fjord; they had been seen by a number of Norwegian Coastguard vessels but ignored. Meanwhile German troops were landed at By Fjord, in anticipation of occupying the Kvaven battery at 0430 hours. Time was running out for the Germans probably in relation to the short nights of northern Norway as summer approached; the German ships entered the fjord and were immediately attacked by coastal defence batteries at 0515 hours. *Königsberg* was hit three times and *Bremse* twice. *Köln,* once she had anchored at Bergen, was fired on by the Norwegian battery at Sandviken. The Germans called in an aerial strike and by 0935 had taken both Norwegian batteries. Bergen itself was captured with no serious resistance.

Events at Stavanger were just as dramatic. Following an aerial attack against the town, the Germans were able to occupy Stavanger using a company of paratroops and two battalions of infantry. A steamer from *Ausfuhrstaffel,* which had been assigned to Stavanger, was sunk by a Norwegian torpedo-boat but three ships from *Seetransportstaffel* (Sea Transport Group) with troop reinforcements arrived in time to save German blushes. Furthermore, the Sola airfield was captured and occupied by the invading Germans. The Norwegian telegraph at Egersund was also captured, without any resistance by 150 Germans troops landed from four minesweepers.

German operations against Kristiansand were carried out using the Light Cruiser *Karlsruhe,* accompanied by three torpedo boats, seven motor boats and their supply ships carrying 1,100 troops. However it took three attempts before the German offensive succeeded. The German force reached the entrance at Kristiansand at 0345 hours in thick fog, but could not get into the harbour until 0600 hours when visibility improved. The Norwegians sounded the alarm and Coastal batteries opened fire on the German ships, causing them to withdraw under a smoke screen. The second attempt included a German aerial attack and again was repulsed by the Norwegians. Following a heavier aerial attack, Norwegian resistance ceased and the German ships entered the fjord after 1100 hours. During the afternoon three ships of the Sea Transport Group reached the harbour at Kristiansand.

The Norwegian capital, Oslo, was assaulted by the Heavy Cruiser, *Blücher*, the Pocket Battleship, *Lützow*, the Light Cruiser, *Emden*, three torpedo boats, eight R-boats (Motor Minesweepers) and two armed whaling ships carrying 2,000 troops. *Blücher* had only recently completed sea trials as

20 *Germany 2*, p. 208.

late as 30 March and originally was designated to take part in the Norwegian offensive. Raeder had severe reservations about deploying *Blücher* but decided to use her in order to leave *Lützow* free for a strategic diversion. The German Naval War Staff had planned to use *Lützow* as the first of two planned merchant raiders, which simultaneously with the invasion of Norway, was to start a new phase of the war against British supply shipments coming across the Atlantic Ocean. However, the Wehrmacht High command ordered that *Lützow* was to be used in Operation *Weserübung*. It is interesting to note that clearly the Wehrmacht had seniority to the German Navy. The original intention had been that *Lützow* was to be assigned as one of the craft for the Trondheim Group and then have her sail into the Atlantic Ocean, after landing troops at Trondheim. However the plan was not realised, as damage was discovered in the ship's engines. This meant that shipyard repairs were necessary before any such long operation, such as an Atlantic patrol; as a consequence *Lützow* was assigned to the operation against Oslo.

On 8 April, slightly before midnight the Oslo force left Kiel and sailed towards the Norwegian capital. A Norwegian patrol boat was met and sunk. Another Norwegian patrol vessel and shore batteries on the islands of Bolärne and Rauøy were passed. The worsening visibility prevented the Norwegians from firing no more than a few shots. German troops landed and occupied the shore batteries, as well as the naval base of Horten, which was largely taken over by torpedo boats and R-boats. Rear-Admiral Kummetz, C-in-C of the force deployed to capture Oslo, had thought that it might be possible to pass through the Drøbak Narrows and the Oskarsborg Fortress without any real resistance: he was wrong. At 0520 hours, the batteries of the Oskarsborg Fortress using 150mm and 280mm guns opened fire on the lead ship, *Blücher*. The German ship was immediately hit and suffered serious damage. A few minutes later, *Blücher* was struck by two torpedoes; these knocked out the German vessel's engines. At 0723 hours, *Blücher* sank with the loss of over 1,000 lives. *Lützow* was also hit and withdrew with other ships. Troops were landed to capture the Drøbak Narrows, while air support was requested. By the end of the morning, 10 April, the fortifications at the Drøbak Narrows had been captured by the Germans, while the German Fleet reached Oslo at 1145 hours. Air landings at Oslo had failed to go to plan, owing to ground fog. Even so at 0838 hours, in spite of spirited Norwegian defences, German transports began to land at Fornebu airfield. By evening, a total of eight companies of German infantry had been flown in to occupy Oslo.

The most serious problem, which faced the German invasion of Norway, had been trying to launch a surprise attack across waters largely controlled by the Royal Navy and then afterwards, try to re-cross the same seas back to Germany. The original plan had been that the German fleet, which sailed to Norway, was to return to Germany with all ships including those detached and sent to Narvik and Trondheim. In the event only *Admiral Hipper* was able to return with two battleships entering the Jade Estuary at 2000 hours, 13 April 1940. It should be understood that the German Navy suffered catastrophic losses at Norway, or more specifically at Narvik. Hewitt observes that the Germans spread their fleet in small groups with warships in 'penny packets,' which was obviously a dangerous tactic for an inferior naval power and so paid the price, once up against the power of the Royal Navy.[21]

Just after the German attack at Narvik, ten German Destroyers were trying to refuel but instead of two tankers being available there was only one. Naturally, this slowed down the refuelling process and made it impossible for the German fleet to put to sea on the evening 9 April. The following morning 10 April, refuelling was still underway at Narvik. There were five German Destroyers in the harbour, of which two were being refuelled, while five more Destroyers were tucked away in side fjords. There were four U-boats on station guarding the Destroyers, but somehow they failed

21 Hewitt.

to notice the entry of five British Destroyers, which had probably slipped into Narvik under the cover of heavy snow. The British ships attacked the Germans at 0530 hours, 10 April and sank two German Destroyers.

When the Royal Navy attempted to withdraw from Narvik; their ships were attacked by the five German Destroyers that had been in the side fjords. The British lost two ships, while a third was badly damaged. It was not all lose though to the British because as they withdrew, they still managed to sink the only freighter from *Ausfuhrstaffel* that had got through to Narvik. The Germans discovered that they were bottled up at Narvik. The senior officer of 4th Destroyer Flotilla was killed trying to break out of Narvik, using two seaworthy Destroyers on the night 10–11 April, as he had been ordered to do. A further attempt to get away from Narvik that night was abandoned, as the Germans realised that the Royal Navy was waiting for them to come out to sea. The next day, 12 April, four German Destroyers were ready to sail but a further attempt to break out was considered to be futile. The British returned to the offensive at noon 13 April, as the Battleship HMS *Warspite* with nine Destroyers entered the fjord at Narvik and sailed into the harbour. There they 'annihilated the German Destroyers,' or at least those which did not scupper themselves after running out of ammunition. It was a disastrous day for the Germans.

There were other attempts by German ships to make the run back to Germany and to safety. Some were successful; others less so. *Admiral Hipper* left Trondheim during the evening of 10 April. The Commander of the Scouting Forces left *Königsberg* and *Bremse* behind, as they were both damaged and put to sea with *Köln,* accompanied with a few torpedo boats during the evening 9 April. To avoid Allied air attacks, the German ships spent the next day in a narrow fjord, before streaking across the seas to Germany and reached Wilhelmshaven at 1700 hours, 11 April. *Königsberg* was fated, as she was hit by bombs twice on the morning 10 April and sank before noon.

Karlsruhe left Kristiansand with three torpedo boats during the evening 9 April. At 2000 hours, the German ship was attacked by a British submarine, but suffered only a single torpedo strike. Even so it was a deadly hit; *Karlsruhe* could not be saved and was finally sunk by a torpedo boat. *Lützow,* whilst returning to Kiel, was torpedoed off Skagen on 11 April, but did not sink. Despite losing her rudder and both propellers, the vessel remained afloat and was towed back into harbour. The damage inflicted on *Lützow* ensured that she was not going to be operating against Allied shipping in the Atlantic anytime soon. There were further German losses. Of the seven ships that had sailed as part of *Ausfuhrstaffel*; six were lost. Of the eight tankers sent to Norway; three were lost at Trondheim and one was lost at Narvik. All of the six ships, which made up *Seetransportstaffen* were lost.[22] Halder writes of *Lützow* (*Luetzow*) as being lost. He also notes that the Norwegian government had fled Oslo to Hamar and that paratroops had been sent out to intercept it.[23] The Norwegian defence of Oslo, as limited as it was, ensured that the Norwegian government and King Haakon could escape the capital before the arrival of the Germans. Halder's diary reveals that German intentions for Norway were not all going to plan; a major threat was British submarines in the Skagerrak and Kattegat, which were disrupting German supplies and reinforcements to Norway, which was becoming increasingly reliant on air supply, until such a time that the British submarine threat was eliminated. It is interesting to note that all German Army signal equipment allocated for the Norwegian Campaign had been lost on sunken transports. This meant that telephone communications had to be routed via Sweden.[24]

22 *Germany 2*, p. 211.
23 *Halder*, 9 April 1940, p. 116.
24 Ibid., 11 April 1940, pp. 116-7.

5

The Allied Response

On 9 April 1940, as the Germans attacked Denmark and Norway, the British governments requested the French government to send mountain troops to Norway, to aid British troops due to land in Norway. The British were specific in their request asking for the crack French mountain regiment, *Chasseurs Alpins* to go to Norway. The British may have been sending eight battalions of infantry but few had any experience or training in mountain warfare, let alone the near polar conditions of northern Norway.

Cecil Aspinall-Oglander in his biography of Admiral of the Fleet Lord Keyes, observed that the original plan to respond to the German invasion was a threefold attack to recapture Trondheim and the occupation of the airfield there which, if captured, would have been invaluable as an extremely convenient base for future Allied operations. There were to be subsidiary landings at the two fishing villages of Namsos (80 miles north of Trondheim) and Andalsnes (150 miles to the south), while battleships of the Home Fleet would attack the outer defences of Trondheim Fjord. After this had been silenced, Cruisers and Destroyers escorting troop escorts would make their way up the 30 mile long fjord, sink two German Destroyers known to be there and then cover the landing of land forces assigned to capture the town and occupy the airfield adjacent to the town and at the time of planning, still occupied by the Norwegian Army.[1] The nature of the targets in Norway should be recognised, as inhabited areas were often tiny compared with the gigantic surrounding natural landscape and features. This is amplified by the enormity of the risks and stakes being undertaken, by both Allied and German force, with the Norwegian caught in the middle of these operations, which often were preceded by an Allied Naval barrage, which often wrecked Norwegian fishing villages and towns if targeted. Churchill in his account of the Second World War, considered that Trondheim was the key to any 'considerable operations in Central Norway.' At Trondheim was a safe harbour with the facilities upon which an army of 50,000 men could be built and based, as well as the nearby airfield, from which several fighter squadrons could operate. Furthermore, there was a direct railway link with Sweden which, in Churchill's opinion, greatly improved the chances of Swedish intervention or a degree of mutual aid, if Sweden was to be attacked (whether by Germany or the Soviet Union, Churchill does not make clear) but the suggestion is Germany. The early days of the Norwegian Campaign were those of optimism, as Churchill discusses how from Trondheim any Germany advance northwards from Oslo could be held, while Narvik was seen as an almost leisurely exercise to come. In the early days it would seem that establishing Allied airpower would be relatively easy but Churchill was correct in asserting that the Allies had control of the seas.[2]

On the first day of the German invasion, it was considered that the Germans had not landed so many troops and the Allies tried initially to get as many men as possible to Norway, before the enemy could land reinforcements. The Allies projected the landing of 20,000 allied troops, which reflected

1 Cecil Aspinall-Oglander, *Roger Keyes* (London: The Hogarth Press, 1951), pp.344-5.
2 Winston S. Churchill, *The Second World War. Volume 1: The Gathering Storm* (London: Cassell & Co, 1948), p. 489.

the eight British battalions and the French mountain troops. Where this force was to be landed was a matter of opinion. The French government considered that Narvik should be the primary landing site; the British government considered that from their point of view, the most important position to be taken should be Bergen, while British Service Chiefs asserted that from their point of view, the main military objective should be Trondheim and that it should be recaptured, as a matter of urgency. The Admiralty arranged for Destroyers to make a reconnaissance tour of first Bergen and then Trondheim and finally Narvik. Eventually it was agreed that the recapture of both Trondheim and Bergen were priorities and were militarily more significant than Narvik.[3]

John Colville in his diary noted on 9 April 1940, that the Germans in seizing the Norwegian ports had acheived a great success and had snatched the initiative from the British, despite that in his opinion the British had '...started the whole business.' However Colville also observed that Churchill was now jubilant that the Germans had shown their hand and made it possible for the Allies to operate in Scandinavia freely. Churchill also considered that the German fleet, even if they had evaded the Royal Navy watch on Norway, owing to bad weather; the German fleet was the weak link in the German chain and that if they tried to leave Norway they would be destroyed by the Royal Navy. This would leave the German garrison in Norway abandoned and exposed to the coming Allied offensive.[4]

The Allied operation in Norway began to take shape and as with many military operations had to change shape and purpose, as events reinvented and reformed the original operation. This can be seen when a report, made after the Norwegian operation, observed that the operation fell into two halves: operations against Narvik and those conducted from the landings made at Namsos and at Aandalsnese. The objective of the first part of the operation was the capture of Narvik and the second half was the taking of Trondheim, using a pincer movement from the south and the north. Detail was supplied on the nature of Narvik. The most important thing about Narvik was that it was ice free and from there it was possible for the supply of iron ore to Germany to continue, even throughout the winter. Narvik was extremely important to both the Allies as well as the Germans and had fallen easily into German hands owing to treachery. The original German force at Narvik numbered about 1,500 troops and this garrison was constantly being reinforced by air and supported by the Luftwaffe. The Germans were also able to entrench themselves in depth in Narvik itself, as well as its surrounding area. Despite the destruction of the German fleet at Narvik, the enemy was still able to maintain its position there. However, once more by examining Halder's diary, it can be seen that the German occupation of Narvik was always slight, with the situation being exasperated by the Royal Navy's two attacks on German warships in the fjord at Narvik. Between 14 and 15 April, German senior staff discussed the German situation at Narvik and it was decided to withdraw from the town area with mountain troops being moved back to the surrounding mountains, but there was no clear decision made to abandon the entire area. Later on 23 April, it was decided by General Keitel that only mountain troops were suited for fighting north of Oslo and Hitler ordered 2nd Mountain Division to be moved from Germany, through Oslo to northern Norway.[5]

By 10 April 1940, the British government had international law on its side and could intervene in Scandinavia. The importance of Narvik was recognised on 9 April and by 11 April, the first convoy of British troops was at sea heading towards Norway. On 13 April, British intervention in Norway was expanding. The War Cabinet considered using part of the British force against Trondheim; Churchill expanded this operation into Operation 'Hammer,' an amphibious assault

3 TNA, CAB 79/3, (COS) 71st Meeting, 9 April 1940.
4 John Colville (Colville Papers) 9 April 1940; War Cabinet: minutes (Cabinet papers, 65/6) 9 April 1940, cited in *Churchill 1*, pp. 991-2.
5 *Halder*, 14 April 1940; 15 April 1940, pp. 120-1; 23 April 1940, pp. 123-4.

on Trondheim, supported by flanking operations at Namsos and Andalsnes. These landings took place on 14 April and 17 April, but Admiral Pound managed to obtain a cancellation of a direct attack on Trondheim, owing to German reinforcements at Trondheim.[6] The commander of British land forces, Major-General Mackesy, also proved to be disappointing to those politicians sitting comfortably back in Whitehall, as he refused to undertake any improvised landings and insisted that the operation against Narvik should be carried out systematically and methodically.[7]

On 15 April 1940, a small force of regular British troops landed north of Narvik. These were later reinforced by two Polish battalions, a number of *Chasseur Alpins* and members of the French Foreign Legion (FFL), as well as members of the 6th Norwegian Infantry Division, commanded by General Fleischer. It was noted that this combined Allied force consisted of good troops and were prepared for the terrain which lay ahead of them (this was not to be exactly true) but were let down by the lack of AAA and artillery supplies. It was also observed that Allied air support was almost non-existent until the assault on Narvik began and a squadron of Gladiators 'did magnificent work against overwhelming odds.' In addition to the area around Narvik, the Germans also held parts of the shore of the Gratangs Fjord and the line from Elvenes Bjerkvik on the northerly point of the Ofoten Fjord opposite Narvik. The enemy held territory ran roughly north and south and dominated all the approaches from the West and backed onto rocky and mountainous terrain, which extended 25–30 miles to the Swedish frontier.[8] It should be noted that the Gladiators deployed were obsolete biplanes and the Germans should have made short work of them, but failed to do so. The initial response was poorly prepared, as witnessed by Sydney Barthorpe aged 19, who served with the Sherwood Foresters in the Norwegian Campaign, before his capture by the enemy in late April 1940. Barthorpe recalled that he and his comrades once in Norway were conveyed in open topped lorries, which of course were appalling given the extreme temperatures met in Norway. It is a wonder than none of them froze to death whilst in transit, while there were no decent maps only Shell tourist maps and a regular shortage of ammunition. The greatest enemy according to young Barthorpe was the conditions that were met with, such as the cold, snow, ice and the overall geography of Norway but he did not overlook the danger that German ski-patrols posed or the use of Storch spotter planes, with which the enemy sought out Allied positions and moves. Barthorpe also remembered that British rations were supplemented by churns of milk left out by Norwegian farmers, who unable to sell their milk at markets owing to the disruption of war, left the filled churns out for troops to use and thus avoid waste. Barthorpe was to spend five years as a prisoner of war and just about survived his ordeal.[9]

The conditions found in Norway were more or less unknown to the majority of Allied troops landing there and this was explained in a letter from Major-General P.J. Mackesy, the Commander of 'Rupertforce,' as the Allied Expedition to Norway was known, to the Permanent Under Secretary of State to the War Office. Even though it was spring in much of Europe, Mackesy remarked on the arctic conditions still found in Norway during April. Mackesy wrote that much of the terrain was covered in snow up to four feet in depth and even at sea level the snow was several feet deep. To add to this hardship, blizzards frequently blew up; there were constant heavy snow storms, bitter winds and very low night temperature. The conditions were so extreme that until the middle of May, even the *Chasseurs Alpins* suffered from snow blindness. Furthermore, there was a dearth of suitable equipment, as Allied troops lacked both skis and snowshoes; as a result it was difficult for them to move over such a hostile terrain. The bitterest enemy according to Mackesy was the

6 *German 2*, p. 213.
7 Ibid.
8 TNA, CAB 44/271, The Campaign in Norway, April, May, June 1940.
9 Barthorpe, Sydney, Liddle Collection 1939-45, Army, Brotherton Library, University of Leeds, Special Collections.

weather and to seek shelter from it was all important. After making a personal reconnaissance of the area, Mackesy was convinced that the topography favoured defence and that any opposed landing was quite out of the question. This was due to a combination of factors: not only snow and the inclement Norwegian winter weather in general, but also the lack of proper equipment necessary for a landing; there were no landing craft or no tanks, artillery support was inadequate while there was no AAA or air co-ordination.

Mackesy reported that the first objectives were to secure the Oljord and Ankenes peninsulas to the north and south respectively of Narvik. Both of these positions were held by the enemy, but even so optimistically, it was hoped that observed artillery fire would begin to degenerate the German positions there. In pursuit of the success of the operation 1st Battalion Irish Guards (IG) moved to the Bogen area and later 2nd Battalion South Wales Borderers (SWB) moved to Ballangen. A detachment of 1st Battalion Scots Guards (SG), under the command of Major L. Graham, MC, which had landed in the Sag Fjord area on 14 April, moved forward to co-operate with 6th Norwegian Infantry Division in the Forsbakken area. However, the problem with these land operations was that the roads were covered with snow between two and four feet in depth. Without skis it was impossible for land forces to move cross-country. Meanwhile, an Allied counter offensive began to build up. On 20 April, Admiral of the Fleet, the Earl of Cork and Orrery, was appointed the sole commander of Allied operations. Four days later the Royal Navy bombarded Narvik while Allied forces stood by to accept the German surrender of the town. This was to prove to be disappointing, as nothing of that nature happened at all.[10] It has to be admitted that the Allies were unlucky with the weather, as on 19 April a 'real Arctic blizzard' blew into northern Norway and the snow fell for a week. This allowed the Germans to consolidate their positions while the Allies were virtually pinned.[11]

This was the first Allied attempt to evict the Germans from their illegal possession of Norway and clearly the Allies were not adequately prepared on land to take on the Germans in Norway. 5th Battalion Scots Guards (SG) had been training a special unit in Scotland for winter and mountain warfare. Some of the members of 5th SG included some of those who had been on the latest Mount Everest expedition, as well as officers from the Indian Army, who had experience of mountain warfare. There were further recruits from across the Brigade of Guards, including 150 officers with skiing experience. The original intention of this force was that it was to be used in Finland but following the Finnish collapse in March 1940, the unit was disbanded.[12] The Indian Army officers, were of course British officers serving in the British Army in India and had no doubt served on the infamous North-West Frontier, which denoted the British India border region with Afghanistan, where hostile tribes occasionally tried to harm British interests in the area and so the British from time to time were forced to deal with such incursions in the mountainous region, which was the North-West Frontier.

General Claude Auchinleck, who was later to command Allied operations in Norway, also made reference to the weather found in Norway that spring. On 2 May 1940, Auchinleck wrote of the climatic conditions, that generally the snow at Narvik melted during the first week of April but that year, 1940, winter did not finish until mid-May. Regarding daylight hours, he noted that during the winter, daylight was short in duration but increased as spring and summer advanced. Auchinleck concluded that operations in Norway, especially in its far north, were only possible between April and October and any other time quite impossible. Furthermore special clothing was

10 TNA, FO 371/56341 1946 Norway, File No. 11144, Letter from Major-General P.J. Mackesy, Commander of 'Rupertforce' to Permanent Under Secretary of State, The War Office, 15 May 1940.

11 Brookes, op. cit. p. 142.

12 Alexander Greenwood, *Field Marshal Auchinleck* (Witton le Wear: The Pentland Press, 1992), pp. 73-4.

necessary for arctic operations.[13] Overall Auchinleck doubted the chances of a success at Narvik, unless things improved. The weather was a huge concern as it favoured the enemy, who could hunker down at Narvik while the Allies would be vulnerable to enemy ski attacks during winter time, as the Soviets had suffered at the hands of Finnish ski troops in the recent war in Finland. The terrain around the locality of Narvik was also hostile to modern motor transport, which according to Auchinleck would have been confined to mountain tracks even between April and October, hence the fear of ski troops and the necessity of the Allies to get up to speed with such troops, in order to counter enemy ski troops.[14]

When he gave his first impressions of Narvik, Auchinleck was clearly thinking of a longer term operation, as he made the point that even if Narvik was recaptured by 1 June 1940, it would be of little use until 1 December 1940.[15] The port had to be cleared of the wrecks of German warships destroyed during naval engagements at Narvik and were blocking the harbour. Auchinleck also noted that 'to hold Narvik by land would require a maximum number of troops between April and October. It is impossible to give a more accurate estimate as this depends on the season.' In his provisional assessment of the situation at Narvik, Auchinleck was not encouraging but sought to be realistic, as well as giving his opinion of how Narvik should be used. Auchinleck saw Narvik as being a defended naval anchorage, that could be used for naval operations in Norwegian waters. The objective of such operations would be to counter German naval assaults along the Norwegian coast, which might originate from bases such as Trondheim and Namsos. Furthermore, Auchinleck considered that Narvik could be used to prevent further raids at Bodo and Mosjoen. But first it would have to be recaptured and the harbour cleared.

Auchinleck observed that any attempt to capture the ore areas at Kiruna (100 miles away) or Gallivare (160 miles distant), would require the necessity of establishing ground bases and air bases at Lulea and Bodo and unless the Allies could establish overwhelming air cover, this was not practical. Even if Sweden did provide military assistance to the Allies, it would not have been entirely useful in the immediate future. It occurred to Auchinleck that it would be best to try to establish a base in anticipation of future operations, perhaps in Sweden or at least towards the east of Narvik and perhaps help the Swedes, should any 'opportunity occur.' In conclusion Auchinleck added that, at the time of his writing this report, the Germans were actually destroying Narvik and so he suggested that perhaps an alternative position might be found for future operations in Norway, as he was not convinced that Narvik was ideal.[16]

Despite Auchinleck's gloomy assessment of the situation at Narvik and the questioning of its value, even if it was recaptured, the Allies continued to press ahead with their ambition to retake it. With Allied troops and their Norwegian counterparts already on the ground in unoccupied northern Norway; the Allies began to make their assessment of the situation. A reconnaissance party of RAF and Royal Engineers (RE) left for Narvik on 30 April 1940. Another reconnaissance party from Namsos was ordered to move with a military detachment to Mosjoen and look to possible sites suitable for aircraft in that area. Heroy Island was of particular interest at the time of this venture. There was also an officers' reconnaissance mission, once more for the purpose of seeking suitable sites for airfields. These men were to fly to Mo and Bodo, by flying boat on either 2 or 3 May 1940.[17]

13 The Auchinleck Papers, GB 133 AUC, John Rylands Library, Special Collections, University of Manchester, AUC/3, May 1-16 1940, Items 3-25, Climatic Conditions, 2 May 1940.
14 Ibid.
15 Ibid.
16 Ibid.
17 TNA, CAB 79/4, COS (40) 105th Meeting, 1 May 1940.

The matter of air support was becoming very important to any Allied offensive in the frozen wastes of northern Norway, as it was not easy to move across its terrain and of course every land manoeuvre had to be supported from the air, as aircraft would spot any movement and it would be aircraft that would attack any such moves first. Not only were aircraft necessary to the Allied expedition to Norway but the right sort of aircraft was also important. Even though the Gloster Gladiator bi-plane was a sterling aircraft, it was somewhat outdated by the German machines and what was really needed in Norway was the Hawker Hurricane fighter plane. This was a much more modern aircraft, heavily armed and heavily armoured. It was to become the workhorse of the Battle of Britain, even if the much more glamorous Spitfire caught the imagination of the British general public in 1940 and still does over 75 years later. In the spring of 1940, as an Allied operation in northern Norway began to explore preparations for air defences, this did include the possibility of deploying Hurricanes from 46th and 501st Fighter Squadrons RAF. However this was dependent on finding a suitable airfield for them to operate from. Reconnaissance parties also ready discussed, were in Norway seeking areas suitable to be built up as airfields, as well as trying to establish a radar station (RDF) station. Some of these parties were already at Scapa ready to go to Bodo and the Loften Islands. The British groups, once in Norway, were to be joined by Norwegian Air Force officers, as they were more familiar with the terrain and localities under investigation.

Air Chief Marshall Sir Cyril Newall was not certain if Hurricanes could be used from the Bodo airfield. All the same both Gladiator and Hurricane ground crews were trained in readiness for operations in Norway, ensuring that they and the aircraft, which they were to serve, were to be able to go immediately, once a suitable airfield had been identified as suitable for operational purposes. Meanwhile, all the paraphernalia such as spare equipment, ammunition and fuel was already en route for Norway.[18] The following day further detail was added to the forthcoming operations, with the discussion of sufficient air cover for Narvik being uppermost in the COS collective mind, as arrangements were being made to embark the forces necessary for the operations. HQ of 'X' Force was reported as being at No 4 Base Area, while No 10 Servicing Flight was at Rosyth, waiting to embark on the Polish ship *Chroby*, which was due to sail to Narvik on 7 May.[19]

The main objective of Operation 'Rupert' was to secure and maintain a base in northern Norway, from which the Allies could deny the Germans their valuable iron ore supplies via Narvik; interfere as far as possible with the supply of iron ore to the Germans from Lulea and preserve a part of Norway, as a seat of government for the King of Norway and the Norwegian people. It was soon realised that this was going to be difficult for two reasons, even if tacit Norwegian co-operation was available and this was described as being a great help; problems remained. The main problem was linked to observation, as the Germans maintained continuous observation by air over the sea and along the Norwegian coast; the continuous summer daylight made it very difficult for the Allies to conceal vessels which carried raiding parties.[20] Given that this report was dated 4 May, it should be realised that the summer daylight was yet to peak and that by late May and into June within the Norwegian Arctic, daylight would be almost 24 hours a day with nothing that suggested nightfall. Obviously, as the British service chiefs had recognised there was no chance of operating under the cover of darkness – there wasn't any to be had.

The question of sufficient air cover was most important if Allied operations could not be concealed from German observation and so the search for suitable air bases continued. There was discussion of using Bardufoss and Skaanland but it was also realised that such bases would not be ready for several weeks; that was between two to five weeks. The main problem was that the main

18 TNA, CAB 79/4, COS (40) 108th Meeting, 3 May 1940.
19 TNA, CAB 79/4, COS (40) 110th Meeting, 4 May 1940.
20 Ibid.

annual thaw had not yet set in, while there was also a need to recruit labourers and machinery, such as graders and tractors necessary to improve and enlarge the area, in preparation to receive fighter aircraft. While decisions about Allied air cover for Norway were being debated in the UK, the Germans continued to reinforce their garrison in the Narvik area, using seaplanes to transport troops. The British COS needed to respond to this and so discussed the use of fighter planes fitted with floats rather than wheels. It was learnt that such aircraft would not be available until 18 May, but there was a chance that naval aircraft from the Fleet Air Arm (FAA) could be used to prevent German reinforcements from arriving.

The plans for an Allied offensive with necessary air cover were beginning to take shape, as it was asserted that the aircraft carrier HMS *Ark Royal* was to arrive at the theatre of operations on 6 May, which would be a great boost for morale. Furthermore, HMS *Glorious* and HMS *Furious* were being made ready to take RAF Gladiators and Hurricane fighters to Narvik. In the meanwhile, the plan was that FAA fighters were to be used, until the above craft were operational. The main thought was the preparation of the airfields in Norway and that the necessary machinery was sent to Norway to get the airfields ready. Manpower was not seen as a problem as local Norwegians could be employed as labourers and amazingly, there was some thought given that 'possibly the battalions of Poles might be employed.'[21] This rather suggested that the British Service Chiefs did not consider Polish soldiers to be anything other than labourers or at best pioneers. It would seem that this was not made public, as there was no complaint from the perpetually thin skinned Polish government-in-Exile or from any Polish quarter at all; there surely would have been if they had heard the British suggestion. It does however rather reflect just how the Allies really viewed their Allies, especially the French, who prior to their own defeat and loss of country considered the Poles not to be very good soldiers and of little value militarily.

Difficulties at Narvik were best expressed in a telegram to the Flag Officer at Narvik sent on 5 May. It ran thus: 'Following is policy for operations south of Narvik. It is not possible to maintain large forces in face of enemy's air superiority at any place well in advance of an established fighter aerodrome and even adequate air cover protection would require forward landing facilities. Only place south of Narvik at which it may prove possible to establish forward landing ground is BODO. Hence at MO and MOSJOEN only small bodies can be maintained. Role of such bodies is to carry out extensive demolitions on road leading North from Namsos, which is already in bad state, and reported impassable for wheeled vehicles, and to delay advances of the enemy as long as possible and prevent landings from sea and by parachute. It is however highly likely that Bodo should be included in the forward defences of Narvik if reconnaissance shows that a fighter forward landing ground can be developed in the area, and provided that the provision of necessary AAA defences and maintenance of necessary forces does not prove too expensive and drain our resources. In the meanwhile, reconnaissance report from Bodo is awaited. Company of Scots Guards, should not, repeat not be withdrawn until further orders. Intended that all military forces in Northern Norway shall eventually come under the command of General Officer Commanding troops in Narvik, at a time to be decided by War Office.'[22]

That was the view of the British Admiralty working 1,000 miles from Narvik. The Flag Officer at Narvik quickly sent his response, observing that there were not enough assault landing craft (ALC) and that it was anticipated that local boats might be used for any projected amphibious assault. A further problem was daylight – there was too much of it – while the frozen rocky terrain made digging an impossibility. This meant that Allied troops landing on hostile terrain would be

21 TNA, CAB 79/4 COS (40) 111th Meeting, 5 May 1940.
22 Ibid., Telegram to F.O. I/C Narvik from Admiralty, 5 May 1940.

Men from the Podhalian Brigade training France, early 1940.

General Sikorski addressing the Podhalian Brigade in France, shortly before their departure for Norway.

Embarkation for Norway from Brest, late April 1940.

Members of the brigade aboard the convoy taking them to Norway, late April 1940.

Members of the brigade photographed as the convoy moves up the Balangen Fjord.

Troops from the Podhalian Brigade shortly after landing at Harstadt, in the Lofoten Islands.

The nature of the rocky terrain illustrated by this photograph, taken on 13 May.

An anti-aircraft machine-gun of the Podhalian Brigade.

Motorcycle despatch riders provided one of the main lines of communication in Norway.

Troops from the Podhalian Brigade photographed in the frontline on the Ankenes Peninsula.

A Polish medical team during the fighting for Narvik.

Some of the German troops captured by the Poles at Narvik.

The Polish evacuation from Narvik.

The Norwegian General Fleischer received the silver cross of the Virtuti Militari from General Sikorski.

General Bohusz-Szyszko, the commander of Polish forces in Norway.

Members of the Podhalian Brigade receive gallantry awards after the conclusion of the campaign.

exposed and had no way of taking cover.[1] However, after a couple of days those on the ground made the following assessment to the Admiralty as on 7 May, it was decided that an assault on Narvik was a risk worth taking. It was asserted that even though Narvik town and harbour were wrecked and that the harbour was actually full of sunken ships, it was still worth recapturing. The reasoning was that the recapture of Narvik would be symbolic; an Allied victory because to date German propaganda was making capital of their possession of Narvik.[2]

Even if political point scoring was on the table, there had to be some reality over the Norwegian campaign. The British armed services had already identified that there was a lack of sufficient Allied air cover, while the terrain was hostile to troops landing in Norway, which was made worse if any such landings were opposed by well positioned and well trained troops, who were also well supplied. There was another problem in relation to the Norwegian Campaign, which concerned the Royal Navy. Out of a force of 110 Destroyers; the Royal Navy had 48 deployed off Norway. This meant that western convoys had no destroyer convoys and the eastern convoys had had their destroyer escorts reduced. The Mediterranean Fleet had had its Destroyer numbers reduced from three flotillas to a single flotilla. Therefore it became essential to source local craft in Norway.[3] The overall impression was that too many Destroyers were being tied up in operations off Norway and for an uncertain profit, if any at all.

By early May, the Norwegians were sharing intelligence with the Allies and the President of the Norwegian Parliament, CJ Hambro, had shared information with Mr Mallet, the British Ambassador to Sweden. Hambro told Mallet that resistance in northern Norway was of great importance and reliant on the Allies stopping the Germans reaching Bodo. Hambro also told Mallet that the main road to the north, was bisected between Elsfjord and Hemnes by a body of water 15 kilometres in length and had to be crossed by ferry. The Norwegian politician told Mallet that good disembarkation facilities could be found in the Mo area. He also told the British diplomat that if the Allies were able to prevent the Germans from advancing any further north, it would deny them important copper mines in the Sulitjelna district, as well as the rich agricultural land found there. Furthermore, the denial to the Germans of this area would allow the road to Sweden to be kept open via Umbukta.

There was also inside information about the use of Norwegian territory as airfields, as Hambro observed that a landing ground could be constructed in the Bodin area and that orders had been issued in the Bardofoss areas, that it was to be made serviceable for military aircraft. It was underlined that it was most important that Bodoe be denied to the Germans, as it would probably be used as a base for bombing Narvik (if the Allies were to recapture the town). The Norwegians considered that the Germans were probably using Lake Roesvatn as an airfield, until such a time when the ice melted there. Hambro stressed the importance of the Allies keeping the ports of Bodoe and Sandnessjoen open, while Mallet added 'I venture to add that we shall largely be judged here by our ability to hold Northern Norway and open up the Narvik route to Sweden.'[4] The Allies might have had military muscle or at least naval muscle once compared with the Norwegians, but the Norwegians knew their land even if some were helping the Germans.

Preparations were being made at the time, especially AAA defences at Narvik. A situation report timed at 0700 hours 9 May 1940, recorded that at that time in the Narvik area the Allies had 48 Bofors anti-aircraft guns and eight 3.7 inch guns. A further eight 3.7 inch guns were already enroute and were due to arrive in the Narvik area on 12 May. More guns, 10 Bofors and eight more

1 TNA, CAB 79/4, F.O. Narvik to Admiralty, 5 May 1940.
2 TNA, CAB 79/4, COS (40) 116th Meeting, 8 May 1940; FO Narvik to Admiralty, 7 May 1940.
3 TNA, CAB 79/4 COS (40) 124th Meeting, 11 May 1940.
4 TNA, PREM 3/328/2, Special Distribution and War Cabinet from Sweden, Mr Mallet, 4 May 1940.

3.7 inch guns from a damaged ship, were also being transferred to the Narvik area but with no arrival date established. A larger consignment of guns consisting of twenty four 3.7 inch guns, two Bofors and six 25mm guns, were also being prepared and were due to arrive on 18 May. This was to be beefed up with the arrival of two aircraft carriers; HMS *Ark Royal* was already in the Narvik area. At the time of this report the scheduled second aircraft carrier was yet to be sent to Norway.

The problem of air cover in the Narvik area dragged on. Even though there were plans for the establishment of airfields, nothing had been acheived thus far. Much of the delay lay with the weather and the late thaw of 1940. The Allies pressed on with their endeavours to provide airfields and suitable air cover for the proposed operations in northern Norway. There was a suggestion that it may be possible for Gladiators to land on a prepared runway at Bardufoss, but this would not have been possible until 15 May at the earliest. Therefore a decision was made to try to provide a portable runway to enable aircraft to fly to and from Bardufoss, but this did not really help, as it was all dependent on the thaw setting in. A ship to bring the paraphernalia for the airfield would not be ready until 10 May, while 'every effort' was to be made to load this material onto special trains on 9 May, to be transported to the port of loading. Furthermore, arrangements had been made for six tracked vehicles to be shipped with the portable runway. Such vehicles were essential to get the materials to their destination in Norway, crossing the hostile terrain there.

Of course there were no fighter squadrons operational in the Narvik area but squadrons were 'proceeding' there. The units moving to Norway were already at sea and were expected to arrive there during the pm period 11 May. A further number of units were due to sail on 11 May, and included a mixed bag: Hurricanes from 46 Squadron RAF, as well as an observer unit, a mobile W/T (Wireless transmitter) unit and 935 Balloon Squadron to be operated from trawlers.[5] As one can see, for the Allies to launch any counterattack from the sea was going to be extremely difficult, compared with the Germans, who had an easier time moving up through Germany, via Denmark and into Norway from the south. An earlier report put more flesh onto information about Allied aircraft heading towards Narvik: on board HMS *Ark Royal* were 27 Blackburn Skua dive-bombers and 20 Swordfish due on 6 May.[6] The Swordfish was an obsolete biplane whose role was essentially that of a torpedo bomber. Both the Skua and the Swordfish were hopelessly out of date, compared with the German machines.

Despite the initial poor provision of air cover for Allied forces in Norway, an operation against the Germans had already been decided on and measures were in place to ensure that a counteroffensive took place and a strong determined attack to eject German forces from Norway was made. Part of this planning saw the appointment of General Claude Auchinleck as Commander of Anglo-French Forces in Narvik designate. Auchinleck was told by General Sir John Dill, that the overall intention of the British government was that he should become overall commander of Anglo-French Forces once the government had decided to end the system of unified command. At the time there was a shared command between Admiral of the Fleet Lord Cork and Major-General Mackesy, who was technically subordinate to Cork. Once in situ Auchinleck was also to liaise with the RAF and try to link the three services together operationally.

Before leaving London, Auchinleck had tried to get abreast of the local situation in northern Norway; he told CIGS that the main objective in Norway was the establishment of airfields there. Auchinleck considered that an airfield should be established at Bardufoss, another in the neighbouring Harstad and a possible third at Bodo and all would need adequate AAA defences. Auchinleck also noted that a suitable naval base was needed; one with suitable anchorage, but could

5 TNA, PREM 3/328/3, Air Defence of Narvik. Situation Report at 0700, 9 May 1940.
6 TNA, PREM 3/328/3, Air Defence of Narvik. Situation Report at 0700, 5 May 1940.

be defended 'economically' against all attacks ranging from surface attacks, submarine attacks and land attacks. He also said that AAA should also be installed at any such base, as well as observing that any such place selected and occupied, which not only should be defended as already described and would also be developed, in order to supply a force of approximately three divisions through the port at Narvik and the railway line to Lulea. Auchinleck wrote:

> I have estimated that this area would include not only an area south of Narvik at least as far as the Tysfjord (40 miles south of Narvik) but also an area east of Narvik along the frontier. Further that the northern position of the area would have to include Hatten, which lies about 80 miles north of Narvik at the head of the Lyngen Fjord and covers the approaches to Tromso.

Auchinleck further informed CIGS of his estimate of forces required for any such expedition, which did not include air force personnel or troops required for administration purposes. According to Auchinleck the force would require: twelve infantry battalions, one or two machinegun battalions, a regiment of mechanised cavalry and the 'due proportions of artillery and engineers units.' He also suggested that for AAA, the requirements would be a gross of 3.7 inch guns and 112 Bofors light guns.

Auchinleck left with an advanced HQ from Leith on the Polish liner *Chroby* on 7 May 1940 and landed at Harstad on 11 May. Auchinleck met with Mackesy and an officer from his General Staff, Colonel Dowler on Cork's flagship, which was positioned off Skaanland. Mackesy and Dowler put Auchinleck in the picture regarding operations in Norway. Auchinleck learnt of a French landing which was about to take place at Bjerkvik, at the head of the Herjangs Fjord. Lord Cork was personally directing the operation. Auchinleck left for Skaanland with Brigadier Gammell from his Auchinleck's General Staff to meet Cork. By the time Auchinleck arrived at Skaanland, the French landings had just taken place in wet and cloudy weather, during the early hours of 13 May. The landings had been supported by the guns of the Allied fleet, which had laid down a heavy bombardment of German positions.

The French landings had been successful despite the continuous daylight and appreciable enemy machinegun fire on the shore. The enemy was ejected from the north and east of Herjangs Fjord, while the French landings not only allowed for the joining, with their own troops advancing from the north coming from the direction of Gratangen, but also cleared the countryside down to the Oi Fjord, which was immediately across from the Rombaks Fjord from Narvik. Auchinleck was impressed by the entire French operation and expressed his admiration for the work of the FFL, which had been largely responsible for the success of the offensive. It was noted by Auchinleck 'that the operation was not interfered with by enemy aircraft was almost certainly due to the fortunate weather conditions prevailing at the time. At this period there were no land based aircraft available in Norway with which to counter enemy attacks and a bombing raid might well have turned the operation from a success into a failure.'[7]

Auchinleck's observation was important, as it was only bad weather and a fierce naval bombardment, which had prevented the Germans from launching effective countermeasures and repulsed the French. The French offensive made it quite clear that without air cover, the Germans were quite vulnerable to land forces, especially if they were heavily supported from the sea, as the Germans had little response to Allied warships, following the German maritime disaster at

7 TNA, PREM 3/328/5, 1941 Norway, Operations in Northern Norway from May 13 1940 to June 8 1940, Cabinet Paper, Lieutenant-General C.J.E. Auchinleck, GOC C-in-C, North-Western Expeditionary Force.

Narvik. Auchinleck also noted the poor relationship between Mackesy and Cork. Mackesy could not be convinced of the necessity of co-operation between British land forces and the Royal Navy. Therefore, Auchinleck decided to sack Mackesy and informed Cork of his decision. And of course Cork agreed with Auchinleck.[8] Churchill on 22 April 1940, telegraphed to Cork with this strong message 'if this Officer (General Mackesy) appears to be spreading a bad spirit through the higher ranks of the land force, do not hesitate to relieve him or place him under arrest.'[9] Given that this was a personal message from Churchill to Lord Cork, it should be taken that it cannot be seen as policy, but does reflect the fact that Mackesy was causing concern amongst British commanders, which Auchinleck later reflected on and even considered that Mackesy was perhaps having some form of breakdown and removed him from his post in Norway.

On 13 May, the situation in northern Norway was reviewed. In the Narvik area there was a single battalion of *Chasseurs Alpins*. SWB were on the Ankenes peninsula fighting but were yet to drive the enemy from the area. It was noted that the enemy remained in possession of Narvik and the entire peninsula where it stood. In the Bjerkvik-Oijord area were two battalions of FFL and a single battalion from the Polish contingent; these were fighting the enemy to the east. A further battalion of *Chasseurs Alpins* operating to the north of the FFL had advanced from the direction of Gratangen and were fighting the enemy at Hartvigvand. There was further fighting as the Allies hit back at the Germans occupying Norway. The Norwegian 6th Infantry Division (five battalions supported by several mountain guns), commanded by General Fleischer, were to the north and east of the *Chasseurs Alpins* and fighting the enemy in the Graesdalen Valley and to the east of it. Another battalion of *Chasseurs Alpins* was near Gratangen.

There were three more Polish battalions in Norway: one near Harstad, another at Ballangen on the south shore of Ofotfjord and yet another at Salangen. Other Allied held positions included the Mo-Bodo area, where 1st Battalion SG less 1 company and a single Independent Company was at Mo fighting the enemy, which landed on the Hemnes Peninsula, which was 20 miles south of Mo. 1st Battalion SG was commanded by Lieutenant-Colonel Trappes-Lomax and included a troop from 203rd Field Battery (four 25 pdr field guns) and one troop 55th Light Anti-Aircraft Regiment (four Bofors guns). In the Bodo area was a single company from the Scots Guards and 3 Independent Companies. En route to Bodo on *Chroby* was 1st Battalion Irish Guards (IG), HQ 24th Guards Brigade and detachments of 230th Field Company RE and 137th Field Ambulance.

Harstad became the base for Allied operations. Forward units in contact with the enemy, were supplied by locally procured boats, which transferred stores to the head of the fjord at Harstad, where about ten days of stores were held. The French system was shambolic, even though it was supposed to work in unison with the British supply system; this was never realised owing to the French dragging their heels and refusing to co-operate. Indeed the French established a separate supply base at Ballangen and had their own transport for fjord crossings. The administrative staff responsible for the French supplies was very small in number, with very little in the way for checking and issuing stores. Once stores arrived in Norway there were no personnel designated to unload or load stores, therefore, there were great delays in unloading supplies for French forces. Five French ships remained in the Base Area only partially unloaded for over 16 days. Reserves of supplies, ammunition and general stores remained low in the French force, while the situation was aggravated by the fact that the French failed to arrive with 60 days of supplies, as had been arranged, while motor transport (MT) facilities and spares were almost non-existent.

8 Ibid.
9 Winston S. Churchill to Lord Cork, telegram Admiralty Papers, ADM 199/1929, 22 April 1940, (personal) p.1118, *Churchill 1*.

At Harstad the number of quays available for the unloading of ships was sufficient for the amount of stores going through the Base Port at that time, but facilities for clearing and holding stores up to the scale of reserves to be held was quite inadequate. Medical facilities were also mixed, as the medical plan for evacuating Allied casualties through British medical units back to base worked effectively, but the number of beds available in the General Hospital at Harstad was inadequate, as it only had 500 beds spread through three buildings.

Overall the Allied situation in Norway was not encouraging. The Allies had plans of what to do in Norway, which were more or less to salvage some dignity out of the wreckage of misinterpreting German intentions in Norway. Therefore an attempt was made to stabilise an Allied position on the southern front in the region of Mo and Bodo, as well as to establish land based Allied aircraft. This was becoming more and more urgent, as the enemy more or less had mastery of the skies and launched constant aerial attacks of varying intensity against Royal Navy ships and other vessels in the area. Daily there were air attacks against anything that floated in the Ofot Fjord and off Narvik. There also had been several attacks on Harstad and on the shipping in the harbour there. On 20 May enemy bombers succeeded in setting alight to an oil storage tank at Harstad; two oil tankers moored in the vicinity were also set alight and left to burn out. The damage caused by this raid to shipping and the subsequent fires was considerable, but little harm was done to the town of Harstad itself, while human casualties were few. However the effect on military and civilian morale was considerable and wholly negative.

Despite the arrangements made to try to co-operate with local military and civil officials by Mackesy and his Staff prior to the arrival of Auchinleck, nothing had come of it. This was due to a failure to seek some form of regulation through diplomatic channels. This made work with the Norwegian armed forces difficult, as nothing official had been made on a political basis. Auchinleck decided to resolve this problem and on 16 May, had a 'cordial and satisfactory' interview at his HQ with General Ruge, C-in-C Norwegian Army and with General Fleischer, whose 6th Norwegian Infantry Division had been working closely with French forces to the north of Rombaks Fjord. The two Norwegian Generals insisted that Mo and Bodo should be protected and prevented from falling to the enemy. They also stressed the need to move from defensive and go over to the offensive and recapture Mosjoen.

There had also been some diplomatic moves in the pursuit of joined up thinking regarding inter-allied work in Norway. On 15 May, Colonel R.C.G. Pollock MC, Head of the British Military Mission, set out to assist Auchinleck's HQ maintain a close relationship with the Norwegian government. Sir Cecil Dormer, the British Minister in Norway, also arrived back from the UK and discussed with Cork and Auchinleck the situation in Norway, before taking up his post with Haakon VII, the King of Norway and the Norwegian government. The opportunity was taken to impress on Dormer the urgent need of closer control of the civilian population in military controlled areas.

On 23 May, Lord Cork flew to Tromso and discussed the general situation with King Haakon and members of his government. As a result of this meeting and of Dormer's relationship with King Haakon, relationships between the British armed forces in Norway and the Norwegian authorities began to assume a more businesslike and realistic attitude, especially concerning the necessity of providing facilities to establish a base at Tromso. The Norwegians had been difficult over this matter, as they were reluctant to concede Tromso on the grounds that a British presence there would expose the town to enemy air attacks. Indeed they went as far as to stipulate that unless AAA protection was put in place, facilities at Tromso would be denied to British armed forces. Colonel Pollock was able to help overcome Norwegian reservations about a British presence at Tromso but

Auchinleck ruthfully bemoaned that 'my already inadequate allotment of anti-aircraft artillery' had been diverted to Tromso, as the WO could not spare him any more for this purpose.

On 16 May, Auchinleck sent a complete report to the COS. The situation at that time, as described by Auchinleck, had remained largely unchanged since previous reports. Serious aggression was developing from the Soviet Union via Finland and from Germany via Sweden. Auchinleck considered that it should be possible to maintain the integrity of northern Norway, using the forces he was to outline in his report. Furthermore, he was in favour of a limited offensive, in order to deny the enemy the airbase at Mosjoen. Auchinleck sent his requirements back to Whitehall and they were quite substantial. For the Royal Navy he requested: four Cruisers, six Destroyers, four Escort vessels, 12 anti-submarine vessels, two submarines, as well as auxiliary vessels. For land forces he demanded: one division of cavalry, one squadron armoured cars, one mounted infantry unit (Lovat's Scouts), five batteries of field artillery, two batteries of medium artillery, 13 batteries (104 guns) heavy AAA, eight batteries (96 guns) light AAA, five companies engineers, 17 infantry battalions and one machinegun battalion. Auchinleck also requested two squadrons of Hurricane fighters, one bomber squadron and one Army co-operation squadron. Quite a list!

Auchinleck's primary objective was to deny the Germans their supply of iron ore via Narvik. This had been successful, up to this point, owing to the wholesale destruction to the facilities at the port there. Much of this had been done by the Royal Navy but also the Germans had also been destroying the place. The secondary objective, the disruption of iron ore supply to Germany via Lulea, did not seem to be practical, unless active and full co-operation was made from Swedish armed forces. The third objective, the maintenance of the integrity of northern Norway, seemed to be the only one of the three objectives that required immediate consideration.

The demands of the third objective included the possession of Tromso as a base, in addition to Harstad. This was urgent for many reasons, as was the arrival of some adequate arrangement with the Norwegian government, in order to ensure sufficient control of the civil population in the theatre of operations, as well as placing all Allied armed forces under a single C-in-C. The defence of northern Norway was challenging from a strategic point, in view of the fact that Bodo, Narvik and Tromso were all interdependent and it was impossible to treat them as separate issues or in isolation. Another headache was the defenceless state of landing grounds in northern Norway, especially at Laxelvn and other such places. During this period the French commander, General Bethouard, perfected his plans for the realisation of the objectives assigned to him by Auchinleck. French troops under his command, assisted by Fleischer's Norwegian troops on the eastern flank, had continued to steadily press back the Germans north of the Rombaks Fjord and south of the Beis Fjord. This was not easily done owing to the considerably difficult terrain in this region.

However, events on the European mainland were beginning to hot up, as Germany, on 10 May 1940, had finally attacked Western Europe through Holland and Belgium. This had consequences for any allied operations in Norway, as a telegram (no. 1129/7) dated 17 May 1940, received by Auchinleck from the COS, underlined the problem. Simply owing to the German advance into Belgium and France, Auchinleck's force was to be limited to 12 French and three British battalions and ten independent companies. This force was to receive the proportional artillery, engineers and service units. Forty-eight heavy and 60 light AAA guns were to be sent, while for air cover a single Hurricane squadron and a single Gladiator squadron and a possible single Army Co-operation Flight would be sent to Norway. This telegram also stated that the objectives of operations in Norway were to be the denial of iron ore through Narvik to Germany and the preservation of northern Norway. It was suggested that possession of a base in Narvik might make it possible to deny the Germans iron ore via Lulea, but this was not seen as a priority at the time. Auchinleck's views regarding the retention of Narvik were sought by the COS.

After consultations with Cork and Group Captain Moore RAF, Auchinleck sent his reply on 21 May. He considered that land forces might be able to manage with some additions but AAA provision was unlikely to be adequate in the face of heavy and determined enemy aerial attacks. Auchinleck maintained that the original air estimates for a successful campaign could not be altered and that he still required two Hurricane fighter squadrons, one Gladiator bomber squadron and one Army co-operation Squadron and nothing less will do. Auchinleck reported that the installation of AAA defences, consisting of 48 heavy and 58 light AAA guns had been pushed forward with 'skill and energy' by Brigadier Rossiter, who commanded AAA defences. The disembarking of AAA guns and equipment had been difficult, as except for at Harstad, everything had to be transferred from the ships bringing them from the UK into smaller vessels and ferried ashore. Finding suitable sites for AAA was also very difficult owing to the extremely mountainous topography of Norway, while the indented nature of the Norwegian coast furthered already complicated matters, especially the supply of isolated AAA detachments. However in spite of these problems, Auchinleck observed that the establishment of AAA was made with 'considerable speed and efficiency' and contributed greatly to the security of the force and its bases.

Owing to the limited number of guns available for AAA defences, guns were allocated on the principal that it was only possible to give a maximum degree of protection to extremely vital areas and that small or less important areas had to manage without. The position was that on 20 May, the allocation of AAA was as follows: Bardu Foss eight heavy guns rather than the preferred 16 heavy guns and 12 light guns rather than 24. At Harstad and Skaanland there were 12 heavy guns but 18 light guns and not 36. At Bodo, eight heavy guns and not 16 but a full complement of 12 light guns, while at Tromso there were only eight heavy guns and not 24 as required and 16 light guns rather than 20. In total 48 heavy AAA guns were deployed, rather than 104 as required and 58 light AAA out of a suggested 96.

In addition, there were demands for AAA protection for French troops in the forward areas around Narvik, as well as at Lodingen at the mouth of the Tjelsundet Fjord, in order to protect the coastal and naval anti-submarine defences and to cover the RDF station to be installed on the Lofoten Islands and elsewhere, as well as the protection of the third landing ground being prepared at Elvenes near Salangen. These proposals never happened; only Tromso got any further guns, following a Norwegian request for guns. Events in France overshadowed the entire venture from May onwards.[10]

Despite the ongoing situation in France and the German advance there; Allied operations in Norway were still to be undertaken. Part of the preparations included the reinforcement of Bodo. This was linked to the holding of Harstad and area, upon which the success of Allied operations depended. Harstad was endangered by the threat of an enemy advance from Mosjoen and necessitated a check to its advance. Therefore it was essential to hold the port of Bodo as it appeared to Auchinleck, that it provided depth to his defences. Bodo was the only port available to the Allies for use as an advance base, as Mo was already threatened by the enemy. Therefore an adequate force had to be established in the area and so a British contingent was sent to Bodo. The French, assisted by the Norwegian troops, continued to maintain pressure on German forces in the Narvik area. On 14 May, Auchinleck issued instructions to Bethouard relating to the operation in the Narvik area. Basically, the French were to destroy enemy forces in that area and capture Narvik.

As we have seen throughout this narrative, the Allies suffered many disadvantages including trying to land forces from the sea onto a difficult terrain and eject a well positioned, well trained and well equipped enemy. Movement from the sea was fraught with danger, especially as the Allies

10 TNA, PREM 3/328/5, 1941.

did not enjoy anything like air supremacy and as a consequence Allied ships were vulnerable to enemy aerial attacks. An example is the attempt to move members of 1st IG and others from Harstad towards Bodo via sea on the *Chroby*. The Polish ship was attacked by German aircraft as it was nearing Bodo and sunk. Six IG officers were killed in this attack but luckily most of the Irish Guardsmen were rescued by British naval ships and the ship *Wolverine*.

As the situation in Norway began to unfold, it was realised that the position at Mo was grave and so it was arranged that 2nd SWB be sent to Bodo as soon as possible, but this was dependent on the French being able to replace 2nd SWB at Ankenes. 2nd SWB was able to leave for Bodo on 17 May, sailing on HMS *Effingham*. However disaster struck within an hour, as HMS *Effingham* struck an uncharted rock and sank. Troops from 2nd SWB and others were rescued by naval ships, but much of their precious equipment was lost. Even so the Royal Navy did manage to save quite a lot of equipment including Bren gun carriers, which were taken to Bodo in small craft. A duplicate consignment of equipment (stores and ammunition) was immediately despatched to Bodo in small Norwegian fishing boats, known as 'puffers'.

The Germans remained on the offensive and on 15 May had outflanked the Scots Guard's position south of Mo. Colonel Colin Gubbins, CO of all troops in the Bodo-Mo area and replacing Brigadier Fraser, ordered the Scots Guards to withdraw from their position. The next day, the Scots Guard's detachment commanded by Lieutenant-Colonel Trappes-Lomax, under enemy pressure, evacuated Mo. Meanwhile Gubbins hastened to Mo to acquaint himself with the situation there. He immediately asked for fighter aircraft support but none could be had. The only aircraft available were those operating from aircraft carriers and not available at the time.

On 16 May, the HQ of 24th Guards Brigade and half of SWB, for the third time, set off in Destroyers to Bodo. This was safely reached on 20 May. The Irish Guards also began to arrive at Bodo on 21 May. Two companies had travelled by local 'puffers,' which meant a 24 hours delay, rather than the nine hour trip by Destroyer. A further two companies also arrived at Bodo; they were lucky and had travelled by Destroyer. They were accompanied by General Dowler of the General Staff. Auchinleck had sent Dowler to make personal contact with Brigadier Gubbins. On arriving at Bodo, the Allied troops were bombed by enemy aircraft.

At the time, Gubbins had a reasonable force at his disposal, which consisted of three battalions from 24th Guards Brigade, three independent companies, one troop of Field Artillery and one troop of Bofors Guns. Gubbins seemed satisfied with his group, however overall things in Norway remained difficult for the Allies. The sinking of *Chroby* and HMS *Effingham* had adversely affected the chances of the Allies being able to stop the Germans, in the narrow defile north of Mo. Enemy air attacks on the long and attenuated Scot Guards' communication line at Messingletten, caused great anxiety to Brigadier Gubbins, who was also in urgent need of small armed vessels to prevent the enemy landing parties at will to his rear. Gubbins told Auchinleck that he considered 'the enemy's comparative freedom to move troops by sea the most serious feature of the situation' in Norway.

The arrival of Gubbins gingered up Allied operations in the Bodo area. On 22 May, a new group 'Bodo-Force' was established under the command of Gubbins, who had integrated his Staff with that of 24th Guards Brigade. Lieutenant-Colonel Trappes-Lomax had been sacked from his command of the Scots Guards, as Gubbins was not satisfied with his conduct during operations or that of his battalion during and after the fighting around Mo. Gubbins also requested reinforcements: infantry, field artillery and AAA. He also asked for motorised transport. Gubbins more or less got what he wanted and arrangements were made for embarkation at Harstad; he did not get infantry reinforcements immediately. Auchinleck learnt that three independent infantry companies were to arrive from the UK on 30 May and then sent onto Gubbins as reinforcements. The French loaned a company of 25mm anti-tank guns to Gubbins and they too were embarked for Bodo.

On 23 May, from 'reasonably reliable information' received, it was learnt that the Germans were concentrating in the Mo-Mosjoen area. The German force consisted of 4,000 troops supported by tanks and artillery. On the same day, the Scots Guards withdrew from their position. Gubbins decided to have them relieved by the Irish Guards. On 24 May, under orders from Gubbins, the Scots Guards withdrew towards Rognan. The following day, there were hints that the British government intended to evacuate northern Norway. Dowler was sent out to acquaint Gubbin's of the new situation and to draw up plans for an early withdrawal of all his troops from Bodo. Operations for the stabilisation of the position in the Bodo area had been marked by unrelenting pressure by the enemy from the air and on the ground.

The sinking of *Chroby* and HMS *Effingham* caused problems in many ways, as not only did the troops being moved need rescuing but they also needed re-equipping from scratch. All of the men and officers needed new clothing. Both the Irish Guards and SWB plucked from the sea were required immediately for action and so their immediate equipment stocks had to be replenished. Reserve stocks were not enough for this and so equipment had to be drawn from Base Units. Even so equipment shortages remained. The main deficiencies included mortars, signalling equipment, webbing, revolvers, field guns, compasses and Bren guns. Luckily the Norwegian government made good the shortfall.

Even so, supplying Bodo remained difficult. Naval Destroyers could transport personnel but only limited quantities of stores. The local puffers could carry stores but not artillery guns or vehicles and naval guards had to be on board the puffers. Furthermore, it was deemed by the British authorities that local Norwegian crews were politically unreliable. There was only one coastal steamer capable of carrying guns and vehicles and it was in constant demand in the Harstad area. Any vessel larger than a puffer had to proceed with a naval escort and that was not always possible. The problem of supplying Bodo-Force remained unresolved throughout the Norwegian Campaign.

The problem with air cover or the lack of Allied air cover, remained a problem as well. On 13 May, it was recorded that the Germans already had a powerful air force based in southern Norway, with several excellent air bases to operate from. The Allies had not a single airfield or landing ground fit for use in Norway. This left the enemy with complete air superiority with only the occasional FAA fighter flying from aircraft carriers intervening against enemy air attacks. Snow remained deep in the Allied held areas, which were in the mountainous regions, which denied them accommodation for airfields.[11]

Despite consideration being given for the evacuation of Norway; the next stage of the Allies strategy there was the recapture of Narvik and the hope to retrieve something out of the disaster, that was rapidly becoming the Norwegian Campaign. The Germans had caught the Allies on the hop, on land at least. It is true that the Royal Navy had devastated the German surface fleet at Narvik but it was of small consolation if the Germans could not be rejected and perhaps the Allies had to face the fact that perhaps all of Norway was about to be lost to the Germans. However an Allied force had been built up in Norway; part of which was Polish and it is to the Polish contingent and to Narvik that we must now turn.

11 Ibid.

6

Narvik Examined

For the Poles languishing in exile, the expedition to Norway was a chance to prove themselves and show that Poland was still very much in the war. Immediately General Sikorski recognised that the Polish Highlanders, the Podhalians, a mountain brigade, would be able and available to fight the Germans in Norway.[1] Churchill had argued that it would be desirable symbolically for the Poles to be incorporated into the Allied expedition to Norway, but the British War Cabinet questioned this zeal of both Churchill and Sikorski, as it was considered that perhaps it might be unwise to break up the Polish Army, which was in the process of reforming and send a 'considerable number of partly trained troops' to Norway.[2] From this small exchange the idea that the Podhalians were a mountain brigade in reality was not really true, as they were not even fully trained troops. Borkowski described the Independent Podhale Rifle Brigade, to give it its correct title, as being composed from battalions separated from 1st and 2nd Infantry Divisions, which were at the time in Brittany or elsewhere in France. The composition of the Brigade was diverse. Some of the officers were combat veterans from the September Campaign but nearly 90% of the rank and file were volunteers from the Polish émigré communities in France, Holland and Belgium and none of them had combat experience.[3] But who amongst the Allies had any experience in fighting Arctic warfare? The Norwegians had not fought a war for over a century or more but they were the only troops amongst the Allies and come to that, the majority of the Germans, who really understood the conditions they were about to fight in. Even so the Allies, including the Podhalians, would have fought in Finland but for the end of the Winter War in Finland.

And so the Podhalians began to form up. The Brigade was composed of Staff, communications, a motorized section and two Demi-Brigades. Each Demi-Brigade, in turn, was made up of a Staff company, an auxiliary weapons company and two rifle battalions. The Commanding Officer of the Podhalians, General Bohusz-Szyszko, was an experienced officer. During the September Campaign he had commanded 16th (Polish) Infantry Division.

A problem for the Podhalians was that it was totally dependent on the French for its equipment and therefore despite being described as an 'Independent' brigade, it was far from being so. The Poles lacked artillery, armoured vehicles and anti-aircraft guns. When the Podhalians set off for Norway, French vessels, *Mexique*, *Chenonceaux* and *Columbie*, transported them. On the night of embarkation, 23–24 April 1940, the brigade consisted of 4,778 officers and men. It was armed with twenty-five 25mm armour piercing guns, fifteen 81mm mortars, fifteen 60mm mortars and 68 heavy machineguns.[4]

1 Władysław Dec, *Narwik i Falaise* (Warsaw: MON, 1972), p. 46.
2 War Cabinet: Confidential Annex, CAB 65/12, 5 March 1940, *Churchill* 1, p. 849.
3 M. Borkowski, 'Polish Forces in the High North' in Rommetveit, op. cit. pp. 146-165.
4 Ibid.

The reliance on allied equipment was to frustrate the Polish armed forces throughout the war, especially when it came to aerial support. This became most acute during the 1944 Warsaw Uprising, when the Allies did not support by air the uprising, just as the Poles thought it should be supplied. Furthermore, during the uprising the Poles were also denied the use of the Independent Polish Parachute Brigade, as they had been earmarked for the ill-fated assault on the River Rhine at Arnhem. And of course the Poles also lacked the aircraft to take paratroopers to Warsaw. It was a running sore between the Allied and Polish High Commands.

However, as we have seen, the Allies and the Germans were to clash in Norway but the Allies were not in place, as ships originally consigned to transport land forces to Norway had been reassigned to join in the pursuit of a German naval column in the North Sea. This German naval force was actually the German expeditionary force heading towards Norway. The Allies had been caught on the hop, even though Norway had been considered a valid military objective, since the outbreak of war. The Germans had certainly taken Norway seriously because as Rommetveit notes; Operation *Weserübung* was the only German joint operation, involving all three branches of its armed forces; the army, navy and air force, working in unison.[5]

On 9 April 1940, Edmund Ironside (CIGS) lamented the dilly-dallying of the British government. At 0630 that day, Ironside was in a meeting of Chiefs of Staff (COS). The early hour gave a sense of urgency of what was happening in Europe. In the meeting it was confirmed that the Germans had actually sent troops and ships to Norway and had already occupied the Norwegian towns of Bergen and Trondheim. It seemed that this was accomplished fairly easily. Ironside also was critical of his political masters, as he referred to them, as they seemed to work a 9–5 day and could not be raised until 0830 that morning and so time was wasted. By midday it was learnt that Denmark had been overrun by German troops and was already being administered by Germany. The Norwegians were fighting the Germans and were refusing to surrender. The Norwegian government had already left Oslo for central Norway.

Ironside had been impressed with the speed of the German operation and began to think of how to counter the German offensive. Ironside thought that a naval counter-offensive might be the best retort. He also considered what the next German move might be and correctly predicted that it would be an advance on the Western Front, through Holland and Belgium; both countries being overrun and with little that the Allies could do. Ironside was clearly, by this time, totally fed up with dealing with the British War Cabinet and their perceptions of how war should be waged, as Committees sat 'wobbling and havering'. Furthermore, Ironside was curious as to how Narvik had fallen to the Germans so easily and considered that it was inexcusable that the port at Narvik had fallen so easily to the enemy. He conceded that nothing could have prevented the enemy landings at Oslo, but the German landings at Narvik were quite something else.[6] Later it was established that Narvik was easily captured by the enemy, owing to the treachery of Narvik's pro-Nazi Norwegian commander, who allowed the Germans to land unhindered.[7]

At the time of the German landings, Ironside was unaware of the treachery at Narvik and thought that it was just that the neutral states were 'terrified of the Germans and their brutality.' He remained equally frustrated with his own people, as the British had to wait for the French to arrive for a meeting of the Supreme War Council, which did not begin until five o'clock that afternoon. At this belated meeting it was agreed that the Allies had to launch a counter-offensive in Norway and to strike against Narvik, Bergen and Trondheim. But it had taken all day for this to be arrived at and Ironside lamented the loss of time. He remarked in his diary that a war cannot be waged in

5 Rommetveit, op. cit, p. 7.
6 *Ironside Diaries*, 9 April 1940, pp. 249-250.
7 TNA, CAB 44/271, 'The Campaign in Norway, April, May, June 1940'.

this manner. Decisive action had to be taken as events unfolded. Ironside noted that if the Allies were to win the war, they needed to have proper control.[8] Clearly Ironside was tired of reacting to events, rather than setting the agenda.

It would seem that not only were the German landings in Norway successful owing to the treachery of individual Norwegian commanders but also the Royal Navy had been lax. Churchill, chairing a meeting of the Co-ordination Committee, said that the German landings at Narvik had been easy work and had been able to land 4,000 men there. It seemed that the Royal Navy after laying mines in the area had stood off and somehow had allowed six German destroyers, a submarine and ten other ships to slip in. The supposedly empty German iron ore ships, as previously mentioned, had made their way up the Norwegian coast; the reality being was that these ships were full of German troops. The Norwegians had either failed to notice them or had turned a blind eye to their presence. In this way the German vessels and their occupants made their way to Narvik quite unmolested, seized it and set about making their positions secure. Churchill told the meeting that Narvik was being made into a fortress complete with pill-boxes, guns and anything else needed to secure the port. Ironside commented on the situation at Narvik in his diary: 'Now we have to go and take this on. A poisonous proposition and something which cannot be done in a few minutes. Luck is so far against us and we have bungled badly.'[9]

The next day, Ironside was more conciliatory towards the Navy and he noted that the weather had been bad but even so the Allies had been completely outwitted by the Germans. It had been agreed by the Allies that Narvik had to be taken from the Germans, but the planning for such an operation had not even started. Ironside understood the necessity for speed but was also aware that any attack on Narvik would 'bring every German aeroplane to the place like a lot of bees or hornets.' The only Allied effort being made towards Norway at the time, was being made by the Royal Navy. Even so two large German ships could not be located, which caused Ironside to doubt British command of the seas. The RAF claimed to have hit a German Cruiser in the stern at Bergen, as well as hitting another in the North Sea but overall the situation for the Allies remained bad. The Royal Navy did not have control of the North Sea and the German Navy was roaming at will. A meeting of the British War Cabinet concluded that the Germans had acted very boldly and had risked everything to seize Norway.

Ironside later addressed a meeting of the Co-ordination Committee and told it that if there were 3,000 Germans in Narvik, it would require a major operation to turn them out and such an operation could not be rushed into. He considered that an operation against Narvik could not be reached until certain criteria had been met. The most important thing was that the enemy should not be able to reinforce Narvik any further by sea. There was also a requirement for an advanced base near Narvik, for the British to assemble their forces. Furthermore, it would be advantageous if the port of Tromsö, to the north of Narvik, could be seized and then establish an oiling base for British Destroyers.

A further requirement was that of intelligence. Ironside called for officers to go to Norway and discover what enemy forces were actually in Narvik and from their reports an offensive could be planned. His final demand was for time, in which to make plans and to carry them out. Ironside had already begun to formulate some embryonic plans for an offensive in Norway but again lamented the tardiness of any British response, compared to the lightning speed and boldness, which the Germans were operating at.

8 *Ironside Diaries*, 9 April 1940, p. 250.
9 Ibid.

Ironside was more upbeat in his assessement of naval action off Narvik and considered that it had gone better, than he had previously thought. The Royal Navy had lost two destroyers but had sunk a German destroyer, blown up an enemy ammunition ship and set three German destroyers alight. However, three enemy destroyers were still operating outside of Narvik and this had to be halted. Furthermore, the Royal Navy had to ensure that Narvik was not reinforced by the enemy via the sea. Ironside's immediate plan was to place a battalion of British troops (600–700 men) to the north of Narvik, allow it to establish itself and if necessary prepare reconnaissance patrols towards Narvik. It was also thought that there were Norwegian troops at Harstad, to the north of Narvik. Ironside said somewhat patronisingly that he hoped 'to get a man over to this place to buck them up.'[10]

On 10 April 1940, the British War Cabinet decided that the Germans should be expelled from Norway: one position at a time, beginning with Narvik. Ironside's plan fell largely into the remit for the coming operation, including the establishment of a British advanced base at Harstad, an island about 33 miles north-west of Narvik. Two battalions were immediately made available with another six to come. The question of operations against Trondheim or Bergen, after the recapture of Narvik, was raised the next day, 11 April 1940, by the Chief of the British Air Staff at a meeting of the Military Co-ordination Committee. It was decided that the Chiefs of Staff might study this project but not prepare for it. On 12 April 1940, the British War Cabinet was being badgered by the Norwegian government to recapture Trondheim. The suggestion seemed to be that if this was not done, both Norway and Sweden might have to capitulate to the Germans. The War Cabinet agreed that even small scale landings on the Norwegian coast might be of value from a political point of view. In response to the Norwegian government's request, the Military Co-ordination Committee ordered a plan to be prepared.[11] It was noted that without skis or snowshoes troops would be 'absolutely incapable of operating tactically at all. Shelter from the weather was of vital importance.' An early analysis of the Narvik area suggested that the enemy held the area in considerable strength, as all the existing defences had been handed over intact by the Norwegian garrison to the Germans. This assessement was reinforced by personal reconnaissance, which suggested that the topography in the Narvik region favoured defence. An Allied landing at Narvik, which would be opposed by the Germans, was quite out of the question. This was not only because of deep snow and the appalling weather but also because the Allies lacked landing craft, tanks, adequate artillery support, as well as anti-aircraft defence and air co-ordination. Even so the Allies continued to plan a counter-offensive.

As plans were being worked out, there was an alternative voice for the offensive, as General Claude Auchinleck, who took over from Mackesy, considered him to be 'unbalanced'. Auchinleck made his opinion of Mackesy quite clear in a letter to General John Dill, Vice Chief of the Imperial General Staff. Auchinleck considered that Mackesy was not fit to command troops at the time of writing and claimed that Mackesy was being too cautious in his approach in Norway. According to Auchinleck, Mackesy was more concerned with how the world would view him, rather than get on with fighting the way, as Auchinleck commented of Mackesy 'cleverness and cynicism completely outweighed his reason'.[12] Auchinleck had also investigated the conditions at Narvik and agreed that they were quite bad and indeed the annual thaw of snow at Narvik was late in 1940, May rather than in April, but he considered that operations were possible and that there was a narrow window

10 Ibid., 10 April 1940, pp. 251-2.
11 Ibid., commentary, pp. 250-3.
12 The John Rylands Library, John Rylands Special Collections, The University of Manchester, GB 133 AUC, The Papers of Field Marshal Auchinleck, GB 133 AUC, File III, May 1-16 1940, Auchinleck to General Dill, 14 May 1940.

of opportunity, April to October, to carry out such work. He agreed that an operation against Narvik was difficult, but it was the only time that an offensive against the enemy could be carried out.[13] Basically, Auchinleck considered that counter-operations had to begin sooner rather than later and that the entire venture ran a risk and it was better to commence operations rather than allowing the enemy to reinforce further. Mackesy was too worried about the future to be of any use at Narvik, in Auchinleck's opinion.

The presence of Allied troops near Narvik on 20 April 1940, might have been the result of a previous naval success on 13 April 1940. Ironside wrote up that day in his diary recording how nine British Destroyers and the Battleship HMS *Warspite* had sailed up the fjord into Narvik and had wrecked the German naval force there and further on: a total of seven enemy destroyers were sunk or wrecked. The Royal Navy force also destroyed an enemy field howitzer, while it was considered that enemy ground forces had been evacuated from the area, owing to the destruction of the British naval gunfire. Ironside considered that it would not take much more to mop up the scattered German forces: all of this at the cost of two British Destroyers. The Royal Navy according to Ironside was 'bucked up' by their success at Narvik and wanted to do something similar at Trondheim. However, as Ironside noted, such an offensive called for a completely new plan, which would then have the disadvantage of taking time to execute.[14]

Trondheim as a military objective, had been studied by the Military Co-ordination Committee but no preparations had been made for its seizure and no troops set aside for this, as the question of how big a force was required for the recapture of Narvik had not been settled. Suddenly Trondheim had become an attractive target, as it had a large and excellent harbour and a railway line, which ran northwards and connected to the iron ore source at Gällivare, the original bone of contention in Norway. To the south, both Oslo and the Swedish capital, Stockholm, could be reached by rail. Trondheim was the ancient capital of Norway and so it may have been that if the Allies could have liberated it, the historical significance may have heartened the Norwegians to fight on, as well as perhaps encouraging the Swedes to make some form of resistance to German aggression.[15]

The offensive against Tronheim was controversial at the time and there were different opinions of how the campaign in Norway should be conducted. During the early hours of 14 April 1940, Churchill with the Deputy Chief of the Naval Staff, Admiral Tom Phillips, came to Ironside's room at the WO. Churchill asserted that the Allies were going to the 'wrong place'. Instead of going to Narvik, there should be an assault on Trondheim. Churchill's plan was that the Royal Navy should make a direct attack on Trondheim and then a small military force of 'good troops' should follow up the naval assault. Churchill also wanted landings made north and south of Trondheim, one at Namsos and the other at Andalsnes. He claimed that the military strikes combined with the naval assault would develop into a pincer movement on Trondheim. Churchill was yet to work out the dates for the naval attack. Ironside was unimpressed with Churchill's idea and protested that he had no troops available for Namsos, until Narvik had been taken. Churchill insisted that the rear half of the convoy heading for Narvik, which was transporting 146 Territorial Brigade, should be diverted to Namsos.

This time with passion, Ironside insisted that Churchill should know, from his own experience, how impossible such a diversion would be. Basically if half of the troops earmarked for the Narvik operation were diverted for other operations, the entire Narvik operation would be compromised. Ironside observed that troops and equipment had been loaded and the administration prepared for a single operation only. Everything would be wrecked if half of the convoy was detached. He also

13 John Rylands Special Collection, GB 133 AUC, File III, May 1-16 1940, Climatic Conditions, 2 May 1940.
14 *Ironside Diaries*, 13 April 1940, p. 256.
15 Ibid., pp. 256-7.

noted that there was no commander for the rear half because it presumed commander, Brigadier Phillips, had been quite correctly, taken ahead by General Mackesy. Ironside considered that it would be better to abandon the Narvik operation, but was overruled.[16]

Without doubt Ironside was referring to the ill-fated 1915 Gallipoli Campaign, which was largely Churchill's brainchild for the invasion of Turkey. General Sir Ian Hamilton, GOC of the force at Gallipoli, was constantly denied the necessary men and equipment to successfully conclude the offensive at Gallipoli. Within a year the Allies were obliged to evacuate the limited territory captured on the Turkish mainland. This campaign ruined Hamilton's career (Hamilton was close to its end anyway) and nearly ruined Churchill's political career. Churchill felt obliged to serve a term of penance on the Western Front in France before returning to politics. Between 1915 and 1940 Churchill was seen by many as a warmonger and a political liability.

In 1940, Churchill once more got his own way and the force designated for Narvik was split in two and 146 Brigade was diverted to Namsos. Ironside took this directive to the COS Committee, which met later that morning. There it was decided that 146 Brigade would indeed land at Namsos, once naval and marine parties had landed. Furthermore, another naval party was to land at Andalsnes to coincide with the Namsos landing. It was agreed with the French government that the first demi-brigade of *Chasseurs Alpins* should be detached from the original Narvik force and deployed at Namsos as reinforcements. Ironside was virtually alone in his view that the Narvik force should not be split and that Narvik was not going to be a 'walk-over'. As he had anticipated, 146 Brigade landed at Namsos during 16 and 17 April 1940, less most of its equipment and its commander, Brigadier Phillips. It was entirely without anti-aircraft cover, which was on one of the lead ships heading for Narvik. Ironside had reluctantly accepted these changes for the Narvik operation and had misgivings about the entire venture once the force was split and diverted.

Ironside was correct to be concerned by the detachment of 146 Brigade and the rather cavalier attitude of Churchill towards the planned Allied assault on Norway. Troops heading for Narvik were already at sea, when these meetings at Whitehall took place and were steaming towards the small port of Harstad. This was not directly on the Norwegian mainland but on an island about 33 miles to the seaward and north-westerly side of Narvik. It was at Harstad that Allied troops were to establish a base from which to attack Narvik.

There was to be further confusion and altering of plans at sea. The British naval commander, Admiral of the Fleet, Lord Cork and Orrery, had not sailed with the original convoy but had sailed about 12 hours later. His intention was to meet with General Mackesy at Harstad and finalise the Narvik operation. Whilst he was at sea, Cork received a signal from Admiral Whitworth, whose fleet was already in the north, informing him of the destruction of the German convoy at Narvik and that perhaps Narvik could be taken by a direct assault. Lord Cork altered course and steered for Narvik. He also tried to contact Mackesy, sailing on HMS *Southampton*, in hope of diverting Mackesy and his troops from Harstad to Narvik. Cork's signal failed to reach Mackesy in time and so his expedition continued onto Harstad, rather than Narvik. The rear half of the convoy had already started for Namsos and so the expedition was already running into trouble.[17]

During the Norwegian Campaign, Ironside recorded his frustrations with Churchill, who seemed to think that war could be run by committee and by meeting everyday at 5:00 p.m. Ironside was well aware that the momentum and speed of enemy attacks precluded such leisurely and gentlemanly attitudes. In his diary, Ironside noted that the COS was receiving 'frantic telegrams' from various Norwegian Commanders in Norway, including the 'so-called C-in-C'. All these telegrams pointed

16 Ibid., p. 257.
17 Ibid., pp. 258-60.

to one fact: that Trondheim must be captured immediately or Norway would collapse. Ironside was equally frustrated with the Norwegians, who previously have been slow to take any measure of co-operation with the Allies but once they faced defeat and occupation, demanded an Allied counter-offensive almost immediately. Ironside claimed that it was 'natural for all neutrals' to want immediate assistance from the outside world. A bit similar to some NATO allies today expecting everything from the British and Americans, especially once Putin's Russia reasserted itself.

Ironside asserted that the most urgent things required for Norway were 'pace, audacity and speed.' Ironside decided that delay was unthinkable and that the Allies needed to take chances. He identified the biggest handicap for the Allies, especially the British, was the lack of trained troops. Ironside considered that the Germans had not sent their worse troops to Norway. Ironside was further motivated once Lieutenant-Colonel Edward King-Salter, the British Military Attaché, arrived with the Norwegians. King-Salter wired that Norwegian morale was 'deplorable'. It was clear that British landings at Trondheim were essential to save Norway. As Ironside began to mentally formulate plans for the salvation of Norway, he made an important observation: that the COS still had to get approval from the Co-ordination Committee. He noted ominously that this civilian led committee had usurped the functions of the General Staff.[18]

This was an important observation as the function of the General Staff, which comprised of senior and experienced officers from the armed services, was to advise elected civilian politicians of how to proceed in matters of defence. During wartime it is often expected that COS would drive the agenda and that civilian politicians should demure to the experience of Staff Officers, unless a certain course might be deemed unpalatable or unnecessary, if not best. The needs for the Norway Campaign were quite straight forward: a unified rigorous response in the face of German and quite possibly Soviet aggression. However Churchill, who was not even Prime Minister yet, as ever liked to call the shots and so dominated proceedings while Norway burnt.

Even so, a meeting of the COS was convened to decide on the Namsos landings, which were due to take place on the night of 15–16 April 1940. A major decision was to get General Adrian Carton de Wiart to Norway, in order to meet the naval officer who was to lead the naval landing that night. Ironside was clearly unhappy with combined operations, as he noted the problems which had bedevilled the Norwegian expedition since its beginning. The most obvious problem was one already seen; Brigadier Phillips, who was supposed to have been Mackesy's Second-in-Command, and so had been taken away from his own troops, 146 Brigade, and put with the leading Brigade going into Narvik. This left 146 Brigade without its Commander, as it headed towards its own objective: Namsos.

The Royal Navy failed to land at Namsos on 13 April 1940 and was about to try once more on 14 April. There was a delay in information concerning this venture and as a result landings were not to be attempted until late evening 14 April 1940. This delay was annoying but there were also niggles regarding supplies, even back in the UK. An example being the movement of Bofors anti-aircraft guns, which were to be transported to Rosyth, Scotland, ready for loading onto naval craft to go to Norway. Even before these guns were moved to Rosyth, it was discovered that there was a broken coupling on the train, which was to go to Rosyth and so their departure was delayed by four hours. A small niggle perhaps, but an example of the problems experienced by the Narvik operation.

However, the most vexing of frustrations had to be the confusion of the Co-ordination Committee and the waiting for decisions from it. Ironside wrote that it made any decisions made by the COS 'impossible'. Ironside was no fool and he knew that combined operations required careful planning and preparation. In the case of Norway in 1940, time was not on the side of the

18 Ibid., 14 April 1940, p. 260.

Allies and so haste was required. This meant that risks had to be run in order to try to save the country from complete occupation by Germany. But the Germans had risked all to take Denmark and Norway, however they had been preparing for some time to carry out this operation.

Almost immediately it seemed that there was a measure of confusion at the top of the command chain regarding Narvik. Churchill phoned Ironside at 2300 hours 14 April 1940, grumbling that Mackesy had landed 300 men at Salangen, near Narvik, 'without consulting Lord Cork.' Ironside corrected Churchill's perception of who was in charge of what at Narvik; informing him that the military landing was under the command of Mackesy. If Cork was going to make a naval attack, all well and good, but he needed to work with Mackesy, to ensure that such joint operations worked well in tandem. After that, Ironside began to scrutinise naval signals to ensure that the Royal Navy was not doing anything which might upset or endanger Allied military operations in Norway.[19]

Ironside had previously stressed that modern warfare was a matter of rapid action, boldness and possession. The Germans had achieved this in Norway, having outwitted the Allies, capturing Denmark in a single stroke, as well as taking much of Norway and various strategic points in northern Norway. Ironside meanwhile was hampered by the ignorance and lethargy of the Co-ordination Committee, which in his opinion was good for long term strategy but hopelessly inadequate for improvisation during on-going operations against a very determined enemy. However by 0700 hours, 17 April 1940 the Allied offensive in Norway had began in earnest and the COS met to consider what next.[20]

At Narvik Mackesy and his force were faced with heavy snow and below zero temperatures at night. A wire had been sent to him to co-operate with the battleship HMS *Warspite,* in an attempt to capture Narvik, occupy the port and then mop up the remaining Germans. It would seem that Ironside was correct in his assertion that the enemy had not sent its worse troops but had indeed sent genuine winter warfare troops, who on the whole came from Bavaria and Austria.

At Namsos, General Carton de Wiart, who had arrived in a Sunderland flying-boat the day before, had got two battalions ashore and was in contact with the local Norwegian commander. The Norwegians held an arsenal at Steinkjer, as well as having troops at Levanger, which was within 15 miles of Trondheim. Allied troops were moved to the Norwegian positions in order to 'stiffen' them, as well as preparing them for guerrilla warfare. Given that the British had very little, if any, experience in winter warfare or guerrilla tactics, one can only wonder what experience they were going to pass on to their Norwegian counterparts. At the same time it was confirmed that the French were to land three battalions of *Chasseurs Alpins,* who were to move inland immediately, so that pressure could be put on Trondheim from Levanger. The French were to have their own commander but were overall under the command of Carton de Wiart.

In the Trondheim area, a force under Major-General Hotblack was to be sent directly into the fjord there together with naval support, in order to capture the airfield at Vaernes and then join up with Carton de Wiart's in order to 'mop up' Trondheim. Troops involved included Berney-Ficklin's Regular 15th Brigade from 5th Division, 1,000 Canadians and as a reserve Lammie's Brigade of 'Terriers' (Territorial Reserve Troops). Allied progress, such as it was, was severely hampered by enemy aerial bombing raids. Ironside received reports that the Germans had persistently bombed all along the fjords, while at Harstad nine enemy aircraft bombed the area for five hours. Luckily the enemy aircraft failed to hit either ships or the town itself. Furthermore, there were no Allied casualties. Carton de Wiart, on the *Empress of Australia* at Lillesjona and later at Namsos, had been harassed by five enemy aircraft for two hours but the Germans achieved nothing with their attacks.

19 Ibid., pp. 260-1.
20 Ibid., 16 April 1940, 17 April 1940, pp. 263-5.

As ever Ironside drummed in the need to push on directly from the sea and not to delay or rendezvous after debarkation. He insisted on boldness and risk. Ironside also laid down some guidelines on what he hoped would be the short term results in Norway. Regarding Narvik Ironside's view was that it was to be strongly defended with AAA and from the sea. It was, in his opinion, to be garrisoned by Norwegian troops with a small British garrison under a British commander. Ironside also wanted the traffic of iron ore from Sweden continued. This meant repairing the railway line to Sweden. Ironside saw Trondheim as being the HQ of the Army, as well as the probable seat of the Norwegian government.

The future of the Norwegian Army seemed to lie in some form of guerrilla warfare, with Ironside harking back to the days of guerrilla warfare in Portugal during the Napoleonic War, over a century before and quite a different age, terrain and climate. He considered that perhaps Admiral Evans and an Army Staff could reorganise the Norwegian Army. For the long term Ironside considered the supply and use of armoured cars, as well as supplying the proposed guerrilla force with arms and equipment.[21] However, as with many Western democracies, Norway, during the 1930s, had been steadily reducing the size of its armed forces. Incredibly in 1933 the number of regular officers and NCOs was reduced from 3,750 men to a paltry 470 and the number of units available for mobilization fell from six divisions to only six brigades, while mobilization was very slow and compulsory military service extremely short, even if it was increased from 48 days to 84 days.[22] Therefore given the size of the Norwegian Army and its lack of obvious martial promise, did not seem to be the right stuff for what the British had hoped, for a promising plan of Norwegian resistance. There was one piece of good news for the Allies, as the Admiralty claimed that the Polish submarine *Orzeł* had on 8 April 1940, sunk the 10,000 ton enemy transporter *Rio de Janeiro* off the Norwegian coast, causing great loss of life amongst the enemy aboard, which included units of the German Army and Staff, which were heading to Norway.[23]

By the end of April 1940, Ironside's vision of how operations in Norway were to continue became British policy. General Ruge at the Norwegian HQ was informed of this. Ironside confirmed the firm resolution of the Allies to continue the fight for Norwegian independence and that the strategic withdrawal did not represent a weakening of Allied determination. It was stressed that Allied forces were already operating in northern Norway and were being rapidly reinforced. Norwegian co-operation would doubly ensure Allied success in Norway. Pencilled marginalia suggested that holding the area north of Narvik could well be a preliminary to southward moving Allied-Norwegian counterattack. Maurice Hankey considered that the idea was that operations in Norway would be like 'a running sore just as the Spanish Peninsula was a running sore to Napoleon.'[24]

It would seem that Ironside had no idea about modern warfare and there was another inconvenient truth, which no doubt some might have wanted to bury, as Auchinleck within a week noted that Narvik was unlikely to be of any use. Reporting on 3 May 1940, he stated that the Germans were actually destroying Narvik, as he made his report. According to Auchinleck, Narvik would not be viable until 1 December 1940, assuming that work on repairing it began on 1 June 1940. This applied to the Germans as well if they wanted to use Narvik. Overall Auchinleck considered that unless more men and he meant a lot of men, were deployed and adequate air

21 Ibid. 17 April 1940, pp. 265-7.

22 Adam Claasen (2004) 'The German Invasion of Norway, 1940: The Operational Intelligence Dimension' *Journal of Strategic Studies* (27) pp. 114-35 in *The Second World War. Volume 1, The German War 1939-1942*, Jeremy Black (ed.) (Aldershot, UK, Ashgate, 2007), pp.69-90.

23 PISM, A.IV. 11/54, 20 April 1940.

24 TNA, PREM 1/419, Invasion of Norway, Chief of Imperial General Staff (CIGS) to General Ruge, Norwegian HQ, 29 April 1940.

cover provided; Allied operations in Norway were going to be extremely risky; he had already highlighted the limited period for operations in Norway as being between May and October and that was every year.[25]

It is interesting to note that the Poles had briefed against considering that the Germans were all conquering, owing to their military methodology. As early as February 1940, the Polish military in exile was preparing plans, which dealt with paratroopers and other novel methods of rapid mobile assault. The Poles also gave thought that, if necessary, in order to preserve the future, during an age of barbaric and total war, perhaps all thoughts of a civilized war should perhaps be forgotten. The Poles thought in the terms of that, perhaps a fight to the death might be necessary if not inevitable, in order to defeat Germany and that the Allies should not be overawed by German tactics.[26]

Perhaps this was what Ironside was seeking in Norway: troops, which were not intimidated by the Germans and would fight fire with fire and so return the game to the Germans. However prior to Churchill taking over in the UK as Prime Minister, but this was not until the fall of Norway, British political and military senior circles seemed dazzled by the capabilities of the German armed forces and, as a consequence, seemed incapable of fighting a war well. It took the near defeat of the UK before this was remedied.

25 John Rylands Special Collection, GB 133 AUC, File III, Climatic Conditions, 2 May 1940; Narvik: Appreciation of Situation, 3 May 1940.

26 PISM, A.VI.11/19, *Wytyczne Specjalne*, 23 February 1940.

7

The Poles in Norway

The Podhalian Brigade, which in 1940 served in Norway, disembarked at Harstad on 7 May 1940. The Podhalians were detailed to operate with the North-Western Expeditionary Force (NWEF), the official designation of the Allied troops serving in Norway. The Poles came under the direct command of General Bethouart, Commander of the French 1st Division *Légère de Chasseurs*.

Auchinleck gives the most reliable information when he narrated events concerning the Norwegian Campaign, in an account dated 18 July 1940, and therefore not long after the return from Norway and when events were still fresh, if not raw but not yet subject to any mythology that might make up the history of the Norwegian Campaign. Auchinleck reported that on 13 May, 2nd Battalion Podhalians marched from Ostevik to Bjerkvik during the day and linked up with FFL already in that area. 1st Battalion Podhalians moved inland from Harstad; 3rd Battalion moved to the Ballangen area and 4th Battalion to the Salangen area. Auchinleck also relates events around the ill-fated Polish ship *Chroby,* which sailed with the HQ of 24th Infantry (Guards) Brigade, mainly Irish Guards, at 1500 hours on 14 May, from Skaanland to Bodo. During the night 14–15 May, *Chroby* was bombed and set alight, 25 miles north-west of Bodo. It is interesting to observe that Auchinleck considered that there may have been a breach of security relating to *Chroby,* before the vessel had even set sail. The CO of 24th Infantry Brigade, as well as five other officers, was killed, as well as a few ORs. The remainder of the force was rescued by the Royal Navy.[1] Auchinleck's remarks relating to security are interesting and necessary, as it was quite clear that there was an element of Norwegian society which had no sympathy for the Allied cause and were quite pro-German, whilst events later seemed to indicate that the minor European allies had a somewhat curiously lax attitude towards military secrecy and so were excluded from planning, unless it directly affected them.

Auchinleck gives some idea of how the Norwegian Campaign was carried out, warts and all, as he related that Bethouart had wished to postpone the relief of SWB by the Poles at Ankenes coming from Bjerkvik, which actually was an integral part of the operation. The problem was that the Poles in turn could not be relieved by *Chasseurs Alpins,* who were exhausted by fighting and marching. However events overtook Bethouart's concerns, as small craft necessary to move Polish troops across the water to Ankenes had already been collected and assembled and the Royal Navy had also already made their preparations for moving the Poles. Bethouart had already ordered a postponement of 24 hours before the Polish troops should be ferried over to the Ankenes peninsula but by the time these orders arrived, the Poles were already moving out and so the original plan was kept to.

Events in Norway moved swiftly, if one follows Auchinleck's narrative, as on 29 May, the French had captured Narvik, Ankenes, Fagernes, and Forsneset and were advancing towards Sildvik and Beisfjord. Auchinleck received a report that suggested that 6,000 people were still living in Narvik

1 Special Collections, John Rylands Library, MUL 82, Narrative of events by Lieutenant-General C.J.E. Auchinleck, 18 July 1940.

following its capture by the French, while casualties remained unknown and provisional estimate indicated that the French had suffered 30 dead and 80 wounded.

As ever, the military in Norway found it difficult to work with journalists owing to secrecy, while the press considered that they had a right to inform the public of how operations were going. Auchinleck was particularly incensed by a BBC broadcast at noon 31 May, which announced that 'Bodo had been evacuated owing to enemy air action.' Auchinleck considered this to have been 'an act of criminal folly,' as a final evacuation was due to take place that night. Auchinleck asked Lord Cork to send a strong telegram to the BBC requiring an explanation from them, regarding this foolish and dangerous report. Stupid reporting by the BBC was one thing but as already observed throughout this narrative, many Norwegians could not be trusted and were quite capable of compromising Allied operations in Norway. Auchinleck reported that on 2 June, several Norwegians, including a local chief of police, were arrested by the British at Skaanland. The Norwegians had been interfering with the British telephone system in the area. At the same time, the Norwegian civilian telephone system was disconnected by Commander Congreve, Royal Navy on the south shore of Ofotfjord, in order to prevent further security leaks to the south. It was noted that on 10 June 1940, after the Allied evacuation of Norway, the Norwegian Army finally surrendered to the Germans during the night of 9–10 June.[2]

Auchinleck's frustrations were quite clear: it was one thing to deal with military matters and the changing fortunes and needs of an operation being carried out locally and under one's control, but dealing with distant civilians who have no idea of what the local situation is, exasperated him and of course Lord Cork. BBC reporting was also another bugbear for commanders in the field, until Churchill took over and stricter censorship was introduced and accepted. In 1982 the BBC World Service was accused of reporting 3rd Battalion, the Parachute Regiment position at Goose Green, during intensive fighting during the Falkland War. The report meant that 3 PARA had to move, as the Argentinean enemy also received the report and so the paras were imperilled, in that they had remained at the reported position. This incident made for bad relations between the BBC and British Armed Forces. The question of Norwegian treachery was not that incredible, as every country, no matter their historical mythology, throws up traitors and collaborators and it is part of the task of an opposing force to deal with such matters. Auchinleck's narrative illustrates most of the problems relating to the Norwegian Campaign of 1940.

Between 13–14 May, the Polish Brigade was disposed as follows: one battalion with the French holding area Bjerkvik-Oijord; one battalion at Harstad; one battalion at Ballangen and finally one at Salangen. The battalion in the Bjerkvik-Oijord area arrived on 13 May at around noon. Even though the Polish advance had been unopposed, the troops had been hampered by heavy snow drifts and had reached their destination weary and nearly exhausted after two nights without sleep. Detachments had protected the left flank of the advance towards Haugen; the right flank of the march was towards Meby and the rear of the move towards Gjeisvik. Two companies moved to Oijord to hold that area.

In order to relieve 2nd SWB and 12th *Chasseurs Alpins* another Polish battalion moved to Ankenes on 15 May; arriving there on 16 May. At the time of the changeover, the enemy attacked the area but was beaten off with relative ease. By 19 May, a further Polish battalion arrived on the Ankenes peninsula and so the Podhalian Brigade was disposed in the following manner. The HQ of the Polish Brigade was at Borkenes, while the HQ of 1st Polish Demi Brigade was at Skjomnes, while that of 1st and 2nd Battalions of the 1st Polish Demi Brigade was on the Ankenes Peninsula. The HQ of 2nd Demi Brigade was at Sjoveien, as was the HQ of 4th Battalion/2nd Polish Demi

2 Ibid.

Brigade, while the HQ of 3rd Battalion was at Ballangen. 4th Battalion was actually en route for Harstad, where a Polish Liaison Officer remained with the Expeditionary Headquarters. There were strong enemy detachments in the Ankenes area but they remained mostly inactive. The only really strong enemy attack came from the air on 21 May, causing an unrecorded number of Polish casualties amongst those holding the ridge east of Storvand. On the same day, 2nd Polish Demi Brigade HQ arrived at Tjelbotn.

On 22 May, Bethouart issued Operational Order No 38, which called for the retaking of Narvik and the Narvik Peninsula. The Poles had been allotted the important task of clearing the enemy from the Ankenes area and of cutting the enemy's lines of retreat towards Sweden, at the head of the Beisfjord. For this purpose they were given a section of three tanks and four artillery pieces, two of which were British and two were French. AAA protection was provided by the British but mainly to do with inadequate air cover postponed and before the original plan was carried out an important modification was made: the Podhalians were to advance without delay to Beisfjord and capture it.[3] And so the question that now lies before us; just how did Polish troops end up fighting in Norway? The answer is that the Polish government in exile in France wanted to make Poland relevant to the war and show that Poland was still fighting.

Polish plans for a return to the field against Germany had been going on since October 1939, when thousands of Polish troops managed to escape the clutches of the Germans and the Soviets and make their way to the West, principally to France. During the winter of 1939–40, the French had largely ignored the Polish experience of a German invasion, as they considered it to have been irrelevant; dismissing the Polish Army as being a poorly led, poorly equipped mass peasant army that could offer no lessons in modern warfare. Then suddenly out of the blue the Poles were requested to form infantry half-brigades or 'demi-brigades,' earmarked for service in Finland. Colonel Kedzior (Chief of the Polish General Staff) in a letter to Colonel Gubbins, told his British colleague who was requesting information of how the Polish Army was reforming in Poland and how many troops it had; that it was impossible to say, as the request had queered all of the Polish plans for its army in France.[4] Even if Polish plans for the re-establishment of a Polish Army had been interfered with by the French request for troops to be sent to Finland, the Poles would have been delighted to have received it as there was a chance to return to the war against its enemies: in this case the Soviet Union. However, it should be noted that Churchill was also reluctant to go to war with the Soviet Union, which he made quite clear during December 1939.[5] It should also be considered that the British and Soviet governments were equally capable of pragmatism, in order to further their own agenda. Evidence of this is the relationship between the British, American and Soviet governments during the period 1941–45, which saw this trio ideologically opposed to each other but focussed on the military defeat of Germany; once this objective was achieved the relationship collapsed within weeks, as the Soviet Union returned to its ideological and revolutionary agenda, which demanded the vanquishing of states such as the UK and the USA.

During February 1940, the Poles had indeed been preparing a rifle brigade, as a report dated 15 February 1940 clearly illustrates. The infantry brigade in question was being well trained in all aspects of infantry warfare, including the use of rifles, machineguns, mortars (60mm and 81mm calibre) as well as the 25mm light artillery gun. Other aspects were also being taught including defensive measures, such as the digging of trenches and how to defend against armour using anti-tank guns and the building of anti-tank defences. Anti-tank warfare was something that the Poles actually had a lot of experience in and during the September Campaign had acquitted themselves

3 TNA, CAB 106/1160, The Polish Brigade in Norway, 1940.
4 PISM, A.IV.1/2, Correspondence with the Allies, Colonel Kedzior to Colonel Gubbins, 20 February 1940.
5 Winston S. Churchill, note, Admiralty Papers, ADM 199/1929, 3 December 1939, *Churchill 1*.

when engaging German armour. It might have been more beneficial if the French had asked the Poles about their experience of engaging German armour; until 1940 no other army had actually fought against German aggression and therefore the Polish experience was unique and there were lessons for the British and French to learn from their Polish counterparts. However there was an element of the training in France, which had been neglected in the Polish Army; how to work independently and to keep an operation moving.[6] Traditionally Polish troops had always looked to their officers for leadership, whilst there was scarcely any effective backbone of senior NCOs who might have stepped into the breach in the absence of officers for whatever reason. The training in France was thorough and important for future actions concerning the Polish Army in the West.

Borkowski notes that the order to create the Independent Podhalian Rifle Brigade was issued on 9 February 1940 and as we have seen from primary sources, it was originally designated to serve in Finland but was not deployed, as Finland capitulated to the Soviet Union. Initially one might be forgiven for thinking that the Podhalians were some kind of crack mountain brigade but the reality was somewhat different. The brigade had been set up quickly from those battalions separated from 1st and 2nd Polish Infantry Divisions scattered in France but mainly located in Brittany. The composition of the brigade was varied; the officers who had escaped from Poland to France were mainly professional soldiers and owing to the September Campaign had combat experience. This is in contrast to the rank and file of which 90% were volunteers from Polish émigré families living in France, Belgium and Holland and had little or no military experience. The final formation of the brigade prior to embarking for Norway was the General Staff, communications, motorised section and two demi-brigades. Each demi-brigade was composed of a Staff Company, auxiliary weapons company and two rifle battalions. Before leaving France, Colonel Zygmunt Bohusz-Szyszko was promoted to the rank of Brigadier-General and made commander of the Polish force going to Norway.

Bohusz-Szyszko was a good choice, as he was an experienced officer and had been in command of 16th Infantry Division during the September Campaign. Despite the training received in France, Borkowski observes that the Podhalian Brigade was unable to conduct independent operations, owing to the fact that it lacked its own artillery, armoured weapons and AAA. They were completely dependent on the largesse of the Allies – a perennial problem for the Polish armed forces throughout the Second World War. The Podhalians embarked on the French vessels, *Mexique*, *Chenonceaux* and *Columbie* for eventual service in Norway on the night 22–23 April 1940. The Polish force consisted of 4,778 men and officers and were equipped with twenty-five 25mm anti-tank guns, fifteen 81mm mortars, fifteen 60mm mortars and 68 heavy machineguns, in addition to the standard infantry equipment carried by infantrymen.

After arriving in Scotland from France, the Poles were put ashore for several days in the port town of Greenock. Finally the convoy carrying the Poles with detachments from 13th Demi-Brigade FFL, accompanied by Destroyers left for northern Norway and across into the Arctic on the night 2–3 May. 13th Demi-Brigade FFL and the Podhalian Brigade together formed 1st Light Rifle Division commanded by General Bethouart. The Poles made up 33% of the Allied armed forces, which operated in the Narvik area and 50% of the troops actually involved in the battle to recover Narvik, once British troops were moved to the Bodo and Mosjoen regions.[7] This was clearly a substantial input by the Poles and risky, as they found it difficult to recruit, owing to the enemy occupation of their homeland.

6 PISM, A.IV.11/52, Training of the Rifle Brigade, Colonel Kedzior, 15 February 1940.
7 M. Borkowski, 'Polish Forces in the High North' in Karl Rommetveit (ed.) *Narvik 1940. Five Nations Fight in the High North*, Oslo, Institutt for forsvarsstudier (IFS), 1991, pp. 146-65.

Apart from primary sources, the best account of Polish participation in the Narvik offensive is a memoir left by Colonel Władysław Dec, who served with the Podhalians in Norway and is an extremely relevant source for the narration of the campaign. Dec considered that the chance for action in Norway was a significant step towards returning to Poland, with the Podhalian Brigade being the first Polish troops from what he described as the 'New Polish Army' (*nowej armii polskiej*) to be sent out to fight the Germans. Sikorski claimed that the presence of Polish troops in the force going out to Norway, illustrated the right of Poland to be considered part of the alliance against Germany; Sikorski also demanded the right to have a seat at the Council of Allies.

Sikorski's demand for Poland to have a seat at the Council of Allies is an interesting point and morally Sikorski was probably right but morality has nothing to do with politics or reality. Furthermore, the Marquis de Sade is said to have said 'what is more immoral than war.' Sikorski was wasting his breath, as he only seemed to speak to his countrymen while the Allies acknowledged the Polish presence in the Alliance when it suited them to do so, otherwise the Poles were ignored. Even so the chance of action in Norway brought to an end the frustration of being unable to do anything against the enemy, as well as bringing to an end the boredom of garrison life and the minor irritations of life away from the battlefield.[8]

Dec makes an interesting observation about the relationship between the French and the British. From his observations of Rennes, the capital of Brittany, by April 1940, had more or less become a British town owing to the large number of British soldiers there. According to Dec, there was a sense of hostility between the British and the French. The French considered that the British Expeditionary Force (BEF) sent to France at the outbreak of war, was of little value whatsoever and more akin to a toddler being sent out to fight. The phlegmatic British, as far as Dec could judge, merely ignored the French. The Poles, whilst in Rennes awaiting transport to embark them for their eventual voyage out to Norway, were bemused onlookers.[9] It did not bode well for future relations between the Allies. It's an interesting observation but perhaps the Poles should have learnt from, it had gained a sense of perspective when trying to gauge their ranking in the alliance against Germany.

Dec recalled that finally on 23 April 1940 in pouring rain, the battalions of the Podhalian Rifle Brigade set off for war once more. Of the 4,778 Polish troops sent to Narvik, 227 were officers and cadet officers, 742 NCOs and 3,809 riflemen. At five past midnight, 24 April, the Poles set sail. Some of the more optimistic Cadet Officers declared that from Norway they were to 'jump' over the Baltic Sea and back into Poland. Dec being a more mature man settled to sleep in his cabin when suddenly he was woken up by the 'hellish' firing of naval guns and automatic weapons. He quickly went up on deck thinking that a German air attack was in progress, but discovered it was the routine testing of guns, as practised by Allied navies as they set out to sea. Dec recalled that like many of his comrades, travel was a novel experience. After an incident free but boring trip, the Podhalians arrived in Clyde on the evening 25 April.[10]

On 30 April, even before they had left the UK, the Podhalians were to witness a tragedy. During the loading of ammunition a mysterious explosion occurred; supposedly owing to a stack of wood catching fire. The flames quickly took hold and threatened a French Destroyer due to escort the Poles to Norway, as part of Convoy X-91. The French ship became endangered by a huge column of flame, despite the presence of smaller vessels around the Destroyer trying to extinguish the raging fire. The blaze caused ammunition to explode and intensified the inferno, to such an extent, that

8 Dec, op. cit. p. 47.
9 Ibid., p. 48.
10 Ibid., pp. 54-6.

not even a heavy downpour of Scots rain could douse it and finally the stricken ship sank.[11] In the long run, this incident was fairly trivial – thousands of ships were sunk before the end of the war and some quite illustrious compared with this unknown and unrecognised French Destroyer but what is interesting is that Dec hints that the entire episode was the work of saboteurs or even enemy agents; later in his narrative, Dec discusses the activities of German spies in France.

Dec is quite clear that security in the French port of Brest was lax and German spies very active. An example being that despite French security, the Germans were fully aware that the Podhalian Brigade and FFL were leaving Brest, despite it supposedly being a secret. The Poles came to no harm during their passage to the UK but the Germans played another game, when they broadcast on 23 April that a brigade of 'Polish bandits' had left Brest. The Germans knew the exact day of sailing and so deliberately advertised that nothing was a secret to German intelligence.[12] Security in the early stages of the war was compromised by both the British and the French. The French seemed compromised from the top down, as even the French leader in exile, General Charles de Gaulle, let the cat out of the bag regarding operations in West Africa in 1940. The Poles were no different and it illustrates why minor allies including, after 1940, the French were often excluded from high level meetings, which did not concern them. Simply the European allies leaked like sieves and could not be trusted.

A further consideration, which the British do not like to discuss for two reasons, was British sabotage in support of the Soviet Union before 1941. In April 1940 the Soviet Union was very close to becoming an enemy of the UK, owing to the Soviet invasion of Finland and had angered a large part of British society; an attitude that lasted until June 1941, when the Soviet Union was invaded by Germany. After that until war's end, support for the Soviet Union led by Churchill was massive. However before that time and at a time when the Soviet Union was still an ally of Nazi Germany, British communists and their supporters portrayed the war as a capitalist war, with little reason for the working classes anywhere to support it. Therefore in a politically charged environment, such as a Scots dockyard where many of the workers were likely to have been sympathetic towards the Soviet Union, it was not impossible for an act of sabotage, such as the firing of the French Destroyer on its way to prevent a possible Soviet annexation of Norway being carried out. Dec is certainly sceptical of the events, as they were explained, as he wrote '*niby*' while describing events. This suggests that he was not totally convinced by the official version of events as set out before him.[13]

On 1 May 1940, the Poles were once more on the move; they knew that they were bound for Norway but speculation was rife as to where they might land: Trondheim, Namsos and Bodo were all distinct possibilities. Clearly the Polish force was abreast of the situation and possible objectives in Norway. Even so the commander of the ship taking Dec to Norway did not know where he was to land. On 5 May after an uneventful voyage the Poles discovered their destination: the fishing port of Tromso, where they landed the same afternoon.

The arrival of the Polish Brigade was a great shock for the Norwegian authorities, who coldly received them. For the first couple of days it seemed that the Poles had nothing to do and so just wandered around taking in the local sights along the nearby fjord, which led them to be dubbed the 'unemployed Polish Brigade.' On 7 May, the Poles were sent to the port of Harstad on the Hinnøya Island. Before the Poles were able to embark they witnessed a German aerial bombing raid on Harstad. AAA positions in unison with naval guns were able to disrupt the raid and their bombs fell into the sea and out of harm's way. It was a beautiful sight according to Dec, to see the Germans struggling and failing in this attempted raid.

11 Ibid., p. 57.
12 Ibid., pp. 58-9.
13 Ibid., p. 57.

Dec noted the topography; the rocks, fjords and mountains. He described the scenery as beautiful and also recognised that it was going to be difficult to fight a military operation over it. Incredibly Dec was moved to consider the living conditions of the average Norwegian fisherman or peasant, as he saw a small holder. Dec wrote that they enjoyed comforts such as large homes, which were light and heated by electricity. He noted every home had bathrooms and kitchens. Dec was impressed that ordinary Norwegian folk had books on their shelves and pianos in their drawing rooms. Such style he reflected would not have disgraced the home of a Polish intellectual. No doubt, this caused him to consider just how backward Poland really was and how poor it was and furthermore, how unfair and divided Polish society was, as many people such as industrial workers lived in single rooms and many peasants lived in nothing more than mud huts, while the Polish upper classes, such as the military officer caste, lived in relative luxury. However British cities until the 1960s were equally of such poor repair.

There was a distinct problem for the French and the British, as Norwegians accustomed to a long tradition and experience of peace and prosperity were reluctant to fight an invader. Indeed sections of Norwegian society, and not just pacifists, considered that it would be better to enjoy peace under German rule than to go to war. Clearly they were deluded regarding German occupation and rule and seemed to have ignored the terror of Nazi governance, if one can call it that rather than the simple gangsterism that it actually was. Finally after displaying quite an understanding of conditions in pre-war Norway, Dec began to outline the military situation as he saw it there.

Dec began to access what had happened prior to the Polish arrival in Norway. Analysis of the original German attack on Norway was made available to Dec. He learnt that 6th Norwegian Infantry Division could be found in northern Norway and that they had been halfway through mobilization when the Germans invaded. At the time of the German invasion, 6th Norwegian Infantry Division were at Elvergårdsmoen, the supply base of the Norwegian Army, which was in the Bjerkvik area. General Fleischer, commanding this area had anticipated a German attack on Narvik and had on 8–9 April sent 1st Battalion 13th Infantry Regiment Norwegian Army to Narvik. He was able to draw on another battalion from Bardu but unfortunately these battalions delayed in setting out, owing to a blizzard blowing up. As a consequence of this delay, the Germans were able to reach Narvik first and occupy its town and port.

The fall of Narvik was fortuitous for the Germans, as the Norwegians had neglected to destroy its equipment there. The Germans owing to this negligence, were able to capture 300 heavy machineguns, as well as about 8,000 rifles and uniforms. Indeed enough equipment to equip an entire infantry division. However, as we have seen, German success (with Norwegian collaboration) was short lived, as the Royal Navy on 10 April and again 13 April swept into the waters off Narvik and the fjord there and wrecked the German surface fleet found there. The Germans dubbed 13 April 1940 '*Unglückstagiem*' or the 'day of destruction'. The port at Narvik, according to Dec, was truly the graveyard of the German fleet.

Once the Germans had been defeated at sea, Allied land forces began to land in earnest. The first troops to land in northern Norway were those from 24th Guards Brigade. Between 15 April and 25 April, individual battalions from 24th Guards Brigade were widely dispersed around the Narvik region, holding territories in the regions of Liland, Lenvik, Salangen and the summits of mountains 295–405 on the Ankenes peninsula. The Guards were waiting for the arrival of the Poles. Hard on the heels was the French 27th Demi-Brigade, of which was part of the *Chasseurs Alpins* arriving on 27 April. On 8 May, the Podhalians and 13th Demi-Brigade FFL arrived. In the ranks of FFL were hundreds of Poles and Italians.

On 10 May, General Bohusz-Szyszko came to Dec's position at Sörvik. Bethouart had ordered Bohusz-Szyszko to do so. A flotilla of puffers had been made available to transport Dec's battalion, 2nd Battalion Podhalian Rifles from Harstad to Bogen-Lenvik area. It was there that 2nd Battalion was to link up with British forces. During the night 12–13 May, Dec and his battalion were to cut across country from Lenvik to Bjerkvik, to the north of Narvik and then attacking from the west German defences in that area. The FFL was to make an amphibious landing, supported by naval gunfire, while from the north *Chasseurs Alpins* was to attack enemy positions. Bohusz-Szyszko said that 2nd Battalion was to leave immediately. Dec knew that the timing was not ideal, as the battalion was at sixes and sevens owing to its rapid move from Brest earlier that spring. The Podhalians had no stretchers for the wounded and no ammunition for heavy machineguns. Even so, 2nd Battalion had to be ready within 24 hours.

During the evening of 11 May, 2nd Battalion were in the port at Harstad. Puffers were under steam and ready to go. Amazingly there still seemed to have been time for a protocol visit to *Chroby*, which was in port and a delegation came from the vessel with an invitation for supper aboard *Chroby*. Owing to the pressure of time, as it was not long before the Poles would have to leave the fjord and go to war, the visit was brief but emotional, as once more Polish soldiers were on a Polish ship complete with the symbols of their homeland. It was with great regret that the Poles learnt of the sinking of *Chroby* on 17 May.[14]

The Podhalians had received movement orders on 10 May. 2nd Battalion 1st Demi-Brigade was to move from the Melvik-Nordvik area to the Ostervik region on the northern shore of Ofotfjord. They were scheduled to be supplied from Harstad during the night 10–11 May. The Polish formations were prepared for action, having been supplied with ammunition, weapons, rockets, snow goggles and sledges, as well as enough food for three days. Once in Ostervik, 2nd Battalion was to seek out the enemy in the direction of Ostervik-Trondviken and Bjerkvik. It was suggested that 2nd Battalion should seek out the guidance of Norwegian ski-troops operating in the Ostervik area. After making contact with the Norwegians, 2nd Battalion was to strengthen holding positions, as well as isolate areas of enemy opposition and prevent them from linking up. There was a consideration that Polish units operating along the shores of Ofoten fjord, might well be supplied from small fishing boats belonging to locals. General Szyszko-Bohusz told Major Leopold Krizar that the primary objective of the Podhalians in the Landgöy area was observation and the prevention of enemy paratroops from landing.[15]

At 2100 hours 11 May 1940, a flotilla of 21 puffers took the Podhalians out to sea and made their way to Bogen-Lenvik. There was a constant fear of enemy air attacks. Even though the Royal Navy had more or less destroyed the German surface fleet in the area, the Allies were yet to master the skies. Dec noted that on some of the puffers were coffins, but he decided that fate was decided by God and did not let the sight detain his thoughts for long. In the event the voyage was quiet and the Podhalians arrived safely at their destination. The following day after finally receiving all of the necessary ammunition by 2200 hours, 12 May, the Poles moved to Bjerkvik; a distance of about 19 kilometres (Borkowski claims 25 kilometres) but the route lacked roads and was covered by snow. The Polish troops found the going very hard, as they were unused to such hostile terrain and were not equipped to deal with it. Every 20 minutes or so they had to stop to rest, which made for some very slow progress and called for great endurance. Dec remarked that not only was the snow deep but it was also wet. Snow drifts impeded their progress and made the already difficult march, that much harder.[16]

14 Ibid., p. 67.
15 PISM, A.IV.11/6, General Bohusz-Szyszko to Major Krizar, 10 May 1940.
16 Dec, p. 67.

Borkowski notes that the Norwegian ski-troops were absolute life savers for the Poles. The snow that covered the terrain, over which the Poles were trying to pass, was deep, melting and lay in heaps. Furthermore, to add to the Polish misery; the Germans had destroyed all bridges over ravines and streams. The Poles carried all of their equipment on their backs, yet somehow managed to cross their destination in less than 16 hours. Borkowski mentions the testimony of Private Wojciech Lipinski, who recalled that the Norwegian troops gave invaluable help and advice to his platoon on their march to Bjerkvik. Lipinski's platoon was to march on to the shores of the Ofotfjord. The terrain, as ever, was difficult and some of the Polish troops were forced to crawl over the snow, putting snowshoes over their hands; many were exhausted and some fell asleep while on the march. Seeing the Polish plight, the Norwegians made them snow shelters and let them sleep. As the Poles slept, the Norwegians stood guard over them. Lipinski's platoon rejoined their battalion a day later. Their sudden appearance hastened the enemy withdrawal from Ofotfjord. Lipinski and his comrades also heard the first salvo of artillery – the offensive had begun.[17] A further report noted, that in the Narvik area German paratroopers in Norwegian uniforms were being dropped and reinforcing the enemy area.[18] This method of underhand fighting was not the only lawless action of the enemy, as reports of the Germans burning down homes with wounded people in the Ankenes area were received.[19] So much for the German 'clean fighting' – it was not just the SS, which committed atrocities.

Meanwhile Dec's battalion could hear the firing of naval guns and shells exploding in support of FFL troops landing at Narvik. It was 1000 hours and the offensive was going well; it seemed that the port and town might well fall quickly. At the time of the German capture of Narvik, it had been captured intact owing to treachery and of course the Royal Navy had wrecked the place since. When the FFL assault against Narvik began, Dec's battalion was still six kilometres away from its objective at Bjerkvik and the fastest they could move was only 1.5 kilometres an hour; as once more difficult terrain had to be covered. At Trondviken the Poles took over the warm quarters which the Germans had recently vacated. The Germans using good patrol work had withdrawn to safety in nearby mountains. Then Dec received new orders.

The bridge at the position had been blown up and Dec's men had to provide an alternative route out of the area. The Germans had made a thorough job of destroying every bridge, large and small in the area and so the Allies had to improvise some form of bridge through thickly forested areas and over every stream. Dec's battalion managed to defeat weak enemy opposition on the axis of the Polish advance and by midday had reached the countryside to the west of Bjerkvik. Fighting had died down in the area; smashed houses on the coast bore testimony to the severity of allied naval gunfire. What had not been blown up by shells from large naval guns, had been set alight. The flames had spread from other buildings also set ablaze by the allied naval bombardment.[20]

During the night 12–13 May, the Poles and the FFL worked together to draw away German patrols that covered the section of road between Bjerkvik and Øyjord. During the evening 15 May, 2nd Battalion Podhalians was relieved by 14th Battalion *Chasseur Alpins* and as ordered by General Bethouart, made for Bjerkvik in readiness to embark for the Ankenes peninsula. As a result of the three Allied offensives, the Germans under Dietl had deteriorated considerably. The taking of the Øyjord peninsula by the Allies gave them complete mastery of the Narvik garrison from the north. Only the waters of the Rombaksfjord lay between the Allies and Narvik. As the Royal Navy reigned supreme on the local seas, this did not seem to be an obstacle.

17 Borkowski, op. cit. p. 149.
18 PISM, A.IV.11/13, Information Bulletin No. 11, 19 May 1940.
19 PISM, A.IV.11/13, Information Communication, 24 May 1940.
20 Borkowski, op. cit. pp. 149-57.

On 17 May, the Narvik operational area was divided into two regions: Ankenes – from the north bordering on Ofotfjord and from the west on Aefjord under the command of the CO Independent Podhalian Rifle Brigade. The second area was the Bjerkvik area under the command of the CO 13th Demi-Brigade FFL. On 16 and 17 May, 1st Podhalian Demi-Brigade relieved British and French troops on the Ankenes peninsula. The Poles were reinforced by the arrival of the 4th Reserve Battalion (Podhalian) on 19 May. Only 3rd Battalion remained in the Ballangen area to secure the supply bases. Detachments of 1st Podhalian Demi-Brigade defended the ridge of the Ankenes peninsula, from the village of Baetberget to Hill 295, 405, 677 and 734 until 27 May. The demi-brigade established two battalion defence regions – 1st Battalion on the right flank and 2nd Battalion on the left. Colonel Benedykt Chlusewicz, CO 1st Demi-Brigade held 4th Battalion in reserve and during 22–24 May, when it was transferred from the Tjelbotn region (HQ 2nd Demi-Brigade) to the Ankenes peninsula.

Once the enemy became aware of the Allied threat to Narvik, the initial German force of two companies of mountain troops (*Gebirgsjager*) was increased to two battalions. Bethouart issued an operational order on 22 May, which called for 1st Light Rifle Division to use part of its force to attack the Narvik peninsula from the Øyjord peninsula. This attack was to go in at midnight on 27 May, timed to avoid enemy counterattacks. The Podhalians (1st, 2nd and 4th Battalions) supported by a detachment from the *Chasseur Alpins*, two tanks from 342nd Company, a battery of French 75mm guns, two British field howitzers, as well as supporting fire from the big guns of the British Cruiser HMS *Southampton,* was to seize control of the remainder of the Ankenes peninsula, as well as stopping the Germans from withdrawing along the shores of the Beisfjord. East of Beisfjord the Poles were to join up with the FFL, who were approaching from the north and so encircle Dietl's troops on the Narvik peninsula. 3rd Battalion, Podhalian Rifles, were at the time in the Ballangen region and with two battalions of *Chasseur Alpins* made up Bethouart's reserve force. They were to go onto the offensive in the final stages of the operation and were to try to prevent the Germans from escaping encirclement.

Szyszko-Bohusz looked at Bethouart's operation orders and decided to amend them, as he considered that it would be best to launch an attack in two different directions. Colonel Chlusewicz's forces (1st Battalion Podhalians and a detachment from 4th Battalion) were to attack east, in order to capture the village of Beisfjord, while Dec's 2nd Battalion was to work independently of the demi-brigade and launch an attack northwards towards Ankenes and Nyborg. This was not quite what the French General had in mind when he issued his orders and had insisted on the seizure of Beisfjord. Szyszko-Bohusz however, had divined that the capture and occupation of Beisfjord would prevent the withdrawal of enemy troops from Ankenes and allow the Podhalians to get around to the rear of the Narvik corps.

Before attacking along the right flank, Chlusewicz's troops carried out a reconnaissance patrol. This was carried out by 4th Battalion, which at 1400 hours, 27 May, secretly left Mattisjorden and encircled the enemy from the south. After marching for 12 hours, 4th Battalion reached the area of Iverdalryggen Hill, in the early hours of 28 May. From this position after receiving a prearranged signal, flashed to them by light; 4th Battalion was to attack the enemy's rear position on Hill 606. They waited all day in vain – no signal was made or received. At 1800 hours still without the prearranged signal, it was noticed that the enemy was beginning to withdraw. Without any orders the CO of 4th Battalion launched an attack and Hill 606 was captured.

Even so, 4th Battalion's successful operation did not coincide with 1st Battalion's operation, which began at 0001 hours, 28 May. This was a hard fought battle taking nearly all day, but by 2130 hours, 1st Battalion succeeded and captured Hill 773. 1st Company supported by a heavy machinegun platoon then set out for Beisfjord but only got as far as Lakselven Valley. The Polish troops were exhausted with climbing and no doubt fighting, all while ascending Hill 773 and so it proved impossible to take advantage of the success of 4th Battalion and the idea of 2nd Reserve Company pursuing and cutting off German troops escaping through Beisfjord towards the Kvanta Pass and onto Sildvik was abandoned. The march was resumed on 29 May and at 0500 hours, patrols of 1st Battalion entered Beisfjord, now clear of Germans and where the rest of the battalion joined them at 1500 hours. Later they moved into the Kvanta Pass without meeting any significant enemy forces.

Dec's troops launched an attack on 28 May. 2nd Battalion's attack began at 0001 hours, following a 20 minute supporting artillery barrage to soften up the enemy. 3rd Company supported by a heavy machinegun and mortar platoon attacked both sides of the main road leading to Ankenes. However tanks sent to support the attack were immediately halted, as soon as they went into action. Despite this setback, 3rd Company continued to attack very aggressively, so their endeavours were rewarded by reaching the south-western outskirts of Ankenes. It was there however, that they encountered heavy enemy machinegun and mortar fire; after heavy losses, the Poles had to withdraw at about 0300 hours, 29 May. The Germans immediately counterattacked and took advantage of a gap between 1st and 3rd Company. At 0500 hours the enemy captured Hill 295, which disorganised Dec's detachment's command and communication systems. The overall danger was averted, as 3rd Company 4th Battalion moved forward from the Brigade's rear and took up positions on the southern and western slopes of Hill 295. Despite three attempts to capture Hill 295, it proved impossible. However during the night the Germans withdrew, as after the loss of the Ankenes peninsula, there was little if any point in remaining on the hill. During the morning 29 May, 3rd Company entered Ankenes and occupied it without any fighting.

1st Company, supported by fire from its heavy machinegun company, began its attack from Hill 295 towards Haugen at 0200 hours, 28 May. Slowly and systematically 1st Company moved forward until its left flank came under fire from the enemy. 1st Company were forced to lie doggo until the morning of 29 May, when the enemy finally gave up and left. The only real success was from 2nd Company's right flank, which supported by fire from 2nd Demi-Brigade's heavy machinegun and mortar platoons and half a battery of British howitzers, forced its way through German defences and seized the high ground at the village of Nyborg. From this position the Poles using machineguns were able to harass the Germans trying to use the main Nyborg-Fagernes route to withdraw along. The occupation of Beisfjord by the Poles eased the situation in the Ankenes area and went someway to improve the position of the FFL, as German resistance on Hill 457 subsided and accelerated the German defeat on the Narvik peninsula and the eventual capture of Narvik itself. The seizure of the Nyborg and Lyngenes region on the south side of Beisfjord and of the southern side of Lakselven Valley denied Dietl's support on the Ankenes peninsula.

Driving the Germans from the Ankenes peninsula was beyond doubt a major fillip for Polish military integrity, at a time when it was needed. For many of the Polish troops it had been a baptism of fire but they had passed this major test with flying colours. The Polish losses at Narvik were 97 killed, 189 wounded, seven captured and 21 missing. The Germans facing the Poles suffered estimated losses of 190 men and officers, including 60 Germans being taken prisoner by Polish forces. The fighting and the German defeat on the Ankenes peninsula was not the end of combat for the Podhalians. On 30 May, the Staff of the Podhalians received another order to remain in combat readiness for an attack on Hundalen via Sildvik. The entire 1st Demi-Brigade in preparation for this offensive concentrated at Beisfjord. However 2nd Battalion was exhausted and were for a time incapable of any further combat service. 3rd Battalion was transported to Salangen and received an order to cover the region of the airfield at Bardufoss. During this time 1st Battalion, ignorant of plans to abandon northern Norway owing to an error in the command system, managed with the help of 13th Demi-Brigade FFL to move their defensive lines further east. When 1st Battalion joined detachements of 13th Demi-Brigade FFL along the Klubnes Line and on Hill 675 and 660, they received a new order, which required them to cover the evacuation of the entire brigade.

The operations of Independent Podhalian Rifle Brigade, even though it enjoyed great success and fulfilled its tasks, as set by the Commander of 1st Light Rifle Division, its conduct had been criticised by military historians. Command errors are often the source of their criticisms. The main objection is that often Polish commanders neglected the objective of an offensive. The tendency to alter troop dispersal was noticeable in the difference between Bethouart's operational plan and Szyszko-Bohusz's actual orders to the Podhalians. From the point of view of the Narvik operation, Ankenes was of secondary importance and should have only received protection. But a decisive solution, not only for the fighting on the Ankenes peninsula but for the entire Narvik operation, could only have been brought about by the Beisfjord-Sildvik operation. That was to attack the enemy's rear positions where the main attack was to be concentrated.

The failure of the attack carried out by Dec's troops was due to shallow, linear grouping and a poor choice in the direction of the strength of the action. Dec launched three companies in a single line along a five kilometre line; distributing them amongst all of the battalion's howitzers, but neglecting to leave any reserves and without focussing on the seizure of the enemy's main defensive point. Szyszko-Bohusz accepted Dec's plan but it led to a crisis after 3rd Company's defeat. Equally Chlusewicz's group moved too slowly (3–4 km per day). This was the result of excessive exhaustion and a lack of experience in mountain warfare. The Brigade's Commander had a groundless fear of a German attack from the direction of Ankenes on Chlusewicz's positions. This fear had the effect of slowing down even further an already too slow an advance.

These criticisms can be partly countered when one looks at Polish problems on the Ankenes peninsula. The Poles had inadequate supplies of armoured and artillery equipment, lack of air support, while most Polish troops lacked military experience let alone combat experience especially mountain warfare. The terrain and climate of northern Norway was particularly challenging. However much of the confusion during the Narvik campaign was that Bethouart had his attack orders in one pocket and his evacuation order in the other. But overall the Poles performed well at Norway in 1940.[21]

Borkowski might well analyse events at Narvik decades later and only Dec can put the flesh on the story of offensive. A joint offensive between the FFL and the Podhalians was beginning to tell on the Germans and Dietl's all conquering force, of only a month earlier, was beginning to break down due to the relentless Franco-Polish pressure, as they moved against enemy positions in the Narvik region. Bethouart and other allied commanders were impressed at the speed and determination of much of the Podhalian force, as it advanced towards its objectives. Indeed Bethouart had a job to keep pace with Polish moves. At one point, Bethouart had tried to contact the Poles and order them to take the town of Lenvik, which was to be attacked by Royal Navy Destroyers, but there was a breakdown in telephone communication and an inability to catch up with the Podhalians, as they advanced towards Ankenes.

As the Poles closed in on Bjerkvik, they could hear the commotion of fighting in the town. A patrol was sent out to assess the situation in the town. It was learnt that there was AAA in depth at the lake area, as well as in other positions and that the highroad had been cut. The situation was far from what had been anticipated. The Poles were exhausted after marching for nearly two days;

21 Ibid.

something which the Allied Staff considered to have been a great feat. Now it could be seen that the situation which lay before them at Bjerkvik was not going to be easy; not that it was ever considered to be an easy target, but the offensive to come was going to be harder than anticipated.

Dec recalled that despite the 'hellish' tiredness, from which the Polish troops were suffering, they were still expected to get on with their new operation and move onto the offensive. Orders were received to attack German positions in the mountains to the north of Bjerkvik and their occupants removed and positions captured. The Polish battalion was also ordered to clear the Oijord Peninsula of the 'Bosch' and herd them towards the Swedish frontier. If this operation was successful, the result would be that the main route from Bjerkvik to Oijord would be cleared of the enemy and their ability to use automatic weapons to prevent movement along this route. Orders for the offensive were issued and at the very end of the published orders, it was written 'the battalion was to drive the Germans away like a flock of sheep.' After receiving their orders, the Podhalians prepared to carry them out. However, Dec relates three incidents, which occurred during the offensive on the Oijord peninsula. The first was quite unpleasant, as it was a case of desertion.

Cadet Officer Smagacz, an outpost commander from 2nd Company (Dec's battalion) deserted his post; Dec received a report on the matter from his Adjutant. In relation to the matter, Dec considered that if the wretched Smagacz was apprehended, he would be tried by Court Martial and as he had deserted in the battlefield, as with every army in the world, desertion in the face of the enemy would be treated quite severely and Smagacz would have to face the consequences of his own actions.[22] Dec washed his hands of the whole affair; what else could he do? He was serving on a fighting front and could not make enquiries about Smagacz's health or other social enquiries. These were questions to be asked in the rear lines; the Podhalians were on a battlefield and Smagacz had deserted in the face of the enemy.

The second incident related by Dec, is recalled in a sarcastic vein as 'How lovely war is' (*Jak to na wojence ladnie*) and concerned the multitude of international war correspondents, which had arrived at Bjerkvik. As with all journalists, they were searching for copy and sensational stories to send back to their editors. Several of the journalists were quite determined to see war at close quarters and so Dec took them along the shores of the Rombaks Fjord. There Dec showed his guests nests of enemy defences, set up in railway wagons along the track of the electric railway, which ran from Narvik to Sweden. On the waters of the fjord, British Destroyers patrolled and kept the Germans (*Szwabów*) in check and did not permit the enemy to 'gad about along the tracks'. The correspondents having brought cameras naturally wanted to take photographs of the war in progress and the Germans seemed to oblige by opening fire with anti-tank artillery. This satisfied the pressmen, who then went out to inspect any damage made by the German shelling. Dec however considered the German barrage to have been desultory and of little consequence. The desire for sensational report had left the British, French and American correspondents sprawling in the muddy snow when the Germans had shelled them. It must be admitted that the journalists recognised just how absurd they had been and their panic comical, but they saw the funny side of it. Several days later an account of the incident was published in full in a British newspaper and the writer was decent enough to emphasize that the only person not to duck when the Germans opened fire on them had been the Polish Colonel (Dec).[23] As an experienced soldier, Dec knew when to duck and when to maintain his cool and perhaps to the British public he represented the heroic Poles, scared of nothing, not even German artillery. It must have made great copy on the day.

22 Dec, op. cit. pp. 70-1.
23 Ibid., p. 71.

The third incident relates to a raid made on the Ankenes peninsula by Polish troops. On 15 May, even before the Podhalians had settled down in their new positions, they received new orders during the afternoon; they were to relieve British forces already on the Ankenes peninsula the following day. Still halfway through their move to the peninsula, the Podhalians had to improvise transport in order to carry out their new orders. A flotilla of cutters under the command of a British Lieutenant of the Royal Navy Volunteer Reserve was pressed into action to meet the new demands of the new orders received by the Podhalians. There was a clear deficit of information of what lay before the Pole, as the Divisional Staff had no idea of what might be met on the Ankenes peninsula, while Dec admits he had little or no idea of what he might encounter, as he advanced with his men into the area.

Dec was present when the flotilla commander received orders to convey Dec's battalion to Ankenes during the night 15–16 May. After loading and refuelling the cutters or puffers as some called them, the Podhalians sent out from Herjangs Fjord and Ofot Fjord and out to Ankenes, in order to attack the Germans garrisoned there. However the Poles in this little flotilla had another idea and so disembarked near a port road, which eventually led to Narvik and raided German positions in the area. The Germans were incensed by the Polish action, which they considered to have been impudent owing to the use of cutters and so fired on the Poles with great vigour. The retaliatory German fire caused no casualties amongst the Poles. After a while the Poles withdrew from their raid and began to seek a more suitable and hospitable position. The Poles moved to the fishing port of Skjomnes, which was occupied by the British. Later the Poles moved along the coastal road to Haakvik.

During the morning 16 May, the Poles relieved 2nd SWB, to whom Dec refers to as a 'Guards' Battalion,' he was mistaken in this assertion. The Podhalians were received as honoured guests and were given tea and became family almost from the outset. However when the Poles asked about the enemy positions the British Lieutenant-Colonel commanding the British position, with the famous phlegm of his people, pointed out the direction of the Germans and said 'they are over there. Don't go there. The Germans are good shots.'[24] It was not quite a meeting of minds. There was nothing wrong with the report; it was factual if not practical and delivered without any hysterics. I can only hope that the British did not serve the Poles tea with milk, as they drink it black or with lemon, as well as having a collective phobia of cold milk. The British and Poles might well have been Europeans but were so far away from each other in many things. Dec was certainly learning a lot in Norway.

The Podhalians had originally arrived on the Ankenes peninsula during mid-April and in the grip of an Arctic winter. The SWB had established their base along the shores of the fjord in hamlets, which looked onto Hills 295 and 405, however the safety of these positions was weak. The greatest danger was surprise attacks from German ski-troops, who seemed to be able to conduct hit and run attacks almost at will.[25] To try to counter such attacks Dec established outposts on the summits on both hill tops and had them linked up. This meant that Dec's units were in communication with each other, could observe enemy movements and report on them. Dec noted that the bare terrain, which had little in the way of forest or any cover meant that the Polish outposts, especially the one on Hill 295, had very good clear views of its surroundings, which at nearly 300 metres in height meant that the waters of Beisfjord could also be seen. To the fore of the Polish positions Dec could see the masts and communication masts of the sunken ships destroyed in the naval battles of April poking out of the water at Narvik. On the Narvik peninsula outlined here and there were the

24 Ibid., p. 72.
25 Ibid.

massive heights, which were so typical of the Norwegian terrain. From a western hill a massive Nazi swastika flag flew and was flapping in the wind. Allied Destroyers patrolling the Ofotfjord fired on the flag before withdrawing. It seemed that the presence of Allied ships was taunting the Germans, who had seen most of their surface fleet sunk before their eyes only a few weeks earlier.

During the early period of the Polish occupation of the Ankenes peninsula Captain Laurentowski, a Company Commander, was observing enemy defensive formations from Baatberget by the fjord beyond Hill 295. Laurentowski kept in communication with his base and waited for instructions of how to proceed. He wanted information of where to reconnoitre and in particular to where he should direct a forthcoming offensive and fire, as another company was to attack the area between Hill 405 and the Bartoszk Mountains. During the afternoon of 17 May, this company began its offensive. Hill 405 was climbed to reconnoitre the area. Basically the Poles were checking the reality of their position and of local geography, compared with the fiction of their operational maps. In the distance between Hill 405 and Hill 295, which was an area of about three kilometres and could be described as 'no-man's land'. The Poles found that they could only control a small part of this land via outposts on the summits of Hills 405 and 295. The outpost on Hill 405 became an observation post from which patrols were sent out to reconnoitre throughout the area, by climbing the summits of various nearby hills in a bid to learn of the whereabouts of the enemy and what they were up to. While engaged in this activity, one of the reconnoitring companies came under heavy German mortar and machinegun fire. Members of the Polish company hit the deck: hard! All around them was the sound of enemy automatic fire.

Szaszkiewicz, the Company Commander, related that casualties were heavy: four dead; Cadet Officer Kowalski, Corporal Gołębiowski, Rifleman Skonet and Medical Orderly Gołąbek, while Riflemen Kotliński and Stalica were wounded. Szaszkiewicz ordered his men to keep moving and not to present themselves as targets. In order to dig in, it was obviously necessary to actually be able to bite into the earth with shovels – in Norway everything seemed to be rock. The small shovels supplied to infantrymen made no impression at all on the frozen and rocky ground, while pickaxes merely bounced off the unyielding earth, complained 18 year old Corporal Burlik.

The trapped Polish company had to remain where they were pinned down and wait for the arrival of nightfall, which in Scandinavia in May lasted for a little over two dark hours and then it was dawn once more. One of the company, Gruda, recalled that they had to keep quiet until morning and he also remembered that ammunition was running out. Gruda said that he had been in a similar situation before in Spain, which suggests that he had served in the Spanish Civil War of 1936–39, but on which side was not given. Dec recorded the conversations that night, as the company hunkered down for the night; Gruda must have reported it to Dec later. One infantryman, Rifleman Bojko from Argentina considered that the air was getting warmer and then, as if to prove this, a mass of melting snow broke the cold of the night. Szaszkiewicz meanwhile hankered for a Rum to warm himself; Sowiński threw a jacket to his commander. The Polish patrol remained where they were, cold and trapped. At 0200 hours, it became very obvious that the Germans were wide awake and on the move as firing began from both sides. To the rear of the Polish positions and to the left, Second Lieutenant Bobul's heavy machinegun squad was firing at advancing Germans, who were still some way off in the near distance. Suddenly out of the pines from the German side came the whine of bullets and then from behind rocks in front of the Polish position were dozens of *Gebirgsjager*.

Immediately a firefight broke out: groups of Germans sent out to destroy the Polish position were cut down by Polish automatic fire. The Germans then brought up a tank to support their offensive. It was during this fighting that Cadet Officer Natanson rapidly grew up and using inspired leadership and with good and accurate firing, he and his men were able to reduce the German line of advance. Meanwhile in front of the Polish position there was more outstanding and inspired defence work by Polish troops and the advancing *Gebirgsjager* were stopped in several places, while the remainder of the enemy force was reduced to sheltering behind the supporting tank.

The next day the foreground in front of Szaszkiewicz's position was quiet. His platoon's machineguns had made sure of that. Then to the right of the Polish position, people could be seen moving. Cadet Officer Ciemior reported that they were heading towards them. Through binoculars Szaszkiewicz looked at these figures, which were running and leaping towards him and his men and was relieved to recognise 3rd Company coming with help. 3rd Company's Commander, an unnamed Lieutenant, called out 'Hang on'. Immediately the Germans attacked throwing in everything they could muster including mortars and heavy machineguns. Natanson's machinegun squad immediately replied to the German fire. Szaszkiewicz saw that 3rd Company had dealt with and had broken the German counterattack, but without additional support was still unable to get to Szaszkiewicz and his trapped patrol.

It was tempting to stay put and not place oneself in any further danger but Szaszkiewicz knew better than that and furthermore, duty was duty and so a reconnaissance mission was to be carried out, to be certain of the German positions. Once he was certain of his target, Szaszkiewicz gave the order to attack and with simultaneous and accurate fire, Messing, Jankowski and Głowacz raked the area, emptying a magazine apiece. This broke the tension and the ejected cases flew, as the guns blazed and the noise of the firing was incredible. German retaliation was swift and the air was rent by enemy mortar fire. The roar of the explosions of the German mortar bombs shook the Polish positions and the ground around it. For a couple of minutes there was a great barrage of mortar and heavy machinegun fire and then silence. Only the groans of the wounded: Messing, Sytego and Wolski broke the renewed hush.

As Szaszkiewicz's testimony breaks here, we rely on Dec's description of what happened next. Zamoyski and his platoon could do nothing to help Szaszkiewicz and so struck out as best he could. Even though the platoon drove the enemy from the valley between Hills 405 and 295, they were still unable to reach Szaszkiewicz's lofty hill top position. Furthermore, Zamoyski's platoon could not even reach the Polish wounded in the foreground and evacuate them. Finally Stańczyk was able to slip away and report to Battalion Szaszkiewicz's critical position on 18 May. Once Stańczyk's report was received, a patrol was sent out to Hill 295 to see the position and how to proceed. It was established that Szaszkiewicz was clearly in great danger, as throughout the night the Germans had continuously attacked his position with mortars and machineguns. There had been a period of quiet but it did not last for long, which was probably because the Germans were waiting for more ammunition. Dec decided after a short period of deliberation that he needed to go and rescue Szaszkiewicz and his men. It was a small episode in the Polish war in Norway.

The overall picture of the fighting in the Ankenes area was somewhat difficult. Initially the enemy force in the area had been limited to only two companies of *Gebirgsjager*, but this was increased as the threat of an Allied invasion of Norway increased and so these two companies was increased to two battalions. Polish reports spoke of strong enemy detachments west of Ankenes, which was an area previously held by British troops. There was also a strong enemy company with mortars in Ankenes itself. The enemy had been able to reinforce the area using the ferry, which ran between Fagernes and Nyborg, as well as by seaplanes landing at Beisfjord. The Poles still held high ground on Hills 650 and 773 east of Storvand, while the Skjomen area was cleared of the enemy.[26] Improvements were made to the Polish position in Norway on the following day at 0930 hours,

26 TNA, CAB 44/74, The Operation in Norway, Narvik.

21 May, when the Polish 2nd Demi-Brigade HQ and 4th Battalion arrived at Tjelbotn, furthermore, 'at long last' 16 Gladiator aircraft from 263 Squadron RAF landed at Bardufoss airfield.[27] During the same day in the Ankenes area, the enemy attacked Hill 677, south of Nyborg, but was repulsed with losses. Polish troops were also attacked from the air and suffered casualties.

The first batch of operational orders was received from Staff HQ 1st Light Division (Rifles). The first consideration to be made was the deployment of artillery. A battery was sent to the Gratangen region and was to gradually push forwards in the direction of Bjerkvik. From there it was to put itself at the disposition of 13th Demi-Brigade of the FFL. Two further batteries were to alter their direction and be ready 18–19 May, to move towards the Oijord peninsula, from where they would receive orders regarding operations for a further offensive against Narvik. Reconnaissance suggested that such operations should begin as soon as possible. It was hoped at this stage of the proposed operation that a mechanised British artillery battery would be able to establish an operational post on the Ankenes peninsula.[28] On the same day, the Podhalians were placed under French command, less a single battalion in the Harstad area and artillery units supporting operational areas. The order placing the Podhalians under Bethouart's command also contained details of the next phase of the operation, which called for SWB and 12th Battalion *Chasseurs Alpins* to move to the Ankenes area and land on the southern shores of Bejsfjord.[29]

Further orders were issued for the forthcoming offensive. 1st Demi-Brigade Polish Rifles (Podhalians) and 1st Battalion, not clear who but more than likely French infantry battalion, were to move towards Harstad on 16 May, in anticipation of the capture of the Ankenes peninsula. This move was swiftly executed beginning at 1700 hours and completed at 1900 hours. 1st Battalion was to relieve 12th Battalion Rifles (French), who were to carry out orders that they had previously received. The Commander of 1st Demi-Brigade Podhalians was to be the overall commander of operations on the Ankenes peninsula, while Captain Baudry, Commander 12th Rifle Battalion (French) was to be his deputy for this operation and for any subsequent operations. This was a direct order from Bethouart.[30]

A Polish sitrep for 19 May 1940, gives an idea of what was happening at Narvik at that time. 2nd Battalion Podhalians reported that a French torpedo boat had shelled Narvik during the evening and had set the area alight. A Polish platoon advanced along the left flank of 2nd Company and safely maintained their new position. By this time Lieutenant Szaszkiewicz and his platoon had been extracted from their imperilled hilltop position, as narrated earlier and had returned to Polish lines with 16 ORs and their weapons. To rescue Szaszkiewicz's patrol it had been necessary to deploy three 88mm mortars; two 60mm mortars, a smoke screen being laid down by British artillery, as well as nearly 30 infantry men with rifles and machineguns covering the Polish withdrawal. This successful action however, did allow for the seizure of the north-western slopes at map reference R.677. Overall the Polish casualty rate was six dead and 21 wounded.[31]

An information bulletin for 10 May discussed the various scenarios developing in northern Norway. In the Gratangen area, it was reported that the ice was melting and breaking up in Gratangsbotn. Hill 694 had been captured and that the French Army had seized Hill 1013. Storvand was under fire from enemy heavy mortars, positioned on the western slopes of Roasme. It was reported that communications for individual operations in Labergdalen and along the Elvenes-

27 Ibid.
28 PISM, A.IV.11/59.
29 Ibid.
30 Ibid.
31 PISM, A.IV.11/4, Daily Situation Report, 0800 hours, 19 May 1940.

Bjerkvik were limited. A German counteroffensive at Loeiganstind remained stubborn, but a strong German force from the south of Loeiganstind could only be supplied with the help of paratroops.

Further reports pointed to great allied activity. In the region to the north between Herjangs Fjord and Rombaks Fjord, the following was reported. There was German activity north-west from Holmvand and in the south-east from Skatvand. Machinegun posts on the summit of Herjanghl were reported, while most of the bridges at Bjerkvik had been mined by the enemy along the southern route from Meby. It was reported that there was an enemy ammunition dump at Kufiskhl. No changes had been reported in the Narvik area. In the Ankenes operational area, the following reports were received: the French had occupied Hills 295, 405, 677 and 794, as well as securing Traadvand. The British area of operations had been heavily bombed by German aircraft on 10 May, while a German seaplane landed a unit of between 12 and 22 troops with heavy machineguns in the Aefjord area. On the same morning four Heinkel bombers flew over Bogen. A major problem for the Allied operation was that maps, issued for the operation, were actually incorrect, once compared with the topography presented before Allied troops trying to make sense of the region they were expected to operate over.

In the southern sector of the operational area, it was reported that French units in Mosjoen had been replaced by British troops. The enemy, including armoured and motorised units, were 30 kilometres from Mosjoen. Two enemy transport planes, escorted by three fighters flying towards Mo, had been sighted on the morning 10 May and were later seen at Baren Fjord.[32]

A report dated 11 May 1940, noted that during the morning 10 May, the Germans were able to resupply their forces in the Herjangs Fjord and the northern Rombaks Fjord area using 12 aircraft. It was considered that there was a German command post either at Andersh or nearby. There was also an enemy ammunition dump, which was guarded by machinegun and mortar positions at Camberg. The Germans had reinforced this position with the use of aerial resupply and possibly Norwegian POWs as labour. Other points of interest to the Allies were enemy command posts: one was thought to be in Kvandalen (north-west Ornej) with a second in the north from Hartvigvand in a local school, which had been pressed into use and marked on an operational map.

In the Skatvand area from the west of the fjord, Polish forward pickets considered that this area had already been evacuated by the enemy. In the Ankenes region, Traadvand, to the north of Storvand, was occupied by French troops, however in central Norway the enemy had been landing more troops in Hemnes. Even so, the Germans were not having it all their own way, as the ships supplying the German reinforcements were sunk, complete with equipment and supplies.[33] This situation was clarified on 12 May, with a report, which made it quite clear that a British warship had attacked German transport ships; sinking them as well as killing a large number of Germans. On the same day, Norwegian units at Mo began to withdraw northwards, as the British landed in the town. It was also thought that the enemy armed with automatic weapons were reorganising their defensive lines between Points 335–409–415 and in Grufjde at Points 676–687. There was also evidence of enemy motorised movements, as in the Lodinven area the Germans were landing reinforcements using transport aircraft and seaplanes in the area of the entrance to the Narvik Fjord. Furthermore, along the Narvik-Beisfjord there was intense movement of enemy lorries.

As the days progressed the two sides in Norway began to firm up and consolidate their lines, as well as draw up battle plans. It appeared that both the Allies and the Germans had recovered from each other's attacks and counter measures and were now determined to finish the Norwegian Campaign as swiftly as possible, as there were bigger fish to fry in Western Europe. In the Gratangen region,

32 PISM, A.IV.11/58, Situation Report, 1800 hours, 10 May 1940.
33 PISM, A.IV.11/58, Situation Report, No.7 Narvik Operation, 2000 hours, 12 May 1940.

the French held lines which ran 500 metres to the north-west from Point 333 to a hilltop located 400 metres to the south-west of Rogne. The Norwegians possessed territory close to the French lines, which ran to the south from Height 836 to the northern valley of Labigastind, one kilometre to the south of the lake at Point 730. The Grakedalen-Buickefjell area was held by Norwegian troops armed with heavy machineguns. Nearby Brattboken was held to the south from Height 856. The same report contained information originating from the British HQ, dated 12 May 1940. It was reported that the Norwegian 1/12 Infantry Regiment had captured Height 676 to the west of Laeigasvand. The Norwegian infantrymen had spread fanlike on the slopes of Laeigastind, while 2/16 Infantry Regiment, Norwegian Army operated in the valley to the east of this position.

The French had pushed on southwards from Lakes Osevand and Storvand but had come under heavy enemy machinegun fire, from a line described as running from Heights 333, 416 and 676. It was further reported that the French were unable to advance any further without artillery support. Norwegian troops moved to Hill 676 by moving along the flanks of the enemy positions, but it was also considered that the Germans might have already abandoned this position. Even though Hill 676 was taken by the Norwegians one way or another, the French still suffered five dead and 15 wounded in fighting in the area. In the Bjerkvik area, individual civilian reports indicated that little had changed in recent days. However, it was learnt that in Andersh, there was a German HQ as well as an ammunition dump heavily guarded with machinegun positions. There was some evidence to suggest that the enemy was not receiving support paratroops, as an airfield was still under construction at Andersh but this was subject to confirmation.

At Mo and its surrounding areas the following situation was reported. The Norwegian infantry battalion operating in that area had withdrawn from Mosjoen, via the mountains towards the north; a special company, under the command of Gubbins had caused the enemy problems, had landed at Hemnes. They were reinforcing a previous landing of troops, which had landed by seaplane on the previous day. A British company had attacked enemy reinforcements at Finneid, as the Germans were en route to Mo. Later Hemnes was shelled by a British warship and the town was left in flames. It was assumed that a Norwegian infantry company from Mosjoen, with a possibility of a British landing at Mo and 1st SG, were already making their individual ways to Hemnes.[34]

About a week later further information regarding the situation in northern Norway was made available. It seemed that the Germans were consolidating their defensive positions, as they had left Vasdalen and were concentrating their forces in the regions of Cirkelvand, Derke, Kerdvand and Lillebalak. The Allies considered that enemy paratroops had landed in Rundfjell and Bjornfjell. There was a report to the effect that on 17 May nine enemy aircraft had bombed Bjerkvik, while the enemy had completely evacuated Cape Oijord. It was also learnt that in the Narvik area, German paratroops had landed but wearing Norwegian Army uniforms. This was not an unusual method of the Germans to wage war, as already noted they sought to sow the seeds of confusion, terror and disinformation: international law meant nothing to Berlin. Furthermore, the Germans were systematically destroying infrastructure especially bridges, of which they demolished so many.[35] The German method of flying false flags or landing paratroops in illegal uniforms was to vex the British authorities later during the summer of 1940, as the UK was threatened with a German invasion leaving the British to ponder in which guises the enemy might come. In the event of course they never did; the Royal Navy, at Narvik, had destroyed any hope of a maritime advantage that the Germans might have tried to enjoy, while British and Commonwealth airman drove the Luftwaffe from British skies between July and September 1940.

34 PISM, A.IV.11/58, Situation Report, No. 26, Gratangen Region, 13 May 1940.
35 PISM, A.IV.11/58, Situation Report, No. 11, Narvik Region, 19 May 1940.

The same report noted other German moves. In the Ankenes area, the Germans had attacked Allied positions using mortars during the night 16–17 May. The Allies put up considerable resistance and beat off the attack, but suffered casualties. In the Ballangen region the Luftwaffe carried out 11 aerial attacks on 16 May, while in the southern area of operations, there was plenty of activity especially in the Mo region, which saw motorised enemy formations close to the town. Enemy infantry supported by four light tanks was spotted in Hatues to the south of Mo; even so in the same region Allied AAA fired on two German aircraft. In the Mosjoen region enemy AAA and howitzers were spotted. It was estimated that in the area of Elsfjorden, Korgen and Bjerra were about 3,000 enemy troops. The Allies were not going to sit back and wait to see what might happen; this led to the German held airfield at Stavangen being attacked by the RAF twice in one day, leaving the runway wrecked.[36]

The German and Allied positions in northern Norway all pointed towards a final showdown between the two sides, as they sought to finish the Norwegian Campaign as quickly and as easily as possible. Norway was very much a sideshow by mid-May and only important to the Norwegians by then, as both the British and French feared invasion and the Germans occupying their homelands, while the Germans knew that real glory was in France and not the frozen wastes of Norway. As the British prepared for an all out assault against the Germans in Norway, the enemy continued to strengthen their positions there. In the Bjerkvik-Gratangen region, the Germans had withdrawn to positions on Hills 648, 572 and 496. There were reports of an enemy presence at Jernvand, but the main German position by 18 May was at Fisklosvand, three kilometres south of Hartigvand. The enemy could also be found on Hill 482 north of the lake in that area, Lillebalak and Hill 648 in the north-east.

It was asserted by the British that the presence of a German HQ at Bjornfjell, possibly had something to do with its proximity to the nearby Swedish frontier. In the Mo region British reconnaissance work tried to establish the actual numbers of enemy forces opposing the Allies. The following figures were produced: Elfsfjorde – 2,000 German troops, Korgen – 300–400 troops, in Bjerka a single company, in north Mosjoen it was learnt that there were six AAA guns and two howitzers, while at Hatnes, 70 miles to the south of Mo, there were 1,500 enemy troops supported by four light tanks. British units in Mo had withdrawn in a northerly direction, fighting a rearguard action. A further report on German activity noted that on the night 18–19 May, 25 Germans had landed from a German warship onto Rørvik Island, 139 kilometres south-west of Mosjoen.[37]

An information bulletin for 22 May 1940, gives evidence of what the Podhalians were doing at that time. For much of the time they were fighting, as the Brigade was involved in intensive patrolling and intelligence gathering. Polish patrols asserted that the enemy armed with automatic weapons occupied Hills 650 and 773. Hill 677 notable for its resemblance to a kidney bean, was also occupied by the enemy in large numbers and well armed. On both sides of the hill were infantry platoons; each armed with three machineguns per platoon; each platoon had a heavy machinegun, as well as a mortar per platoon. In one clash between a Polish reconnaissance patrol and the enemy, the fighting was at close quarters using grenades and bayonets, which saw five Germans killed and an enemy machinegun destroyed. A Pole, Cadet Officer Browarski, the patrol commander, was also killed. Platoon leader, Bogdanek, was decorated for his part in the same action.[38]

Further orders came for the Podhalians. Lieutenant-Colonel Michał Mackowski, CO 3rd Battalion Podhalian Rifles sent orders to the CO 3rd Company of the same battalion. 3rd Company was ordered to reconnoitre in the area of Forsa. Once the riflemen arrived in this area, they were

36 PISM, A.IV.11/58, Situation Report, No.11, Southern Region, 19 May 1940.
37 PISM, A.IV.11/58, British Reports, 30 & 31, 18 May 1940, 19 May 1940.
38 PISM, A.IV.11/58, Podhalian Rifle Brigade Information Communication, 22 May 1940.

to check the situation on the banks of the coast in the Sandwik-Vorset-Kjerringvig areas, as well as surveying the islet at Story and its surrounding areas. To maximise their chances of success the reconnaissance patrols were advised to use hill tops, as far as possible, to make their observations. Furthermore, Mackowski gave detailed instructions to the commander of the reconnaissance patrol, Lieutenant Kontrym. Two platoons were to be sent out: one from 1st Company and another from 3rd Company. 3rd Company's CO was given similar orders. The platoon from 1st Company set out on its objective at 2100 hours, 11 May 1940.

The next day Mackowski gave his orders to the CO 3rd Company. A platoon with a heavy machinegun was to advance to Forsa Skole and establish an outpost there. The platoon was given several tasks and was to observe and reconnoitre around the fjord, as well as close up the entrance from the fjord in the Forsa Skole area. The Commander of the proposed outpost was given a telephone from Forsa, in the event of an emergency. The remainder of 3rd Company were to carry out reconnaissance work to the south-east and to the south-west. Overall, 3rd Company was prepared for combat and had had 15 pairs of skis issued for reconnaissance patrolling.

On 14 May, Mackowski issued further orders to the CO 3rd Company, in response to a report that German airmen had been seen landing in the Lake Grunnbt area. Mackowski immediately sent out a patrol, consisting of an officer and three riflemen, towards the Brukshaasen-Nesel Lake area to check on the report. Second Lieutenant Edward Bednarski, 2/3 Podhalian Rifles, a patrol commander, reported on patrolling and conditions being faced in Norway. With two squads Bednarski set out on patrol at 0240 hours, 14 May 1940. Their task was to reconnoitre and try to assert if the town of Forsa was actually occupied by the Germans or not. After entering the town, the Poles discovered from locals that the Germans, disguised as civilians, had left. Four of the enemy had sailed away from the town and up the fjord, while another five had gone away on skis along the fjord opposite Forsa. Local information told the Polish patrol that the Germans were about 25 kilometres from Forsa. Bednarski must have received this intelligence promptly, as it was only 0300 hours, 14 May, when he was made aware of the German movements. This rapidly developing situation caused Bednarski to do his own rapid thinking, in order not to lose his quarry. Germans on the loose in Norway were quite capable of infiltrating Allied lines and causing mayhem and misinformation.

To try to catch the Germans using motorboats was going to be a problem, given the size of the German patrol but local Norwegians wanted to help the Poles find suitable craft for the pursuit. As the Norwegians set out to find decent and suitable boats; Bednarski after buying breakfast for himself and his men sat down and ate with them. At about 0720 hours, Norwegian civilians arrived with a motorboat that could carry 15, meanwhile the remainder of the Polish patrol embarked in two other boats. The chase for the Germans was on.

At 0830 a Polish lookout on one of the chartered boats reported that he could see the German boats in the distance. As the Poles closed in on the German craft, the Germans suddenly headed for the shore. The Poles had qualms about fighting from boats but for some reason the enemy had made things slightly easier for the pursuing Polish troops, by heading for the banks on the other side of the fjord. Some of the Poles carried on by boat while others disembarked and on foot got to the enemy held fjord shores. Firing machineguns from the stern of their boats the Germans attacked their Polish pursuers, but were outnumbered by the Poles and taken prisoner.[39]

39 PISM, A.IV.11/59, Report, Second Lieutenant Edward Bednarski, 2nd Company Patrol Commander, 14 May 1940.

8

The Capture of Narvik

The main Allied objective in northern Norway was the recapture of Narvik because, as we have already seen, it was significant from the point of view of denying the Germans a constant supply of iron ore, as well as being prestigious politically. Auchinleck gave an account of the recapture of Narvik, when he reported to the British government on the Norwegian Campaign. He began his narrative by linking the successful landings near Bjerkvik and subsequent operations, which cleared the Oijord Peninsula north of the Rombaks Fjord as far east as Lilleberget, to the Bethouart's plans for the capture of Narvik; the French commander had been instructed by Auchinleck to produce an operational plan that would lead to the capture of Narvik.

Auchinleck noted that until the ground north of the eastern entrance of the Rombaks Fjord had been cleared; an assault on Narvik would have to be launched onto difficult beaches, which were thought to have strong machinegun defences along them. Furthermore, an element of a surprise assault on Narvik from the sea would have already been lost, as ships and landing craft necessary for any such landing would have to be mustered in the Ofot Fjord in full view of the enemy. The Allied hold on the northern shore of Rombaks Fjord widened the front on which the attack could be launched and permitted it to be supported by French field artillery, which had been established north of Oijord. The first echelon of troops to be used against Narvik and their landing craft were being assembled in secret, in the cover of Oijordneset Point, eventually these hidden men and craft, according to the planner, would be able to emerge less than a mile from Narvik behind a naval bombardment once the Allies decided to attack the town and harbour.

After careful reconnaissance Bethouard concluded that it would be best to land the first wave of troops on a beach east of Oineset and subsequently transfer three battalions, including a Norwegian battalion, across the Rombaks Fjord from Oijord using motor landing craft (MLC). Once established ashore this force having first blocked the approach of enemy reinforcements from Sildvik, by securing a strong position astride the railway line in the area, was able to advance across the peninsula and take Narvik town from the rear. The assault on Narvik was to be accompanied by an attack towards Beisfjord, by Polish troops established on the Ankenes Peninsula. The Polish objective was to contain German troops in the operational area, as well as threaten the enemy line of retreat from Narvik along the road which ran along the north shore of the Beisfjord.

The landing operation was rendered particularly hazardous by the scarcity of landing craft, which owing to enemy action and mechanical breakdowns had been reduced to three ALCs and two MLCs. This limited the number of men in the first landing party to a mere 290. This numerical weakness caused considerable anxiety to both Bethouart and Auchinleck. The original date for the operation against Narvik was due to have been during the night 24–25 May, but at a conference with Bethouart on 23 May, both Auchinleck and his French counterpart decided that the operation might be delayed. There were several reasons for this postponement: as ever the weather was a factor and it was so foul that the two commanders considered that an operation undertaken in the prevailing weather conditions would be an 'unjustifiable risk'. Furthermore, sufficient Allied air cover was lacking with only a single fighter squadron being available to deal with numerous enemy bombers, assuming that the operation even went ahead. In view of these conditions it was decided that the operation should be postponed until the arrival of a Hurricane Squadron, which was due in the operational area on 27 May. Lord Cork agreed with this decision.

After this decision had been taken, news of the British government's intention to evacuate northern Norway was received, which obviously altered the situation and decision making for and in Norway. Another consultation was called for and so Auchinleck and Bethouart met, after referring to Lord Cork it was decided that Narvik was to be attacked during the night 27–28 May 1940. Auchinleck wrote regarding the operation against Narvik; 'In doing so I considered that apart from the desirability of making sure whether the facilities for shipping ore from Narvik had, in fact been destroyed as thoroughly as had been reported, the chances that a successful attack would do much to conceal our intention to evacuate the country in the immediate future would outweigh the possible disadvantages involved in extending air commitments by establishing troops in close contact with the enemy on the Narvik Peninsula where his main forces was thought to be located.' To be frank, Auchinleck's reasoning seemed to be impeccable.

Auchinleck continued in his narrative as he outlined the naval operation against Narvik. Operations began at 2340, 27 May 1940, when three Cruisers and five Destroyers steamed into position on the mouth of Rombaks Fjord and began to bombard German positions. Admiral Lord Cork flew his flag on HMS *Cairo,* on which Auchinleck sailed accompanied by Bethouard and his Staff. HMS *Southampton* was detached from the bombarding ships and made its way to the mouth of Narvik harbour to support Polish troops on the Ankenes Peninsula. The naval bombardment against the Narvik peninsula was across a wide front with selected targets, such as the mouths of railway tunnels, as well as suspected enemy machinegun and artillery positions. The fire of the naval guns and field artillery was heavy and accurate but close support of the attacking Allied troops was hampered throughout by the 'broken nature' of the terrain, which made accurate observation in the birch shrub, which covered the lower slopes of the hills, very difficult.

The initial Allied landings were quite successful and were hardly opposed and were accomplished with little loss. This meant that the first wave of the Allied landing was quickly able to establish a beachhead on the shores at Narvik. However, subsequent movements of troops moving were hampered for a short period, by a small artillery piece firing further to the east of the south shore. This gun caused some casualties but was soon silenced by naval gun fire. By 0330 hours, a battalion of FFL and the Narvik battalion of the Norwegian Army were ashore on the peninsula. While the operation was in progress the enemy managed to launch a counterattack from the east and the forward Allied troops had to fight hard for a time, in order to maintain their positions. This forward movement of the Germans enabled them to harry the Allies and bring the landing beaches under fire, for quite an appreciable period of time. During this time Commandant Paris, Bethouart's Chief of Staff, was killed in a landing craft. Finally, the Allies were able to launch a counterattack, beat off the Germans and continued the advance inland. During the same period, HMS *Cairo* was hit twice by bombs and 30 men were killed or wounded.

Once the initial landing had succeeded, the progress of Bethouard's troops was steady and continuous. It seemed from received reports that the enemy had withdrawn from Narvik in considerable haste and had moved eastwards along the Beisfjord. By 2200 hours, the entire peninsula west of a line from Fagesnes to Forsneset was in French hands and about 200 Germans had been taken prisoner. Polish troops, after an initial setback, also pressed along the Ankenes Peninsula and had established themselves on high ground overlooking Beisfjord.

Auchinleck considered that the entire operation against Narvik had been carried out with great risk and with the 'barest margin of safety,' and could have well ended in disaster. The first echelon ashore, consisting of 290 men, had had to maintain itself unsupported for 45 minutes and if the enemy had counterattacked once more, the entire operation could have been a disaster. In the face of this, even though the two potential disasters had been avoided, Auchinleck considered that there was a real need for adequate land craft to be made available for the first wave in the future, so that larger numbers of troops can be landed, to be followed by reinforcements. A significant problem was the lack of bombers available to the Allies but overall Auchinleck considered that the risk undertaken at Narvik had turned out to have been justified.[1]

An account of how the Poles fought towards Narvik underlines what Auchinleck's statement said. It was noted that prior to the Allied offensive there were strong enemy detachments in the Ankenes area, but on the whole they remained inactive; the only enemy strong attack was from the air on 21 May, where an unrecorded number of casualties occurred amongst the Polish battalions, which still held the ridge east of Storvand. 2nd Polish Demi-Brigade's HQ arrived at Tjelbotn.

Bethouart's Operational Order No 38 dated 22 May, concerning the capture of Narvik and the Ankenes area and cutting off their line of retreat towards Sweden at the head of Beisfjord. For this purpose the Poles were supported by three tanks, four artillery guns from the French and British, who also supplied AAA protection. The original operation was postponed, as we have seen, due to local weather conditions and a lack of good aerial support. With some modification to the original plan the Poles were ordered to advance without delay towards Beisfjord and capture it.

In Ankenes village there was no enemy west of the church on the night of 24–25 May, but the rest of the village remained in enemy hands. Hand to hand fighting occurred in the immediate vicinity of Ankenes when on 25 May, five of the enemy were killed by either bayonets or grenades, while an enemy mortar was destroyed by a Polish patrol. At this time the Polish Brigade reported considerable traffic on the Narvik railway and troops with light armour moving from Beisfjord by the coast road to Narvik, which was itself being bombarded by enemy aircraft. The report gave a brief description of Narvik and what might be found there. Narvik was considered to be a modern town, while it's unfortunate inhabitants number about 10,000 and were quite dependent on the export of Swedish iron ore for its income. In peacetime Narvik was garrisoned by about 1,500 Norwegian troops, supported by a few 3 or 4 inch guns, while a high wireless mast could also be found on the same site. The German defences were reported to be very strong and had been prepared by the Norwegians. These defences, included concrete pill-boxes and trenches covering landing places around the town and harbour, remained intact and had been without doubt strengthened by the Germans, whose strength was estimated to have been 2,000–3,000 men. The importance of capturing Narvik, as ever was underlined mainly in the power its possession would exercise amounting to depriving Germany of the iron ore, which was necessary to its manufacture of munitions.

At 2340 hours, 27 May 1940, the operation for the recapture of Narvik began and within four hours one French battalion and a single Norwegian battalion had succeeded in gaining a foothold on the peninsula from the sea. As we have seen, the enemy launched a ferocious counterattack, which had no effect. Fierce attacks from the air were also ineffective and so as early as 0700 hours, the enemy hurriedly began to evacuate Narvik, even though it was still in their hands.

The Polish battalions, in supporting operations on the Ankenes peninsula, experienced an early setback at about 1015 hours, but supported by HMS *Southampton* pressed ahead and advanced further forward. By 2200 hours, 28 May, the entire Narvik peninsula west of a line from Fagernes

1 TNA, PREM 3/328/5, Section 11, The Capture of Narvik.

to Forsneset was in French hands; on 29 May the operation to capture Narvik was reported as being successfully completed. The Poles advanced further south-eastwards on 29 May, while French armour and motorcyclists pressed forward to the southern shore of Beisfjord. As this was happening French and Norwegian infantry followed the railway line along the southern shore of the Rombaksfjord to guarantee the Allied flank.

The capture of Narvik had been very difficult, not only because of enemy resistance but, as ever, the terrain was extremely challenging. According to the report 'the wide distances and the broken nature of the country made the operation extremely difficult. The mountain masses are split by deep, narrow valleys; arms of sea, great and small, penetrate in all directions. Movements had to be co-ordinated most carefully. Many comparatively small groups of troops had to play their parts, each with complete success, and exact to the appointed hour. The Polish troops contributed not the least part in the success of the whole operation by which a German force of several thousands had been pushed towards the Swedish border.'

However, the British government had already decided to abandon operations in Norway and had ordered the entire North-Western Expeditionary Force to be withdrawn. French and Polish forces reached Beisfjord at 0130 hours, 30 May and from there the Poles moved determinedly forwards to the Moluelven Valley in the Silduik area, but they were soon to receive the disappointing news that their efforts had been in vain and Norway was to be evacuated of Allied troops.[2]

The above narrative explains why the Polish role was important on the Narvik operation, as it was relatively small units of troops operating over large areas of countryside, which was heavy going and despite its size, the limited viable topography forced operations often meant that battles were fought in comparatively small areas. Polish troops may have been small in number but their contribution should be noted, as often they appeared to be the only Allied troops in Norway fighting, who actually understood what they were fighting for. Even the Norwegians seemed half-hearted in fighting the Germans and all too often it was obvious that many Norwegians at this stage of the war harboured sympathy for Germany but quite rightly feared the Soviet Union with many Norwegians certainly not having much sympathy for the Allies and their objectives.

Polish sources record the fevered attitude in the Polish camp in Norway, as they prepared to go on the offensive once more against the Germans. The days between 23–27 May were quite frustrating, as the Poles were champing at the bit to go onto the offensive, as orders had been issued but the time to go had been put back, owing to the weather and lack of sufficient air cover. The Poles already knew what their task for the forthcoming operation was to be; it seemed simple enough. The basic task was to capture the entire Ankenes peninsula and to deny the enemy any withdrawal route. The Poles were to advance along through the region of the Beisfjord in a north-easterly direction and cut off any German withdrawal towards the Swedish frontier.

FFL artillery operating from the Oijord peninsula with British naval fire was to lead the assault against Narvik, originally on 25 May but put back to 28 May. The Polish operation was to encompass the entire Podhalian Brigade with the exception of 3rd Battalion Podhalians. One company from 3rd Battalion was sent out to the Swedish frontier on a deep reconnaissance mission, for which the communications company had to organise a separate telephone communications line. During the preparation period, before the offensive opened, every commander of every unit, indeed all of the men involved, prepared intensively and were completely prepared for the coming battle and without exception just wanted to do their very best when they once more took to the battlefield to face their deadly enemies; the Germans. However there is more to winning a battle than zeal and this included close co-operation with the Allies. There the work of the commanders was cut out to

2 TNA, CAB 106/1160, The Polish Brigade in Norway.

ensure good quality and effective co-operation with British and French artillery, as well as working closely with warships, which poured in heavy supporting fire against German positions. This called for close and detailed co-operation before and during the operation, to maximise the effect of artillery barrages that were to support the Allied landings and advance from inland, as well as being ready to alter targets for new ones if such an occasion arose.

The Brigade's Staff ensured that everything was closely guarded and a secret, so that there were no leaks and that only those who needed to know were informed of what was to happen, when and where. At 0001 hours, 28 May, the offensive opened with a 30 minute artillery barrage supported by warships firing from the sea. Fighting across the Ankenes peninsula lasted until the afternoon 29 May, with the Poles victorious after breaking enemy opposition in the northern sectors of the Ankenes and Nyborg areas, as well as a series of hill tops and Beisfjord area, in an offensive coming up from the south. The fighting which the Poles had just experienced in the Ankenes offensive was mostly heavy and bloody, while at Beisfjord they had been bombed by German aircraft.[3]

Events in Europe were not lost on the Poles fighting in Norway because as Dec reflects in hindsight, the moment that the offensive began in the Narvik region at one minute past midnight 28 May, was the same time that the Belgian King, Leopold III, surrendered his country to the invading Germans. This act led to the Germans racing towards the English Channel ports of Dunkirk, and Ostend on the coast of northern France and Belgium. As all British people ought to know Dunkirk was a scene of almost miraculous deeds, as the British were eventually able to lift thousands of British and French troops off the beaches at Dunkirk during late May and early June 1940.

As planned at 2330 hours 27 May 1940, the British Cruisers, HMS *Cairo*, HMS *Southampton* and HMS *Coventry* with their sister ships, Destroyers of the Royal Navy, HMS *Beagle*, HMS *Fame* and HMS *Firedrake* opened fire on German positions at Narvik and bombarded the beaches on the Narvik peninsula between the towns of Orneset and Forsneset for 30 minutes. Colonel de Magrin commanding the offensive against Narvik landed punctually from the landing craft, which bore in ashore coming from the port at Oijord and then via Rombaksfjord headed to Narvik.

Taking advantage of the enemy's surprise of being heavily bombarded from the sea, the first wave of troops consisting of about 300 FFL troops waded ashore at Orneset and towards the cover of the suburbs of Narvik, such as they were. There was an immediate need to make a reconnaissance of the immediate area and the most promising point, to make observations of what was ahead, was from the dominant peak of Hill 457–Taraldsvik, but the terrain ahead was difficult and was certainly unsuitable for the use of armour. Two tanks, which had accompanied the first wave of landing French troops, had become immediately immobile.

The next wave of troops landing in the area had been unfortunate to have been met by the enemy, which had by now recovered from its shock of being attacked from the sea and had organised counter measures. The German counterattack caused huge casualties amongst troops landing at Narvik. General Bethouart and Major Paris from Bethouart's Staff were present as French troops were landing and were aware of the plight of the second wave of their countrymen. With the FFL being pinned down on the beaches and taking heavy casualties, co-operation between Norwegian infantry and the FFL came to a halt until the situation could be retrieved and the Norwegians landed at Oijord. The move of the Norwegian battalion to Segnes and then onto the beach at Forsneset was retarded by an hour and even then little headway could be made from the beaches. Meanwhile, the Germans were making some very stubborn resistance using automatic fire and mortars firing from the northern slopes of Hill 457.

3 PISM, C.671, *Oddziały Łączn. Sam. Bryg. Strz. Podn. Historia. 'Historia Oddziałow Łasznosci Samodzielnej Brygady Strzelcow Podhalanskich w Roku 1940'* Lieutenant-Colonel Jozef Morkowski, March 1947. (*History of the Communications Units, Podhalian Rifle Brigade, 1940*).

The situation of the FFL and the Norwegians worsened after 0400 hours, as Hurricane fighter planes, which had been supporting the Allied offensive since it began, had to return to their squadron after four hours of fighting. After the withdrawal of the British aircraft, all that the remaining Allied land forces and warships could do, was to wait for the inevitable German aerial attacks, which could be launched with little fear of any Allied countermeasures.

German bombers come over in large numbers and began to attack the Allied landings, both at sea and on land. At 0430 there was a massive battle between the sea and the air; such was the German aerial bombardment that Lord Cork began to withdraw his Cruisers and left only two Destroyers to support the FFL on the beaches. At 0500 hours the German aerial attack lessened; Colonel de Magrin taking advantage of this lull in the fighting got his men into the northern countryside on the Narvik peninsula.

At 0600 hours the attack on Hill 457 was broken; FFL had taken heavy casualties. Allied attacks against Hill 457 were relentless, pressed forward from the railway track. At 0700 hours the FFL position was critical and the fighting on Hill 457 continued until 1400 hours.

However, the FFL battalion commanded by de Magrin was amazing and pressed home every advantage that they held. De Magrin by linking up the various French units, which could have become scattered or isolated took the beach and pressed along it to the outskirts of Orneset. After a short break the battalions attacked Hill 457 and after taking large casualties both dead and wounded took the hill. The German defenders could not contain such a determined and strong attack. By 2115 hours, the shores of the fjord at Nyborg had been taken by the Podhalians. Furthermore, Fagernes and the road from Narvik to the outreaches of Beisfjord came under Polish fire. Other groups of the Podhalians were able to take hilltops in a line towards the suburbs of Beisfjord and made sure that the German lines of retreat towards the Swedish frontier were imperilled by Polish fire and marauding troops.

Other Polish groups assaulting the Narvik region had problems. Colonel Chłusewicz's group was not adequately supported by Allied artillery, whether land based or supplied by the large guns of the Royal Navy. Chłusewicz and his men had to manage with a half battery of French 75mm guns and two mortars. The resulting artillery barrage made much noise but did little in the way of inflicting damage and cause casualties amongst the enemy during the 20 minute bombardment, before Chłusewicz's opened its offensive. However artillery supplies went to Hills 643 and 773 to supply later artillery support for the offensive.

At 0001, Major Kobyliński's company moved on to the offensive. 1st Company, after only a few minutes, had advanced about 200 metres when they came under heavy machinegun and mortar fire. The Germans had bought the Polish advance to a halt very quickly. The Poles immediately requested French artillery support to take Hill 643. This was readily done and so with excellent firing by the French, as well as some spirited shooting from the Polish mortar teams, the first Polish target, Hill 643, was captured by 0230 hours. The next target was Hill 650 and the offensive against it moved slowly, as it was hampered by heavy enemy fire. It was proving difficult to shift the Germans from the hill top and it took a combination of artillery and infantry from Captain Bogusławski's company to dislodge the German defenders.

On the right flank of 3rd Company was yet another Polish offensive, against an enemy held hill top. This time it was Hill 773 and once more the Germans were very determined in their defence work. The Poles had got within 500 metres of the hill, when it was stopped by heavy enemy infantry fire and pinned down until the afternoon.

This crisis called for renewed thought and plans and General Szczyko-Bohusz ordered Chłusewicz to move towards Beisfjord and relieve the French Battalion. Kobyliński and his men tried to advance further and at 1600 hours, 1st Company once more attacked Hill 650 but German bombers put an end to this particular offensive and the Poles were left hugging the ground, as the Germans bombed and strafed them for the next hour. Even so, by 1845 hours 1st Company captured Hill 650–Skantuva. But Hill 773 remained unconquered.

The battles for the heights in the Narvik area were far from over and the work could be tedious, as the Allies had to enter valleys, climb hills often against determined enemy positions who were also better equipped than most of the Allied troops. The question of the capture of Hill 773 remained outstanding and plans were renewed for its capture. Eventually Captain Brymor personally led 3rd Company in action against Hill 773 and it was taken by 2130 hours. It seemed that at times a bull headed approach was the only way to remove the enemy from its positions and at the same time Polish attacks were causing the Germans to wilt in the face of a determined attack against them.

Having received orders to an energetic advance on Beisfjord, Major Kobyliński moved 1st Company in the direction of the town. At midnight the company moved to the Lakselven Valley, where they were to see action for the following hours. However there was to be a huge mistake. It was clear that along the route between Narvik to Beisfjord via Fagernes and on the hilltops and summits in the direction of Sildvik towards Hundalen, Dietl had hidden his men in their hundreds, as they had come from Narvik and the surrounding areas. Early hours at 0500 hours 29 May, a Polish patrol reported that the enemy had left the surrounding areas of Beisfjord. At 0600 hours, 1st Company moved to the area and later in the afternoon the remainder of the Battalion arrived. At 1500 hours a German patrol shot up the rear of the Polish position, Kobyliński took the pass at Kvanta while the Germans returned to Sildvik and Hundalen.

Much of the important work prior to offensives opening was due to excellent reconnaissance work, which fell largely to the reconnaissance group from 1st Company 4th Battalion commanded by Captain Sulatycki. The reconnaissance group undertook lengthy and deep missions seeking out what lay ahead of any Polish attack and ascertaining hazards and even short cuts, which had not been previously indentified. Sulatycki's group moved deep to the south from Lake Stervd moving for over ten hours. At 0230 hours 28 May, the Polish patrol discovered the German rear lines in the Tverdalryggen 673 area. The Poles lay quiet waiting in vain for a rocket signalling that an attack against Hill 606 was to go in; the patrol waited until 1800 hours. However Sulatycki observing that the Germans were preparing to withdraw from the area took the initiative and led an attack against Hill 606 and by 2100 hours, the hill was in Polish hands. Throughout the day Sulatycki had been trying to contact Chłusewicz's radio position but with no joy, but finally from the summit of Hill 606 he made contact at 2200 hours and reported that he was sitting on the hill and what further orders were there for him and his patrol. He was told to return to base at Sjursheim and then the radio went dead and was as deaf as a post. At 0500 hours 29 May, the patrol rejoined its group.

Dec recalls his own actions during this period of campaigning. He was on Hill 295 having been ordered to go there by Szyszko-Bohusz, with the orders being telephoned to Dec. During the evening 27 May, Szyszko-Bohusz arrived. By 2200 hours, Dec was already involved in the planning for the next operation. Dec knew that once more the new area of operations was wide. In order to take every objective, as ordered, all three companies of Dec's battalion would have to be deployed. Two platoons from 4th Battalion would not be available and there was nobody available to man Hill 405. That was why Stańczyk was later ordered by the Brigade Commander to go onto the offensive. Finally Dec was happy that everything was in place for the next offensive against the Germans.

The extensive preparations for the coming offensive can be illustrated in a small exchange between a young cook, who was probably nothing more than a schoolboy and a veteran of the First World War, as the younger cook questioned if there was enough goulash for the entire battalion and the veteran assured him that there was. The difference in age of these two soldiers should be noted, as well as the concern for the welfare of the men, who are about to risk life and limb for their lost country and their allies. Dec wrote of how later after the supper of goulash, troops were issued with other things such as hand grenades, plenty of ammunition, as well as the necessary clothing in addition to their standard clothing; items such as sheepskin jackets, blankets and capes, anything to keep the troops warm as they moved across the frozen terrain of Norway.

During that evening the platoon commanders informed their men of what lay ahead of them in the forthcoming operation. It was of course the offensive against the Ankenes peninsula and their duty was to secure it and make it safe for Allied operations. The offensive was to be supported by two tanks. There were three hours before the Polish attack was due to begin and the young soldiers' faces were etched with concern and anxiety for what lay ahead of them and one of them asked if they could be permitted to sleep until it was time to go. It was not a problem to allow the soldiers to sleep but it was a question if any of them could actually get to sleep; given what might lay before them once they awoke and it was time to go into battle.

Those who could sleep did so and then at 2320, Cadet Officer Koczul was sent around to awaken those sleeping and at 2330, absolutely on time three Cruisers and three Destroyers began to shell the enemy. The noise of the naval gun fire was horrific and awesome, especially the echoes of the shells screaming and exploding; their reports resounding through the valley, as well as dislodging snow from hill and mountain tops. The first wave of shells to strike the Germans hit a storage depot, which led to a fire and thick columns of black smoke ascending towards the heavens. Suddenly, the 24 hour daylight over Narvik was gone and within a couple of minutes it was as pitch black as midnight, all that could be seen was the blue waters of the fjord. A pair of Spitfire fighter planes were spotted by the Poles (they were probably Hurricanes) while Lieutenant Gałacki observed that enemy Stuka dive bombers dare not show themselves at present, as they would be punished by the British fighters.

The Allied artillery and naval barrage was making inroads on Ankenes and German positions on Hill 295. As the Poles watched and discussed the progress of the artillery, the barrage shifted to the northern slopes of Hill 295. Other targets for the artillery included buildings in Narvik and Fagernes. While other guns were busy bombarding the shores of the port and the wooden buildings in Ankenes. The debris being thrown up by the shelling was incredible and included earth, stones, rocks, branches and even entire fir trees still intact yet blasted from the earth.

Amongst all of the destruction being caused by the Allied guns; the Poles wondered what the Germans were doing. Rifleman Czwojdrak considered that perhaps the Germans might have fled. Rifleman Syperowicz replied that the Germans would just take to their bunkers and sit out the bombardment and furthermore, considered that Czwojdrak was a simpleton in thinking that the enemy would up and run at the first sign of danger. Meanwhile as the Polish infantrymen discussed the likely outcomes of the Allied bombardment, the Royal Navy unleashed another set of salvoes against the enemy. Rifleman Sobczak, a forester from the Beskidy Mountains in southern Poland, noted that the big guns of the Royal Navy were almost making a clearing in a poor patch of forest between Baatberget and the top of Hill 295.

At midnight the final salvo of shells from the British armada fell. Then the Polish infantrymen made their move, making great noise with their machineguns, as the land offensive began. Rifle and automatic noise was muted by the rage of mortar fire heralding the attack overland, while patrol and platoon commanders waited for the signal to move off. Dec noted that on the slopes of Hill 295 through binoculars, the Brigade Commander was able to observe the offensive, especially the left hand side of the Polish attack and those companies fighting through the centre of the operational area.

Then from into the heavens exploded white rockets; the offensive was on!

'Third company – in groups – at the Krauts! (*szwabów*) to Ankenes – jump –quick march!' cried Captain (*Rotmistrz*) Zamoyski. Other commanders of platoons and sections followed the example of Zamoyski; giving fighting commands, ordering their men to the fore, to quick march, anything to get them onto the enemy and past them. The heat of battle was raging.

The attacking Polish troops conducted themselves perfectly, almost as if they were on manoeuvres as they advanced. They worked in groups inching forward on their stomachs as they crossed ground raked my enemy fire. Szyszko-Bohusz watching the operation, was very pleased with the conduct of his troops and how they operated whilst under fire. There was no panic or wavering; the Polish infantrymen just advanced as they had been trained to do so. It was indeed a triumph for Polish arms. There was the chatter of the Polish machineguns of Lieutenant Mostow and Cadet Officer Cłapa, as well as the moans of Polish mortar tubes fighting against the clamour of German automatic weapons. Firing of weapons of many calibres was in evidence but mostly small arm bullets, which also flew over the heads of battalion and brigade commanders at their posts. The fighting was that close. Those noises which sound like singing were not dangerous, but anything sounding snapping like a whip is dangerous instructed Lieutenant Gałacki, via radio. Meanwhile, a squad from 3rd Company swiftly moved into the forests and disappeared from sight. However, soon the sounds of fighting could be heard from the direction from where the squad had moved to, while the remainder of the company moved in the direction of Ankenes.

Dec related what was happening to 2nd Battalion and its offensive. As according to plan, 1st Company moved onto the offensive at 0020 hours and in that moment Zamoyski's company was raised to its highest glory to date, as the cry went up calling for vengeance against the Germans for their attacks against Westerplatte and Hel, where Polish garrisons had held out for longer than the Germans had anticipated during the September Campaign and had retarded the German advance along the Polish coast. 'Quick march!' shouted Captain Laurentowski, as his men moved towards the German positions.

However, despite these heroic dispositions which the battalion strove to obey and wanted to complete, reality set in as the area they were to advance over contained very little in the way of cover, just tree stumps, scrub and hard, hard rock which also fell on to them. General Bohusz-Szyszko could see that the Polish offensive was being hampered by the hostile topography. Despite the problems that were presented by the Germans, 2nd Battalion was determined to complete their operation task and took on the enemy. Already after the first advance made by a group from Laurentowski's company, the Poles had run into a hail of German machinegun bullets, from which they were luckily able to take advantage of nearby rocks to shelter from them. Even so it had cost the Poles, as they had both dead and wounded. This local offensive had come unstuck. The automatic weapons belonging to the group were unobtainable; there were no machineguns or mortars available for the group at that time, as they had been lost in the fighting.

Corporal Dudziak was sent back to Laurentowski to alert him to the plight of the squad, which was now stymied in its advance. To cover Dudziak's departure, a pair of grenades was thrown at the German positions to distract them. However Dudziak's desperate mission was doomed, as he was killed, shot through the head, this veteran of the Spanish Civil War was no more.

Despite the drama of the small group pinned down by the Germans, the overall offensive of 2nd Company continued once more but slowly. A long series of the jabbering of machinegun fire accompanied by the explosions of mortar shells was the soundtrack of the Polish advance, with the occasional report of rifles. The first objective of 2nd Company's offensive was the capture of a small plateau between Hill 295 and the hamlet of Haugen had been captured, as Laurentowski reported by radio.

Bohusz-Szyszko was delighted and ordered a further advance towards Stańczyk, whose company was the nearest to Nyborg. This was not to be easy because Laurentowski's position was in great difficulty. The ground that Laurentowski's company had taken was now under intense enemy attack, as a hail of mortar and machine gun fire rained down on the Poles. On the slopes of Hill 295 were Polish wounded; Cadet Officer Klepacz, Platoon Commander Biały, while Rifleman Lasowski had been wounded in the head whilst taking a wounded German prisoner out of the fighting. Lasowski was a model infantryman; two weeks before the Norwegian Campaign he had been on two weeks leave, as he had just got married. His wound left him blind for the remainder of his life; after the Norwegian Campaign, he was awarded the Virtuti Militari.

Reports from nearby were not promising. One Polish soldier came in and said that there was a devilish battle going on ahead. From the direction of 1st Company, a soldier came running and reported that everybody was dead. The Captain, Lieutenant Kemp and the Cadet Officers. The Battalion lookout cautioned the soldier to speak quietly and calmly and to settle down. The soldier was still in shock and while the lookout post tried to clam him down and convinced him to speak to his own captain, who was indeed alive, but it was true that Kemp, as well as Riflemen Molski and Dutkiewicz and several other riflemen had been wounded. The shocked soldier was spoken to gently but firmly by the lookout, who said to him, 'the rest are alive but are under fire. Now stop being silly, sit behind this cliff and settle down. It's going to be alright'. The lookout may have been a veteran soldier settling a man, who for the first time has witnessed the horrors of war.

The progress of 1st Company's offensive was very slow and lacked any direct communication with their neighbours to the left, 3rd Company. Even so the company pressed ahead towards Haugen. Moving towards Zamoyski from Ankenes was a communications patrol under the command of Sergeant Major Wojciech Lipiński. While Lipiński was making his way to 3rd Company, he had seen Germans moving back towards Hill 295. This was reported to Laurentowski. At 0330, the platoon on the right hand flank was about a kilometre north-east of Hill 295, the left flank protected on the sides of Hill 295, of which the precipice stood at Haugen. At 0500 hours, these companies stormed the German positions and drove them off Hill 295. During this action, contact was lost with the Battalion Command, so Captain Laurentowski organised defence and communications with Stańczyk.

During the period 17 to 27 May, Tkacz andWyganowski's platoons from 2nd Company had a difficult time. Even the smallest movement or action on their part always led the enemy opening fire on them. However, other platoons remained inactive and even got bored waiting for action. There were no attractions as Spring 1940 was late arriving in Norway, so even unknown flora were not available as a distraction. The lads, as Dec referred to the young Polish troops, discussed the nearby towns including Narvik. One wit, Rifleman Kapusta, noted that it would be impossible to go there, as the sea or fjord had to be crossed and that the Poles lacked a Moses to divide the waters and provide a path across the fjord, over which the Poles might march and not get wet feet. Some of the older soldiers went for a walk along the shores of the nearby fjord but this proved to be reckless, as the enemy occupying the opposite shore opened fire on them.

From the north of the Oijord port, which on 15 May fell to the FFL, the French and the Norwegians were en route for Narvik. From Ankenes, 3rd Company were preparing to go onto the offensive supported by three French tanks. 1st Company moved to the summits of Hill 295 towards Haugen; to the right of Dec's was Lewicki's platoon and to the left Lieutenant Wyganowski's platoon. Dec's company was to give supporting fire, which included Mamczarczyk's machinegun platoon, a mortar platoon from 2nd Demi Brigade, as well as two British howitzers. Everybody was ready to go and it was checked that every soldier had two hand grenades apiece. The offensive was to go in, once 1st Company had got halfway to Hill 295. Dec asked if everybody was ready to go and was everything clear. A section leader asked what the objective of the offensive was. Dec replied that will be revealed during the attack.

Captain Stańczyk's company was in the opinion of Pruszyński, the toughest company in 2nd Battalion and moved onto the offensive at 0200 hours. Even so, they did not gain much advancing, only 300 metres over the coming hours. The problem was that from the right hand flank of their offensive, every time the company came under intensive enemy fire. Second Lieutenant Wyganowski was furious but there was nothing that he could do and he could not advance any further. Even so, he looked at events around him and what might be done to save the situation and re-start the Polish offensive. On the right hand side of the offensive and to the fore of the fighting was Captain Kudelski's company from 4th Battalion. Wyganowski pointed out to his 2IC, Cadet Officer Rozenberg, that if a platoon could be peeled off from the main offensive before them and from the cover of nearby bushes engage the enemy, the momentum of Wyganowski's offensive could be regained.

This was how it looked to Second Lieutenant Szewczyk serving in Kudelski's company, who in compliance with orders to attack and destroy the German position moved to do so. Orders were given for a short series of fire against the enemy position and then quick march forward and the Poles, a small group of riflemen, attacked the enemy position. The Germans opened fire with automatic weapons. Wyganowski called for mortar fire to be used against the German position but to little avail as the Germans merely took shelter and then returned fire once more. It seemed that the Germans had a bunker to sit out heavier attacks.

Corporal Gruda said that in such a position, an anti-tank grenade should be put under an enemy bunker, while riflemen shot at the bunker, as well as throwing hand grenades. But it was suggested that the bunker was too far away from the Polish infantrymen discussing how to takeout the enemy bunker. However, the suggestion sowed the seeds of a thought in Szewczyk's head and he began to think of how a similar plan could be undertaken. A plan was formed in the absence of any anti-tank grenades; hand grenades distracted the enemy machineguns and it was discovered that they were positioned in a triangle. Szewczyk's and Wrzeszczyński's sections in a short vicious attack, took the German position. After this brief action Wyganowski was able to move towards the rocky precipice by the fjord and could not see the rear to the right. From the right protecting him was Szewczyk. On the left it was also not easy to move. Second Lieutenant Lewicki called out to Captain Stańczyk that further action was impossible at that moment, but Stańczyk ordered a combined attack by all the companies led by the commander of 2nd Company.

At 0300 hours Dec and his men returned to Hill 295, where he found at the observation point the Brigade Commander. Dec stood by him and watched the centre and right flank of the Battalion's operation. Occasionally rocket shells flew over Hill 295. From the Baatberget to Ankenes road, the sound of battle could be heard. The platoon from 3rd Company fighting along the road, was supported by two French R 35 tanks. One of the tanks stood as sentry at the entrance of the road, while the other progressed along it. It seemed that everything was going to plan and General Bohusz-Szyszko was in a good mood and even telling jokes. Basically the Polish offensive on the left was unfolding as had been planned – thus far there had been no hiccups but all of the commanders knew that the operation was like a bagatelle, especially regarding the local terrain and a well placed enemy machinegun, which could bring any advance to halt, as there was nowhere to dig in, owing to the rocky and still frozen nature of the Norwegian earth and little or no chance of trying to scout ahead or try to muddle through such situations. The commander of the tank making its way up the Baatberget-Ankenes highway was cautious, as he was afraid of mines; the next day his fears were borne out, as the route was indeed discovered to have been mined by the enemy.

As the Poles advanced, it was learnt that not all German positions had been destroyed to the rear of the Polish advance. This caused a crisis on the left side of the Battalion's advance, as the Germans made their presence felt in retaliation against the Poles. However artillery and infantry fire soon restrained and reduced the enemy capacity for further mischief to the rear of the Polish lines.

Finally, Zamoyski's company began to close in on Ankenes and the ruins of houses there and straight away ran into enemy fire, as they engaged the first lines of German defensive positions, as well as attacks to the rear of the Polish lines. The German counterattacks led to some heavy fighting along the highway; in an understatement Dec observing the situation through binoculars considered that the situation was not good. As far as Dec could assert, at the time, the most endangered position was that of 3rd Company, who had been jumped by the Germans from the rear. Individual groups from 3rd Company making their way along the road to Baatberget had to slip along through brush, bushes and woodland. Many of the Polish troops had lost their weapons and helmets and many had been wounded.

Bohusz-Szyszko decided to withdraw 3rd Company and cancel their operation. An artillery barrage supporting 3rd Company had proven to be ineffectual and as could be seen the Germans clearly had the upper hand against the Poles. Hill 295 was about to become a redoubt but from their new operations and new command post, could be established to reorganise the Poles and hold the German counterattack. It was a question of the Poles holding their nerve, however Dec had his doubts and reported to Bohusz-Szyszko that he did not think that Hill 295 was a suitable position from which to defend against the Germans. Bohusz-Szyszko replied quietly perhaps but if the position was abandoned, where were they going to and where would a new command post and observation point be established.

The incident was beginning to unfold at a rapid pace. The Poles lacked any reserve force nearby; Dec placed the Adjutant on the hill Staff and telephone operator. Captain Moreń went to Zamoyski with orders to gather 3rd Company in the anti-tank area in the northern countryside of Emmenes. 3rd Company received their orders but were unable to go into action and Moreń returned to Hill 295. For the best part of an hour, the Poles deceived the enemy into thinking that they were able to hold the hill but the reality was quite the opposite and indeed desperate. At the end of a telephone call to Bohusz-Szyszko, Dec heard the sound of explosions. In the near distance about several hundred paces from Dec, the silhouettes of advancing Germans could be seen. The situation was now critical. The Germans encouraged by the withdrawal of 3rd Company at 0500 hours, counterattacked and stormed summit of Hill 295. Polish troops behaved well as model soldiers in the defence of the hill top and Dec related that he actually stood only a step from either death or capture. Luckily in the nick of time the Adjutant saved Dec's life.

Dec and others were rescued by a small group, who covered them as they withdrew down the rocky sides of the hill and down to the rear. Cadet Officer Buntkowski, inspired by the leadership of Captain Neuman, played an important role in the rescue of Dec. Neuman had also got quite caught up in the fighting and before him lay several dead Germans, but it was Buntkowski who threw Neuman to safety down the rock to the rear of the position, as well as personally covering the withdrawal of his other compatriots.

With Lieutenant Gałacki, some staff and telephonists, Dec moved several hundred metres to the rear of the previous Polish line and organised a small defensive position. Now under the cover of Dec's small group's fire, Neuman and his men were able to withdraw safely. This small band of Polish troops and officers was able to close the German route to the rear of the Polish battalion and Brigade. At 0600 hours, Lieutenant Gazdy arrived with his platoon from the Brigade reserve and was sent out to no-man's land to see what was happening. It was learnt that there had been some

Polish success, as the Germans may have taken the summit of Hill 295 but they could not go any further. It was a success of sorts.

Dec had tasks to perform and made his way to the road and towards Finder. Dec was to access the situation with Jaśkowski, while Dec also had orders to arrange passage for 3rd Company to move to the command post, as well as to swiftly establish communications with Laurentowski and Stańczyk and speak to Neuman.

There was also the question of who was going to report the loss of Hill 295 to Brigade. Dec said that naturally he would report the entire episode to Bohusz-Szyszko. On the slopes towards the road between Baatberget and Emmenes, Dec met with Lieutenant Mostow's machinegun platoon at their post. The anti-tank platoon commanded by 2nd Lieutenant Finder was in the same position, as they had been the day before in Emmenes. Along the road Dec was also able to contact Majors Nowiński and Iliński. With them was Zamoyski, who had seen too much fighting and was not himself and seemed to be an almost reduced man. Zamoyski had tried to save the Polish position and personally had covered the withdrawal of Polish troops by throwing hand grenades at the enemy, taking no heed of his own personal safety. Eighty men had got away but Zamoyski in the meantime was exhausted.

Major Nowiński asked if Bohusz-Szyszko knew of the loss of Hill 295. Dec confirmed that the General did not know, as there was, not as yet, any communication with Brigade. Dec put the two majors into the picture, outlining the positions of Jaśkowski and Finder. After establishing the whereabouts of 1st and 2nd Companies, Dec moved on to make his personal report to Bohusz-Szyszko. Dec got a lift in an empty lorry making its way to the Command Post.

Once Dec appraised Bohusz-Szyszko of the loss of Hill 295; the General remained calm but did not conceal that the situation was bad, because the FFL offensive had also been broken. Only Chłusewicz's group was advancing albeit slowly. Regarding new orders Bohusz-Szyszko ordered that Second Lieutenant Jaśkowski's unit should conduct reconnaissance and see what can be done regarding the retrieval of Hill 295.

A major concern was just where were Laurentowski and Stańczyk? From behind Hill 405 the sounds of heavy fighting could be heard. 1st and 2nd Companies radio networks were silent, so scouts were sent out to try to discover what was going on and to make a report to the commander. Dec returned to Szyszko-Bohusz and made his report; it was not good and was more or less what the General already knew, but his information was confirmed by the latest intelligence gleaned by Dec. Gałacki reported that there was nothing from the radio stations of those companies still out in the field, while the radio station on Hill 295 was of course in German hands. It was impossible to contact fighting Polish companies by radio.

A communications patrol consisting entirely of NCOs was sent out to Stańczyk's position. Stańczyk was given a short briefing of the situation in the direction of Ankenes and how it lay with 1st and 2nd Companies. The Polish commanders sought to try to communicate with the lost companies and were made aware of the situation.

3rd Company from 4th Battalion were alerted to movement in the morning. Reaching from their bivouacs to the buildings in Haakvik, individual platoons moved along the road to Emmenes and two light lorries in line. They had to quickly identify themselves to 4th Battalion; they were Poles including wounded men from Zamoyski's company. From the road Jaśkowski made his report. Lieutenant Gazdy was to the south of the forested section from the top of Hill 295, joined with Second Lieutenant Rydel's platoon. The remainder of the company are positioned astride the road. Major Jaśkowski has sent several patrols out in the area around Hill 295 to try to discover the strength of the Germans on the hill, as well as in the forests on the hillsides leading towards the road.

One of these patrols had been personally led by Rydel. They had been careful in how they had moved across country, moving from bush to bush, rock to rock, the only cover in this bleak territory but despite their caution had run into a German machinegun nest. In the resulting fighting Corporal Pelc was killed and three riflemen were wounded.

Rydel halted the patrol and thought for a moment and realised that he was trying to keep the entire patrol together with only two flashlights. 'Well that's madness' said Cadet Officer Kucharski, as the patrol was probably moving into the jaws of the Germans. Rydel sent out to try to find a way back. As he did this, the Germans opened fire; the Poles were continuously on edge as they waited for their patrol leader to return. Then the patrol Corporal said 'look there's something moving'. Breath died in the chests of the patrol and every barrel was ready to meet what was coming through the bushes. It was Rydel returning at last.

Rydel still had a sense of humour, as he asked the patrol what they were aiming at; were they about to shot him. After a couple of minutes Major Jaśkowski learnt that the Germans on Hill 295 consisted of two platoons with two machineguns. Other patrols had mistakenly reported that Hill 295 was unoccupied. These erroneous reports managed to reach Brigade. This led to the swift decision to recover Hill 295. They made their way to 2nd Company's machinegun's Command Post and the bereaved men there, after the heroic death of Captain Moren. Rifleman Baczyński, Moren's orderly, told Dec that they were to retrieve Moren's body. A group set out and returned after two hours; the Germans were still on Hill 295. Once again in the evening a patrol set out to retrieve Moren's body and this time they were successful.

Troops from 3rd Company 4th Battalion advanced over unknown territory, which was strewn with rocks and ledges as they moved towards the summit of the Hill 295 and again Dec had to protest that the hill was still occupied by Germans and to ignore the incorrect reports, which they were receiving. Between Hill 295 and the group on 2nd Battalion's right flank, was over a gap of about a kilometre, which meant a tiring night march for two platoons of riflemen from 1st Company 4th Battalion. The direction of the march was simple – straight to the Command Post of 2nd Battalion and Brigade.

Dec pressed the space between Hill 295 and 1st Company 4th Battalion, while to have to move across this way was a diabolical situation. Dec moved to 3rd Company, where everyman had been fed and during the afternoon pushed on. Zamoyski was in the immediate centre between Hills 405 and 295. At this time Jaśkowski made a spirited assault against Hill 295, while the direction towards Dec's rear lines was blocked by the enemy. It was around this time that Dec saw the Adjutant.

The coming offensive was being prepared and necessary measure being taken. One thing that Dec desired was that there was communications with Stańczyk, who was positioned in front of Hill 405 towards the direction of the nearby fjord and with Major Jaśowski, who was south of Hill 295. Dec detailed Zamoyski to ensure that these arrangements were made. Zamoyski's men set out during the evening to undertake this order, meanwhile, amongst others, Cadet Officer Stojowski returned with his squad, who had been cut off in Ankenes but had still managed to link up with their battalion.

At 1300 hours, in pursuit of his orders Stańczyk set out with his men; they were not certain of what lay ahead of them but remained optimistic. From 0915 hours every platoon of Stańczyk with Mamczarczyk's machineguns and mortars from 2nd Demi-Brigade, sat on the cliffs overlooking Nyborg. To the right of them was a platoon from Kudelski's company. Laurentowski was positioned on the slopes between Haugen and Lyngenes.

According to Stańczyk's reports, every patrol report that he had received made it clear that 2nd Company's route to the fjord was very difficult and had actually cost 20 men their lives and 15 had been wounded. It was clear that the advance had been slow and only achieved with great and strenuous effort on Stańczyk's left flank. To break the German defences on the reverse slopes of Hill 405a, the Polish platoons moved from one small summit, every man climbing from hill to hill, in order to make towards the fjord. It was just hard work especially for Szaszkiewicz's platoon, who was getting it 'hot' from the German defenders. Indeed everybody was catching it even Stańczyk.

From the direction of Hill 295 came the sound of heavy firing. To the right 1st Battalion's battle could be clearly heard. However, at long last the platoons of 2nd Company had made it to the fjord. Between them as if in the palm of a hand lay houses denoting Fagernes and in the left Narvik could be seen, the town was on fire. It was 0915 hours. Lewicki, Tkacz and Wyganowski's platoons, supported by machineguns and the rest of the strength, moved to the heights over Nyborg. Once more the Polish troops did not have to stop and catch their collective breath, as once more their hands were full and they had even more work to do before they were finished.

The problem was that almost as soon as the Poles entered the fjord area, one of Stańczyk's lookouts had sighted boats heading towards the machinegun platoon; immediately the four machineguns and a platoon of automatic Polish rifles, all ten of them, opened fired on the enemy boats. The lead boat opened fire on the Poles, who initially were inaccurate and almost amateurish in their firing on the boats, but this was a target that they had never encountered before; fast moving boats which fired back, but the next round of Polish fire was more determined and the Poles had their collective eye on and one of the enemy boats was turned into a sieve, forcing the Germans to abandon it, jumping into the water, jettison their weapons and swim back to Nyborg.

From Fagernes the noise of German machinery could be heard but that was soon silenced by mortar fire. Germans swam to the Polish held shores and then surrendered to the Poles there. Tkacz was taking their surrender and asking where their weapons were. The Poles pulled weapons out of the water using a rope. Then Tkacz asked his captive if they knew who they were surrendering to; the Germans did and answered 'Poles,' but they were clearly embarrassed about having to surrender to people of whom Nazi propaganda declared to be 'subhumans'.

The worse of the day came at 1000 hours, when Stukas attacked several Polish held hilltops and the route between them. Hill 677 was attacked, as was the route between Hill 405 towards Hill 295. The enemy aircraft on their return to their own bases via Haakvik also bombed the command post of 2nd Battalion, as well as the positions of Laurentowski's and Stańcyk's companies. A lot of bombs were dropped on the two companies. Even so the Poles only suffered two casualties, with the youngest corporal of the Polish force in Norway, Corporal Dziedziach being badly wounded as was Rifleman Kłosak.

Several of the bombs dropped by the Germans were phosphorus incendiary bombs, which literally burnt their trail and left their mark. The most fierce fires were near to the rear of both Laurentowski's and Stańcyk's companies. The troops there were certainly receiving a baptism of fire from bombs and from fire and even worse, not only were they bombed but the German aircraft also returned to strafe the Polish positions. The Polish troops were left to extinguish the flames as best they could, often using haversacks to beat the flames out.

During the evening, the Commander 2nd Demi-Brigade Colonel Kobyłecki came to Dec's post. It was a social visit in many ways, in which Dec met with Cadet Officer Henryk Jabłonski, who later serving in the French Resistance Movement rose to the rank of Major. Throughout that night Jaśkowski was still unable to take Hill 295 and the Ankenes region. During the morning hours 22 May, his group began to concentrate on defeating the Germans and assaulted the final lines of the enemy defence, said Colonel Kobyłecki. Dec and Kobyłecki by motorcycle went to Jaśkowski, whose position had not changed as the Germans remained on Hill 295 and held Ankenes town.

Kobyłecki and Dec decided that they might look over what had been going on to decide what might be best to do next. However at 2200 hours, after heavy and bloody fighting, it was learnt that the French Foreign Legion had captured Narvik and that the Norwegian 15th Infantry Regiment had taken possession of the town.

The capture of Narvik was not the end of the campaign in Norway, but it pretty much was, as the British were certainly no longer interested in maintaining its presence there if the UK was in peril of German invasion. The Poles were still fighting in Norway and at the time of the capture of Narvik, Chłusewicz's was threatening the German withdrawal route through the town of Beisfjord towards Sildvik-Hundalen. Towards the cliffs near Nyborg near the fjord was a half battery of howitzers, as well as Polish machineguns and mortars from Stańczyk's platoons. A little to the rear of this on the left was Laurentowski's company.

The question of the capture of Hill 295 remained, but once the news of the capture of Narvik was made known amongst Polish troops, there was a renewed energy within 3rd Company 4th Battalion and shortly before midnight they stormed the hill and took it. The Germans seemed to lack the strength to continue defending the hill. Abandoning Hill 295, the enemy made for Ankenes town, while owing to thick fog, Polish action for the night was suspended. This time, reports of the capture of Hill 295 were genuine.

In the clarity of morning it was obvious that Hill 295 had been captured by the Allies, as well as the scenery of a post-battle period, including the heads of 17 soldiers, of which two were French and another was a British Bos'un signaller of the Royal Navy. The body of Moreń was the only one not desecrated by the Germans.

Dec and Kobyłecki went by motorcycle to Jaśkowski's position. Preparations were being made for the coming offensive against Ankenes. At the time of Dec's visit the squads were preparing to move; Jaśkowski's men were supported by a tank, but quickly it was learnt that the way ahead was mined. The tank almost immediately ran over a mine and had its tracks blown off. Jaśkowski fell from the tank but suffered nothing more than cuts and bruises.

Dec considered that it might be possible to enter Ankenes without any fighting. Colonel Kobyłecki returned to the Brigade to make his report and Dec decided to go across to Haugen and straight into a minefield, but luckily his 'lads' realised what had happened. They called to Dec to remain still and wait for a guide, who seemed to have arrived quickly, as within a few minutes he was back with his 'lads' and the genuine victors from the Ankenes area. Apparently these troops had at 0915 hours 28 May, made their presence and remarkable influence felt on the right hand side of the FFL action. The Germans throughout the evening in masses had been heading towards the snowy mountains, which led to Sweden. Even so there was still uncertainty about Hill 295.

Preparations for the Polish offensive were still underway. Dec recounted that bread, cigarettes and jam was provided for the troops, as well as a report for Dec from 2nd Company. The memory of Polish troops moving out and away onto the offensive at Ankenes remained strong for Dec, who also moved along the road by the fjord to Ankenes. The town had been thoroughly wrecked by war and was terrible to see, as beautifully painted homes had been perforated by shells, as had the other houses in the area. Others had been burnt out, while some were still on fire. Dec's troops seemed to have organised themselves well and from the wrecks of the German supply ships, pulled out bread, jam and many, many bottles of beer. Then Dec learnt of further good news, as it was announced that Jaśkowski and his men had taken Ankenes; it was all over but as Dec recalled, the atmosphere seemed very odd, as the debris of conflict was everywhere; fires, destruction, minefields, and the bodies of Allied and German soldiers were still lying around waiting to be collected.

However something that Dec never lost sight of is the fact that once more the Germans had suffered a loss. The fight for Ankenes, according to Dec, had involved 22 hours of hard and bloody heavy fighting, which resulted in the defeat for the first of crack German mountain troops, as the Allies with the Norwegians co-operated and learnt how to defeat the Germans and prove to the world that the German Army was vulnerable. Most importantly the Polish Army was seen clearly as part of the victorious force and not merely hanging onto the coat tails of France and the UK and broadcast by radio across the world. From secret radio stations in Poland, Poles were able to learn that not only was the Polish Army still fighting but it had just taken part in a defeat of German arms.

However, the Allied victory did not come cheap, as the casualties were relatively high. The French carried the highest losses, while the Podhalians suffered 70 dead, 130 wounded, seven taken prisoner and six missing. The Germans had suffered 110 dead, which included 70 who had died when one of their ships was sunk in Beisfjord. But the battle had been won with Narvik, Ankenes and Beisfjord, all captured by the Allies, including the Podhalians, who maintained the highest standards expected of a soldier, even though the Brigade that had gone to Norway had only been in existence for a mere four months.[4]

4 Dec, op. cit. pp.66-125.

9

Evacuation

Even though Narvik was captured by the Allies, it was, as already indicated, events on the main part of the European continent which dictated what happened in Norway. France had all but fallen to the Germans and the UK was preparing to repulse an anticipated German invasion of their shores. A major concern of any Allied evacuation of Norway was the necessity for secrecy. This was very difficult and made relations between the Allies fraught. After the evacuation at Bodo, relations with Colonel Finne, Norwegian Liaison to Auchinleck's HQ became very difficult. Even General Fleischer was kept out of the loop, even though his forces were actually fighting the enemy at Narvik, ignorant of the British government's intention to evacuate the theatre of operations. General Bethouard was extremely uncomfortable with having to keep the Norwegians in the dark, especially as his forces were fighting alongside Norwegian troops.[1]

Other plans for the evacuation of Norway were also extraordinary and illustrated that even after nine months of war, the Allies were still not really clear who the enemy really was. An amusing side of caution being taken by British commanders was that Auchinleck spoke by telephone to Pollock in Hindi, as a security measure whilst briefing him. Pollock saw General Ruge at noon 4 June, who told Pollock that the Norwegians feared that the Soviet Union might invade Norway, very much in the manner that it had done in Poland in September 1939. As a consequence, the Norwegian government was contemplating inviting the Germans through Sweden to stabilise a frontier around Narvik and the Norwegian position in the north, while using all their resources to combat the Soviet Union.

The Norwegians considered that this measure would be accepted by the Germans, as they had commitments elsewhere (the invasion of France!) The Norwegian government was not contemplating inviting Germany to take over Norway, but it was preferable to the Soviet Union annexing the country. In the event of a Soviet invasion, the Norwegian government would be evacuated and the Army surrender to the Germans. The Norwegian government hoped that if the Soviet Union was to endanger Norway and the Germans were willing to defend it from Soviet aggression, then perhaps the British would leave lorries and other materials, which could be used against the Red Army.

Ruge also admitted that the Norwegian government would be glad to see the British leave Norway. As a consequence, the Allies continued to precede with their evacuation plans for leaving Norway and considered that any delay would be dangerous. All the same the British planners still managed to consider the question of decorations and who and how to make awards for the Norwegian Campaign. Fleischer was to get nothing, as he would be upset by events, whilst the French Commander, General Bethouart, should be told of forthcoming events regarding evacuation of Norway and be decorated, as he passed through the UK.[2] One assumes that the

1 TNA, PREM 3/328/5, 29 May 1940.
2 TNA, PREM 3/328/4, FO Narvik to Admiralty in Naval Cypher (NAR) By W/T, 4 June 1940.

reference to Bethouart's passage means as he makes his way to his already doomed country but the Norwegian attitude was gobsmacking and extremely naive. They were yet to discover that Germany may have had the trapping of civilization but it was skin deep, as with most states in a certain set of circumstances. Norway had had the good fortune to have enjoyed peace for decades, but of course this left them vulnerable to reality.

The above events were in total contrast to previous thoughts of how the Norwegian Campaign might go, as only the previous week the following thoughts had been shared. On 26 May there was still consideration that perhaps the evacuation of Norway might be put on hold for a while at least. There were several reasons for hesitation with the main objection being the effect on Allied morale and prestige. It was further noted that the Allied offensive in Norway was tying down German resources, however the toll of using the Royal Navy to evacuate Norway would weaken naval resources, which were more urgently required in the North Sea, which was judged to be 1,000 miles away.

As if to contradict Auchinleck's thesis that any capture of Narvik and its port would take at least six months to repair and clear of wrecked ships, it was asserted that this would not take as long and that its destruction and that of the railway line between Narvik and the Swedish frontier would not amount to that much time to repair. A major consideration was that the Germans had unlimited resources at their disposal and the work would be got through quickly. What was mentioned, was more or less the destruction of the entire Narvik peninsula in the manner of a scorched earth policy. This argument was extended further and if necessary called for the same measures to be applied to Kirkenes, if not the entirety of northern Norway because if the enemy was able to capture the entire area (Norway would be conquered) the German ability to acquire all the iron ore necessary to the German war effort would be completely unhindered, even when Lulea was closed owing to being iced up.

It was further considered that a large proportion of Allied stores, including ammunition would be lost in any evacuation. What was suggested was a swift capture of Narvik and a defensive line being formed in northern Norway by the Allies. It was also thought that to supply an Allied garrison in Norway, would not require a great number of Destroyers, provided they were used properly to bring supplies, as well as troops and there was a warning not to use them exclusively as troop carriers. British planners thought the use of railway tunnels would be extremely beneficial for the protection and hiding of supplies of men and stores against enemy aerial attacks.[3]

However, any attempt to keep Allied especially British troops in Norway was doomed and had been since 24 May 1940, when the British government realised that the UK was about to have to fight for its very existence, as France was on the verge of collapse and the next obvious German target was the UK. Therefore the Admiralty on 24 May sent the following message out to the Flag Officer at Narvik. The message was from the British Chiefs of Staff and ran 'His Majesty's government has decided that your forces are to evacuate Northern Norway at the earliest moment. The reason for this is that the troops, ships, guns and certain equipment are urgently required for the defence of the United Kingdom. We understand that from the military point of view operation of evacuation will be facilitated if the enemy's forces are largely destroyed or captured. Moreover the destruction of the railway and Narvik port facilities make its capture highly desirable. Nevertheless the speed of evacuation once begun should be the primary consideration in order to limit the duration of a maximum naval effort. Two officers will be sent out at once from the United Kingdom to concert the evacuation plan with you and General Auchinleck. Evacuation of all equipment, vehicles and stores will clearly take too long. The following are required to be evacuated in order of importance for the point of view of the defence of the United Kingdom:

3 TNA, PREM 3/328/4, From C-in-C Home Fleet to Admiralty; First Sea Lord and First Lord, 26 May 1940.

Personnel,
Light AA guns and ammunition
25 pounder field guns
Heavy AA guns and ammunition.

Tactical conditions must rule but so far as they permit plans which should be formed accordingly. The Norwegian government have not, repeat not, yet been informed and great secrecy should be observed.'[4] The necessity for secrecy was obviously necessary as many Norwegians could not be trusted, whilst the French security system was not watertight and so only a day after the official notice to evacuate Norway was issued to the Flag Officer at Narvik, there was rapid signalling from him to Churchill at the Admiralty concerning informing the French government of British plans to leave Norway. The Flag Officer at Narvik suggested that he should inform the local French commander of the situation, rather than the French government doing so and that he was alive to the need for secrecy. He also in the same message requested aid, perhaps a light naval force to 'harry' the coast, using aircraft operating off aircraft carriers between Mosjoen and Boco, in order to delay a German advance party, which was heading northwards towards the Allies.[5] Everything in Norway depended on what happened in France and as the Germans steadily advanced into France and headed to the English Channel ports, it became obvious that France was lost and that the UK had to be defended. This was obviously the main consideration of the British government and the British General Staff, informing the French posed its own problems as communications might easily have fallen into enemy hands, as the German Army advanced into both France and further into northern Norway. Not everything can be destroyed in time and so a risk was posed of the enemy discovering plans by chance. The requirement for AAA and 25 pounder field guns that could be used for anti-tank purposes to be returned from Norway, gives an indication of just how the British were preparing for German aerial and later armoured attacks against and on UK territory. The tanks were never landed and the German aircraft were defeated.

However the most important thing as the capture of Narvik, which seemed to have hypnotised the Allies from the very beginning and probably caused them to lose perspective of the overall Allied plan for Norway, was nevertheless the relentless pace of the German advance across Western Europe, which caused the biggest upsets in Allied planning. The capture of Narvik was always going to be a primary concern for the Allies, owing to its capture and retention, would have allowed the Allies to disrupt the supply of iron ore to Germany.

However one can only consider Narvik, despite the impressive victories of the Royal Navy in April and the sterling work of Allied land forces in Norway, to be a failure, as the objectives were not held. The main failing at Narvik was that of timidity. Allied commanders, prior to the arrival of Auchinleck, refused to go where the Germans did, as Churchill observed. A good example was the road between Namsos to Mosjoen, which both the British and French had declared to have been impassable, whilst the Germans traversed in seven days.[6] However, in fairness the Germans were better prepared for any offensive in Norway, but the Allied commanders were found to be wanting. This was something that Churchill was not shy about remarking upon, within a decade of events in Norway, of course he had his own agenda to pursue, but it makes his observations no less relevant for that. Churchill's point was that, as we have seen, the German plan for the occupation of Norway was ruthless and well executed and used airpower to perfection. Churchill also noted the relatively small numbers used by the Germans, as at Narvik for example 6,000 Germans held 20,000 Allied

4 TNA, PREM 3/328/4, Admiralty to FO, Narvik, 24 May 1940.
5 TNA, PREM 3/328/4, FO, Narvik to Admiralty, 25 May 1940.
6 Churchill, op. cit, p. 511.

troops at bay for six weeks. Churchill wrote that even though the Royal Navy had opened the Narvik attack 'so brilliantly,' it was 'paralysed by the refusal of the military commander to run what was admittedly a desperate risk.'[7] Of course this commander was General Mackesy.

The Norwegian Campaign led to a change of tactics by British forces at least, which became known as 'Commando' style warfare. Basically small specialist companies led by inspired and inspiring officers were used to fight vastly larger forces. Such roles are now frequently seen in contemporary warfare, including the Royal Marine Commandoes and the SAS and SBS. The British were not the first to use commandoes, Churchill was inspired by the type of warfare waged by Boer irregulars, during the Second Anglo-Boer; 1899–1902, which saw what were basically farmers fighting from horseback running rings around the British Army. It took some extreme and controversial measures by the British Army against Boer women and children, before the Boer fighters could be brought to heel by the British Army. Within the Polish Army, there was a superb commando and winter warfare expert, General Maczek, who was still in France trying to organise Polish armoured forces, in 1919–20 had led commando raids against Ukrainian forces, as Poland and Ukraine fought to deny each other territory and to try to establish their respective frontiers, at the expense of each other. Maczek was to distinguish himself as a commander of armour between 1944 and 1945 and instrumental to the Allied victory in Normandy during August 1944, but this is quite different to that of Norway. It is interesting that the officer chosen to lead the commando style fighting in Norway, Colonel Colin Gubbins, was to become well known to the Polish Army, as he often worked with them and championed their cause. However the problem of 1940 and Norway was that the Germans had prepared well for the offensive, as it was truly their campaign and the Allies were left behind trying to understand land warfare over such difficult terrain, with only a small Norwegian force available to guide them through the basics of Arctic warfare, at a time when many of the Allies did not totally trust the Norwegians, owing to recent treacheries. However, as Churchill observed after the war, the land warfare was hard going for the Allied in Norway and the Germans seemed champions of it. Churchill may have noted that the Royal Navy, with its allies, were masters of the seas around Norway and could 'pounce' on the enemy anywhere along the largely undefended Norwegian coas, Allied troops were constantly outpaced by German troops during the Norwegian campaign. Indeed Churchill asserts that the 'finest troops' of the British Army, the Scots and Irish Guards were 'baffled by the vigour, enterprise and training of Hitler's young men.' This situation was the result of the naivety and quite frankly stupidity of many inter-war democratic governments, who seriously believed that war could be outlawed by not preparing for it; Churchill especially throughout the 1930s had warned against such foolishness but was ignored. In 1940, Churchill wrote; his warnings were now remembered.[8] The Scots and Irish Guards might well have been the best troops of the British Army but the German Army had been preparing for war for a number of years and had been considerably enlarged after 1934 with the reintroduction of conscription in Germany, contrary to the terms of the Versailles Treaty, which concluded the First World War in relation to Germany. Churchill had warned against this; the fact that Germany was rearming and once more, contrary to the Versailles Treaty was re-establishing an air force. Between 1936 and 1939 this air force had been able to develop, practise and perfect aerial warfare using the Spanish Civil War and Spain as its proving ground. All of this Churchill had protested during the 1930s and except for a small band of loyal supporters, had been ostracised in political circles and denounced as a warmonger. One might have considered that German actions post-Munich might have been evidence enough of German ill-intentions, with the German invasion of Poland being

7 Ibid., pp. 510-1.
8 Ibid., p. 511.

the final proof of German aggression, but for many this was still not sufficient to have faith in Churchill and continued to question his intentions in Norway.

It was to take disaster after disaster to remove Neville Chamberlain from his post, as the Prime Minister of the UK and install Churchill as PM; all in the nick of time as it is unlikely that Chamberlain had the charisma to defy the threatened German invasion, inspire the British people and have upper class leading British fascists arrested and imprisoned. Chamberlain was not the man to command the UK in wartime.

Even so, Churchill had to witness two humiliating withdrawals from the European mainland, as the British and French armed forces were driven from both Norway and from France, having fought a gallant rearguard action from Belgium to the beaches of Dunkirk. The evacuation from France was a series of evacuations, with the one from Dunkirk entering the mythology of British military history: Churchill was never impressed. The evacuation from Norway was a brilliantly executed manoeuvre and was a response to the German overrunning of western continental Europe and the loss of France. Norway had been a success of Allied arms but now these arms were needed to defend the UK. Furthermore, Churchill did not want to go down in history as being linked to landings and then their evacuation, as he had already been held responsible for the 1915 Gallipoli expedition against Turkey; the fault was not his but the blame was to lay with him and his friend General Sir Ian Hamilton.[9]

Churchill speaks of Hitler's assault on Norway as the ending of the Twilight War. It was the end of allowances being made for Germany and perhaps especially once the UK was threatened of some accommodation being made with the Nazis. Churchill supported by a broad church of politicians and other influential figures openly opposed Hitler and his plans and openly challenged the Germans to land in the UK. In his memoir of the war years, Churchill described the period between September 1939 and April 1940 as being a trance, in which France and the UK was held and was most harmful for the Allies. A further concern was that of Stalin and the Soviet Union because, as Churchill wrote, from the minute that Stalin reached an understanding with Hitler, French Communists taking their instructions from Moscow, declared the war as 'an imperialist and capitalist crime against democracy'. According to Churchill, communists did all that they could to undermine morale in the French Army and impede industry in France. By May 1940, the morale of the French, both soldiers and civilians, was lower than it had been at the outbreak of war. Even Churchill makes reference to the activities of British communists, to which Dec also alludes to, as we have seen, Churchill claims that British communists were 'busy,' but British response towards Communism was weak. However, in areas such as Clydeside, where people were more radicalised for a number of reasons, with the main factors being poverty; unfair and uneven work practises, and rule from London, communism was more likely to take root and the mysterious fire, as witnessed by Dec, could well be attributed to Moscow backed saboteurs. However, there was the bigger picture than local saboteurs.

Another aspect of the defeated Norwegian campaign was events on continental Europe. As Churchill mentioned before, the German invasion of Denmark and Norway, the war on the Western Front, had been surreal or a 'twilight war' more often spoken of in the UK as the 'phoney war' as nothing happened. The war was real elsewhere in the east especially in Poland and Finland, as Auden's ogres behaved as ogres must, while at sea British sailors and others were well aware of the war but land forces in the West were left untroubled. Perhaps both the Germans and the Allies thought that something could have been arranged to satisfy honour for all but at the expense of

9 McGilvray provides a good political-military study of the 1915 Gallipoli offensive in: Evan McGilvray, *Hamilton & Gallipoli. British Command in an Age of Military Transformation* (Barnsley: UK, Pen & Sword, 2015).

the Jews and the Slavs. However, once Germany invaded Western Europe there appeared to be no-going back; the Rubicon had been crossed and with the fall of the Chamberlain government and Churchill's assumption to power in the UK, there was to be no doubt, as to the end of the war in Europe, it was a fight to the finish. Both the UK with her allies, were going to have to comprehensively defeat Germany and her allies, or Europe and Eurasia were doomed to experience a neo-dark age, if the Nazis were victorious.

The evacuation of northern Norway, as we have seen, had been on the agenda since almost before Narvik was recaptured by the Allies, but as France fell to the Germans, the evacuation of Norway was sped along, if only to try to prevent the fall of the UK to German forces and the complete subjection of Europe to Nazi rule. A major problem was the need for secrecy and later this was too led to recriminations, as some alleged that not enough equipment had been saved and returned to the UK for defence of the homeland. Colonel Graham at Base Command, Tromso was told on 1 June by NWEF HQ that evacuation was imminent. It was stressed that all British service personnel at Tromso, including members of the British Military Mission to Norway were to be evacuated, with numbers estimated as being 350. Colonel Graham was given quite a comprehensive list of what to do and to expect. The FO Narvik had already instructed the Captain of HMS *Devonshire* to contact Graham and make the necessary arrangements for removing him and his men on, or before, 6 June 1940.

It was noted, that it was expected that not all equipment would be saved from Tromso, other than personal arms and such equipment that might be possible to move onto HMS *Devonshire,* while secret papers, other than those that could be taken aboard the ship, were naturally to be destroyed. The most interesting is that the authorities were determined to keep a tight rein on finances, as part of the instructions issued by Auchinleck's HQ was 'you will hand over to the British consul sufficient money to meet all known liabilities and withdraw the balance from the Bank and take it with you. If this, for any reason, is not practicable you will transfer your credit to the account of the Consul. You should keep a record of your financial action.'[10] So British to keep the accounts straight! Other instructions to Graham were based on involving the least number of people in the knowledge of what was actually happening, while a pretence of establishing an advanced base at Narvik was the fiction to be maintained to those asking why a move from Tromso was necessary.[11]

Further and clearer operational orders were made to the RAF concerning the evacuation and how it was to support it. It was revealed that the NWEF was to be re-embarked (evacuated) over a five day period, beginning at 2200 hours, 2 June 1940. The method of embarkation was to transfer troops via 'puffer' or from the quays to waiting Destroyers, in the four main areas of Harstad; Skaanland; Ofotfjord Sorreisa and Salangsverket. Later, the evacuated troops were to be transferred from the Destroyers to transports, which were lying about 60 miles to the west of the evacuation points. The embarkation was not to be a continuous process but to be undertaken at varying periods, in each 24 hour period. The main task was the provision of air cover for the evacuation. Therefore FO Narvik arranged for Swordfish aircraft, operating from aircraft carriers, to carry out reconnaissance patrols, in order to try to discover enemy movements up the coast along the tracks leading north from Sorfolla to Tysfjord. There were other duties for aviators, which included a daily bombing of the enemy HQ at Hundalen, as well as other bombing raids in the Hundalen area if necessary. Also two Swordfish were to be sent to Bardu Foss at a later date, in order to guide Gladiator fighter-bombers of 243 Squadron RAF to the naval carriers, which would take them from Norway and back to the UK. A schedule of the evacuation was

10 Special Collections, John Rylands Library, AUC/70-120 Southern Command, File V, June 1-30 1940, Items 63-73, MUL 63 HQ NWEF to Colonel Graham, Base Command, TROMSO, 1 June 1940.

11 Ibid.

also released to the air force. The first day (D1) between 2200 hours 2 June and 2200 hours 3 June, saw evacuations from Harstad at 2200–2330 hours and then another between 0745–0915 hours; from Skaanland 2130–2330 hours; Ofotfjord 2300–0200 hours and both Sorreisa and Salangsverket saw evacuations at 0645-0915 hours. D2, 3 June 2200 hours to 2200 hours 4 June, saw evacuations from; Harstad from 2200–2330 hours and 0745–0915 hours; Skaanland 2130–2300 hours; Ofotfjord between 2100 hours and 2359–0200 hours and Sorreisa only 0645–0915 hours. D3, 2200 hours 4 June to 2200 hours 5 June; Harstad 2200–2330 hours and 0745–0915 hours; Ofotfjord 2100–0200 hours; Salangsverket only 0645–0915 hours. D4, 2200 hours 5 June to 2200 hours 6 June; Harstad 2200–2330 hours and 0745–0915 hours; Ofotfjord 2100–2359 hours; 0100–0300 hours; Sorreisa 0100–0230 hours. D5, 2200 hours 6 June to 2200 hours 7 June; Harstad 2200–2330 hours; Salangsverket 2130–2330 hours; Ofotfjord 2200–2359 hours; 0100–0300 hours. Times for evacuation through Sorreisa were to be arranged later.[12] Why some of the operations were scheduled, before the times recommended began, earlier is not made clear. However the clearest instructions regarding the evacuation, as might have been surmised, was given to Lord Cork by the Admiralty, as after all it was his ships which would be responsible for getting Allied troops away from Norway and back to the UK, in order to defend it from a threatened German invasion.

Cork was informed that the forces being evacuated from Norway were needed for the defence of the UK. It seemed that the most important element of the evacuation was manpower. If equipment could be saved and brought back so much the better, but it was feared that this might take too long. Therefore the priorities were in order of importance: personnel; light AAA guns and ammunition; 25 pounder guns and finally heavy AAA guns. However, after the evacuation there was criticism of how little equipment had been retrieved, especially AAA guns, as out of 60 light AAA guns only 16 had been bought back from Norway and of a possible 48 heavy AAA guns only six had been retrieved.[13] Throughout July 1940, there were further recriminations and arguments concerning how the war to date had been run. The Allies had been driven out of Europe and were treed in the UK. The British were on invasion alert, while the Germans were attacking from the air, in preparation for sending land forces across the English Channel, therefore there was an obvious need for the AAA guns, while the 25 pounder field artillery pieces made excellent anti-tank guns if the Germans were to land and deploy armour. But as the world was to see, the Luftwaffe was defeated by the British and her Allies, while it was a matter of opinion that the Germans could have even got land forces across the English Channel, given the mauling that German surface fleet had received at Narvik, during April 1940. However the summer of 1940 was a tense time for the British and it is not surprising that tempers and tetchiness had set in amongst British officials, especially service chiefs, as they licked their wounds and set to begin to plan responses to German aggression and successes since September 1939.

Cork was not slow to respond to the criticism which came his way and he particularly vexed with the criticism concerning the small numbers of AAA guns returned from Norway. As he said, how was he expected to defend the embarkation points without AAA guns? This point is particularly relevant given the fact that the Allies never established air supremacy during the 1940 Norwegian Campaign and that ships being loaded were extremely vulnerable to enemy air attacks. A further concern, as Cork outlined, was the need for secrecy especially since local Norwegians could not be trusted, including some military commanders.

12 Special Collections, John Rylands Library, MUL 64 Operational Instruction, Operational Instruction No. 3, 1 June 1940.

13 Special Collections, John Rylands Library, MUL 74, File VI, July 1-31 1940, Items 74-83, Copy of Letter Addressed to the Admiral of the Fleet the Earl of Cork and Orrery from the Admiralty, 3 July 1940.

So during July 1940, Cork maintained his defence, as those who were not in Norway, and therefore ignorant of the situation there, continued to attack and question him. As Cork suggested none of the embarkation points used were safe, the entire operation in Norway was not safe, no doubt due to pacifist policies of interwar European governments that refused to recognise the true situation in Germany, and so were caught out when Germany finally began its war in the west. Wishful thinking in Western political circles had run its course and had been found wanting.

Cork also made the point that how was he meant to maintain secrecy? Harstad as a military secret did not remain so for long because, as Cork wrote, the enemy made daily aerial reconnaissance and could clearly see that something was afoot there. The trick was to deceive the Germans of what was the real intention of the Allies at Harstad. Cork was quite correct in his reply to the Admiralty, noting that if the AAA defences at Harstad had been dismantled during the last week of May, the enemy would have been alerted to the fact that the Allies were probably planning to leave Norway, given that they had expended so much effort installing the same defences only one week earlier. That was why the dismantling of the AAA defences at Harstad did not commence until 2 June; the day that the evacuations were to commence and, on his own initiative, Cork on the same day informed the Norwegian government that the Allies were about to begin to abandon Norway. The embarkation points at Ballangen, Ankenes, and Bjerkvik designated for French and Polish troops, who were still fighting the Germans, as they made their way to their points from which they were to be ferried by fishing vessels to waiting Destroyers, were actually open beaches. As open beaches these points needed defending from enemy aerial attacks, which actually occurred during the period of embarkation and therefore Cork needed AAA until the very last and that was the very reason why AAA guns had not be returned to the UK, in the numbers anticipated by those sitting at desks in Whitehall.[14]

Auchinleck was also very surprised and dismayed to hear of the problems that Cork was encountering from Whitehall concerning the considered insufficient number of AAA guns returned from Norway. Auchinleck considered that this was due to ignorance on the behalf of the Admiralty. On 7 July, Auchinleck wrote to Cork thus, 'As you know on 24 May, the Bodo situation was critical and unless Gubbins could have been reinforced, he would probably have been pushed into the sea, as happened at Namsos and Andalsnes, or had been surrounded. As you also know, we had reinforcements actually embarked and ready to go down; if the order for evacuation had not come, these reinforcements would have been sent. Similarly, if the general evacuation had been appreciably delayed or postponed, these reinforcements would have had to go, as Bodo could not be evacuated too far in advance of the evacuation of Harstad, for the reason that the enemy was pushing up the coast (as they did so) would have seriously compromised the latter operation. In actual fact, the period between the evacuation of Bodo and the final evacuation of Harstad-Narvik was only just long enough as you will remember. If Bodo had had to be reinforced and a delaying action fought around it, the withdrawal from that area would have been definitely more complicated and difficult and might well have become another Andalsnes or a minor Dunkirk. As it was, owing to the lack of suitable ships and port facilities, the four field guns and two Bofors had to be abandoned there (the other two Bofors were left at Mo as you will remember).[15] Quite simply as with many military evacuations, things were done in haste and plans set by naval and military planners had to be compromised in order to get service personnel away, while some equipment had to be abandoned often owing to the lack of facilities to remove and transport them or the fact that

14 Ibid.
15 Special Collection, John Rylands Library, MUL 77, Auchinleck to Cork, 7 July 1940.

pieces such as AAA were being used until the last possible moment: Auchinleck and Cork knew this and had some difficulty explaining the situation to others.

It was the invasion of Western Europe which sealed the fate of events in Norway in 1940, but was to cost the Germans far more than they had ever anticipated. This was as Churchill depicted in his work about the Second World War. Churchill conceded that events in Norway were going well and that there was a chance of cutting off the iron ore supply to Germany, as well as maintaining a foothold in northern Norway from which King Haakon and his government might operate from. Auchinleck, as we have seen, requested further materials for the campaign of which, even at that time, only half could be promised to be sent. However by 24 May 1940, events in France caused the Allies to focus, because as Churchill wrote, it was obvious that the Allies faced defeat in Europe and so resources had to be concentrated in France and in the UK. The British attitude, not surprisingly, was that the UK should be defended to the outmost, whilst it was preferable not to be driven out from the European mainland. As we have seen, during the period of late May and early June 1940 saw Allied successes in Norway, but they could not be capitalised on owing to events in France.

Naval evacuations from both France and Norway stretched the Royal Navy further than it would have liked. Operation 'Dynamo,' the evacuation of British and French armed forces from France was underway, whilst British troops and aircraft were being positioned in southern England ready to face a German invasion. The Royal Navy also had to be ready to intervene against any German invasion force that might try to cross the English Channel and land in the UK and so many Cruisers and Destroyers were in position, ready to face the German threat. This left the C-in-C at Scapa only having four capital ships at his disposal to cover all contingencies.

The evacuation at Narvik went well and by 8 June all troops, British, French and Polish; 24,000 men in total, with large quantities of stores and equipment, were embarked and sailed in four convoys without hindrance from the enemy. Churchill claimed that the victorious Germans amounted to no more than 'a few thousand' who were scattered, disorganised but victorious. The German victory in Norway was more of a case of default as the Allies had been forced to withdraw because of German victories elsewhere.

The Allied withdrawal from Norway was well run and heroically carried out. Air cover for the withdrawal was provided, not only by carrier based aircraft, but also from a shore based squadron of Hurricanes. This squadron had been ordered to fight to the end and destroy their aircraft if necessary. However the Hurricane pilots fought to the very last and then actually managed to fly and land their aircraft on the aircraft carrier HMS *Glorious*. To cover the evacuations out of Norway, Lord Cork had two aircraft carriers as HMS *Ark Royal* was also alongside HMS *Glorious*, as well as the Cruisers, HMS *Southampton* and HMS *Coventry*, along with 16 Destroyers and other smaller vessels. The Cruiser HMS *Devonshire* embarked King Haakon and his Staff from Tromso and was moving independently of Cork's main force. Cork informed his C-in-C of his convoy arrangements and requested protection from possible attacks by large enemy ships.

Admiral Forbes sent HMS *Valiant* on 6 June to meet the first convoy of troopships returning from Norway, escort it to the north of the Shetland Island and then set out again to meet the second convoy. British naval commanders had been distracted by reports made on 5 June that large German ships had been seen making for Iceland and that the Germans had landed there. These reports turned out to be false and distracting, as the German Battle-Cruisers *Scharnhorst* and *Gneisenau* with the Cruiser *Hipper*, having been repaired in Germany following their mauling by the Royal Navy at Narvik during April, suddenly appeared off the coast of Norway with an escort of four Destroyers. The German ships had left Kiel on 4 June, with the object of attacking Allied shipping and bases in the Narvik area and providing some relief for the somewhat German land forces in that area. The German Admiralty had no idea of the Allied withdrawal from Norway until 7 June and on learning that British convoys were already at sea, the German Admiralty decided to attack them. Early morning 8 June, *Hipper* caught a tanker with a trawler escort, an empty troopship *Orama* and the hospital ship *Atlantis*. The sanctuary of the hospital ship was respected, but the other craft were sunk by *Hipper*. After this during the afternoon *Hipper* and her Destroyers returned to Trondheim, but *Scharnhorst* and *Gneisenau* continued to hunt for Allied shipping and at 1600 hours, 8 June, they sighted the smoke of HMS *Glorious* and her two escorting Destroyers HMS *Acasta* and HMS *Ardent*. HMS *Glorious* had during the morning detached itself from its escort and was proceeding home alone, as it was claimed that it had insufficient fuel to continue as part of a convoy. At the time of its sighting by the Germans, HMS *Glorious* was nearly 200 miles ahead of the main convoy. Churchill is not convinced by the tale of a fuel shortage and maintained that the carrier should have remained with the convoy.

At 1630 hours, the fighting began over 27,000 yards range. HMS *Glorious* with her 4-inch guns, which lacked the range of the enemy's guns, could not hit back at the German vessels. There was an attempt by HMS *Glorious* to get her torpedo-bombers airborne, but this was doomed as the forward hangar was hit by enemy gun fire that started a fire, which in turn destroyed the Hurricanes and prevented torpedoes being bought from below for the bombers. In the following 30 minutes, HMS *Glorious* was struck several times more by enemy fire and then at 1720 hours, listing badly, the order was given to abandon ship and the carrier sank about 20 minutes later. The two Destroyers protecting HMS *Glorious* did their level best to protect her, by making smoke to try to screen the carrier and both Destroyers fired their torpedoes at the attacking Germans, before being finally overwhelmed. HMS *Ardent* was swiftly sunk followed by HMS *Acasta*, which only had a sole survivor, Leading-Seaman C. Carter. As Churchill recorded in this action, 1,474 men and officers of the Royal Navy and 41 men of the RAF died; prolonged searches for survivors only retrieved a further 39 survivors rescued by a Norwegian ship and a further six were picked up by the enemy and taken to Germany. The *Scharnhorst* was badly damaged by a torpedo from HMS *Acasta* and was forced to withdraw and make her way to Trondheim.

While this action was taking place, HMS *Devonshire*, with the Norwegian King and his government, was making its way to the UK and was about 100 miles west of the sea battle related above. HMS *Valiant* coming north to meet the convoy was still a long way off. The only message to come from HMS *Glorious* was corrupt and barely understandable, which suggested that her main wireless equipment had been wrecked in an early stage of the battle. HMS *Devonshire* was the only vessel to receive the message from HMS *Glorious*, but failed to recognise the significance of what it contained and so maintained radio silence, as she proceeded towards the UK. It was not until the next morning that the story of the previous afternoon's action became known to the British, when HMS *Valiant* met the hospital ship *Atlantis* and learnt of the loss of the *Orama* and the fact that enemy capital ships were at sea. HMS *Valiant* immediately signalled this information to the Admiralty and continued on its way to join Lord Cork's convoy. The C-in-C, Admiral Forbes, set out to sea at once, with the only ships that he had; HMS *Rodney*, HMS *Renown*, and six Destroyers.

The damage done to *Scharnhorst* by HMS *Acasta* was significant, as both *Scharnhorst* and *Gneisenau* abandoned further operations and returned immediately to Trondheim. The German C-in-C was in the bad books of the German High Command, as he had deviated from his objectives given to him by Berlin. *Hipper* was sent out to sea, but it was already too late for the Germans to try to gain the upperhand at sea.

On 10 June, Admiral Forbes ordered the aircraft carrier HMS *Ark Royal* to join him. British reports showed that German ships were in Trondheim and Forbes hoped to attack them from the air. On 11 June, RAF bombers attacked this position but with no effect. The following morning 15 Skua dive-bombers attacked the German vessels moored at Trondheim, however enemy reconnaissance had alerted the Germans to the approaching British attack and eight Skuas were lost in the attack. As Churchill observed, so fated was this attack that one bomb from a Skua, which struck *Scharnhorst,* failed to explode. Even so, while these actions from the air and on the seas took place, the Narvik convoys arrived safely back in the UK and the British campaign in Norway ended.[16]

16 Churchill, op. cit. pp. 514-8.

10

Consequences

Despite the apparent failure of the Norwegian Campaign, Churchill himself made an important observation concerning the outcome of the operation. It may have cost the Allies somewhat in men and prestige, but it also had a reckoning for Germany. Britain at the time of the outbreak of war in 1939 was the world's leading maritime power, while Hitler actually had very little interest in a surface fleet. In the sea battles, in and around Norwegian water, between April and June 1940, the Royal Navy suffered significant losses; one aircraft carrier, two Cruisers, one Sloop, and nine Destroyers. The British also had six Cruisers, two Sloops, and eight Destroyers disabled but could be repaired in British dockyards, while overall the power of the entire British surface fleet was damaged but not impaired. However, by the end of June 1940, the Germans were left with an effective surface fleet of only a single 8-inch Cruiser, two Light Cruisers, and four Destroyers. Like the British, the Germans had many damaged ships, which could be repaired but the German Navy was already a spent force, when factoring forces available for the intended German invasion of the UK.[1] The failure of the Luftwaffe to defeat the RAF and its allies in the air postponed the German invasion for 1940; the 1941 German invasion of the Soviet Union cancelled the entire invasion of the UK.

The military ventures in Norway, indeed as Churchill observed, had long term consequences for the Germans despite their victory there but in the UK the perception and reality of failure in northern Norway was causing political rumblings. The British Prime Minister, Neville Chamberlain, had become a figure of mockery, especially after his claim in the House of Commons on 4 April 1940, that Hitler had 'missed the bus' regarding any invasion of Western Europe. It would seem that the German dictator was actually checking the bus timetable to Western Europe, as well as studying the tide tables for Norway.

On 7 May 1940, as the Norwegian Campaign was beginning to intensify a debate on the war situation was held in the House of Commons. The House was packed and MPs from both sides of the political divide attacked Chamberlain and his government. At times, even Churchill as First Lord was attacked, especially when Sir Roger Keyes, dressed in his uniform of Admiral of the Fleet, was extremely critical of the Naval Staff in relation to the failure to capture Trondheim. However the ire of the House was reserved for Chamberlain and those associated with deep cuts in the British armed service during the 1930s; appeasement and the overall failure to stand up to Germany during the 1930s, of which Churchill had long spoken, as Germany rearmed following the Nazi take over there in 1933, but he was ignored. The pigeons of collective democratic wishful thinking had come home to roost and the sight was not edifying. The leader of the Opposition, Clement Attlee, who as a young man had fought in the 1915 Dardanelles campaign, made several points: were the right troops sent to Norway? Was the present War Cabinet capable of leading the war, as well as making the withering assessment of Chamberlain observing that as German

1 Ibid., pp. 518-9.

aggression against Norway had followed that of German aggression against Czechoslovakia and Poland; it would seem that Chamberlain had been missing buses since 1931.[2] Sir Archibald Sinclair, the member for Caithness & Sutherland, made some very important observations of the Norwegian Campaign and how the British armed forces had dealt with the situation. A major criticism was that Norwegian ski-patrols, armed only with rifles, had for seven days held up a German force, which had consisted of tanks, armoured cars and had been supported from the air by bombers. Sinclair said that the Norwegians were critical of the calibre of troops sent to Norway, which on the whole had been territorials and regulars, as well as being withering of the British equipment, which was of very poor quality and unsuitable for operations in Norway. A lamentable episode had seen the British Minister of Supply demonstrating, at a photograph session, a white overall or camouflage smock suitable for Arctic warfare. Unfortunately, it was the only one available to British troops in Norway. There were other observations, such as no snowshoes, even though some of this force had been earmarked for service in Finland, it would seem that no serious thought had been given to winter warfare within the Arctic Circle. Furthermore, the AAA guns lacked equipment. It was noted that the French had sent their best Alpine troops to Norway.[3] The climax of the session was when Mr Leo Amery, a fellow Birmingham MP and friend and colleague of Chamberlain for many years but totally opposed to the pacifism which pervaded Western democracy in the 1930s, standing turned on his hapless Prime Minister and quoting Oliver Cromwell address to the Long Parliament of the 17th Century, said to Chamberlain 'You have sat too long here for any good you have been doing. Depart, I say, and let us have done with you. In the name of God, go!'[4] It was the death knell of the Chamberlain administration.

Amazingly the debate continued into a second day as Chamberlain continued to try to defy his critics, thus enhancing his reputation as a naive fool. Chamberlain tried to appeal to his past record and asked his friends to stand by him and, as Churchill observed, he had the right to do so, as they were part of the problem that stood before the UK in 1940, as during the 1930s they had slavishly participated in policies of appeasement, disarmament and doing nothing, while Nazi Germany rearmed and embarked on an extremely hostile foreign policy. By 8 May 1940, Chamberlain's followers were silent and ashamed at their poor judgements and by the fact that the man, Winston Churchill that they had derided for over a decade was right. Of course Churchill was right; he had looked at evidence rather than rhetoric; even if some of that evidence was illicitly gotten, it was still proof that the sitting government had legally at their fingertips but instead they were ideologically driven and failed to join the inconvenient dots.

The debate of 8 May 1940, saw the last influential intervention of the veteran MP and former Prime Minister, David Lloyd George, who spoke for around 20 minutes and heaped further ashes onto the head of Chamberlain, while defending Churchill and his record. Lloyd George scathing of Chamberlain but of Churchill stated that he did not entirely blame Churchill, as First Sea Lord for the events of the Norwegian Campaign; to which Churchill replied that he took the entire responsibility for everything done there by the Admiralty. Lloyd George's response was to caution Churchill against converting himself into 'an air-raid shelter,' which would protect the government from 'splinters' hitting the government. An apt metaphor. Then Lloyd George turned to Chamberlain and pointed to the failings of his administration and leadership.

In the early months of the war, British political leadership had been woeful. Lloyd George observing that in the past Chamberlain had appealed to the British people to make sacrifices; Lloyd George told Chamberlain that the British people are willing to make sacrifices, but only as long as

2 Hansard Vol. 360, 23 April 1940 – 13 May 1940, London, HMSO, 1940, 7 May 1940, Cols. 1089-1093.
3 Ibid., Cols. 1100-1103.
4 Ibid., Col. 1150.

they were shown clearly what they were aiming for and given a purpose. And for this, the nation needed clear leadership and good governance, in which the British people could have confidence in and could be seen as doing their best. Then Lloyd George appealed to Chamberlain to make the greatest sacrifice of his career and resign the office of Prime Minister of the United Kingdom. Churchill wrote that he and other ministers tried to remain loyal to Chamberlain and volunteered to windup the debate; he felt that he had duty to do, so not only in loyalty to Chamberlain but also he was aware that the Norwegian Campaign in early May 1940 was bordering on catastrophe even if the Royal Navy had all but sunk the entire German surface fleet in clashes off Narvik. Churchill did his best to regain control of the debate and House for the government, but found it hard going, owing to continuous interruptions coming mainly from the Labour Opposition Benches. Even so, Churchill seemed to relish fighting off the Labour Party interventions as he considered their mistakes and hypocrisy and 'dangerous pacifism' over the preceding years. It was not hard for Churchill to recall that only four months earlier, the Labour Party had been united in voting against conscription and this was obviously during wartime. Churchill thought that he might have some support in the House but he had little and for much of the time struggled to make himself heard. However Churchill was able to realise that the ire of the House, from both sides, was not directed against him but against Chamberlain and his Administration. Finally at 11 p.m., the House divided and voted their confidence or otherwise in Chamberlain and his leadership. As Churchill noted, the governing Conservative Party had a majority of 81 but in this crucial vote, over 30 Conservatives voted with the Labour and Liberal Oppositions, while a further 60 Conservative MPs abstained. Chamberlain and his government were finished.

Even Chamberlain recognised the severity of his position and the hostility against him. His career was over and his administration had been a failure; it had not prevented war, while its and other measures prior to 1939 had meant the UK was having to militarily play catch up, as the Germans really had been rearming since 1934 and that Hitler was not going to be cheated of his war. Hitler had failed to invest in a surface fleet and had paid the price at Narvik; what if the British had expanded its army since 1934 and had reintroduced conscription at the same time, perhaps Hitler might have never got going, at least against Western Europe.

Churchill met with Chamberlain in the Premier's office and it was obvious that Chamberlain could not continue and felt that there ought to be a National government, as a single party alone could not continue to government during wartime, especially as the UK faced invasion. It was recognised that a government had to be formed consisting of all parties, or the UK would not survive. Churchill claimed that he did his best to boost Chamberlain's morale but it was clear that the man was broken, even if Churchill tried to use Norway as the case for Chamberlain to continue. It should be remembered that events after the British government's crisis showed that victory over the Germans was possible; that was of course the Allied victory at Narvik but events in France made a total victory in 1940 illusive. Chamberlain refused to alter his stance and so Churchill left him at midnight.

The next morning Chamberlain consulted with his colleague and long term friend, Secretary of State for Air, Sir Kingsley Wood. It was from Wood that Churchill learnt that Chamberlain had decided to form a National government and that if he could not be head of such an administration, Chamberlain would give way to somebody who was trusted to head the British government. By the afternoon of that day, Churchill learnt, that it was more than likely, that he would be expected to take over from Chamberlain. Churchill writes that he was neither alarmed nor excited but merely thought that this would be the correct decision, and so sat back and allowed events to take their course. During the afternoon, Churchill was called to a meeting with Chamberlain and Lord

Halifax and where Churchill discovered that they were waiting for the Labour Party leadership to arrive. Once the Labour leaders arrived, conversation was polite between the two party leaderships but it was quite obvious that the Opposition leaders were not willing to commit themselves to any form of National government without consulting their party membership and it was hinted that it was likely that the response would be in the negative. Churchill then returned to his office at the Admiralty to continue work until late into the night.

It was the next morning, 10 May 1940, that Chamberlain's work was totally undone, as the Germans struck in Western Europe, invading both Holland and Belgium and it became very clear that France was the main target of the entire German offensive. All considerations concerning the campaign in Norway were off; the futures of France and the UK, if not Western civilization were imperilled. Concerns of a country of a dubious alliance were shelved as all resources, as we have seen, were recalled to the UK with a limited offensive against the Germans, with the hope of allowing the Norwegians to hold northern Norway. Amazingly Chamberlain, instead of recognising what a failure he was, told Sir Kingsley Wood that he felt that he ought to remain in office owing to the new crisis. Wood was no fool and told his old friend that on the contrary; he should actually leave office and allow a National government be formed under a new leadership. Chamberlain accepted this view.

At 11 o'clock Churchill was summoned to 10 Downing Street for a meeting with Chamberlain. Once sat down, Churchill learnt that Chamberlain had decided it was clear that he was not in a position to form a National government, especially as the Labour Party's leadership had made it clear. As a result, Chamberlain was about to tender his resignation to the British King, George VI; Churchill saw himself vindicated in his stance of the 1930s, a decade which was indeed 'low' and Churchill vilified as a warmonger, he seemed to have been the only rational man in a body full of ideologues.

Churchill's premiership was marked by victory in Europe, even if he lost the 1945 General Election before the Allied victory against Japan. By 1945 the British had crept back to some form of woolly-minded wishful thinking, before re-electing Churchill at the next British General Election. However Churchill in 1940 led the UK; he knew who the enemy was, some were indeed friends of his but without hesitation he had them arrested and held without trial, in case they endangered the security of the UK.[5] Equally he controversially had enemy aliens interned, regardless of their origin and then had investigations made into their conduct and backgrounds once interned. Many were released and went on to serve the Allied cause against Germany, but Churchill never lost sight that the enemy was the enemy and had to be checked. Diplomacy did not always work and a bully had to be slapped and defeated. His thinking was to have peace, you must prepare for war. Chamberlain could not even prepare for reality, as it was not the vogue.

The events surrounding Narvik prove the points made above, as it can be seen from the narrative that a significant sector in Norway clearly saw that their futures lay with Germany. Indeed the Swedish King saw this as well. The problem was the nature of the Soviet Union, especially under Stalin. Russia, or the Soviet Union under Stalin, was a terrifying place and the rest of the world quite rightly feared it but were all too willing to accommodate Nazi Germany. Even today people still are, but the difference between Hitler and Stalin was that Stalin was more rational than Hitler and up to a point could be worked with, even if he frequently lied, especially regarding Poland and the Poles; he was still willing to work towards the defeat of Germany after June 1941, even if it was in pursuit of the World Revolution. Hitler was quite a different man and the German people were all but destroyed by his maniac policies. However, returning to 1940, it is interesting to note

5 Roy Jenkins, *Churchill* (London: Macmillan, 2001), p. 608.

that the British at one point even contemplated leaving stores for the Germans and Norwegians to use against a Soviet invasion of Norway. The true enemy was yet to be recognised. Once Churchill became Prime Minister of the UK on 10 May 1940, all such nonsense was removed from the dialogue. As the unfortunate Yugoslav leader, Mikolović, found when Churchill asked who was killing the most Germans in Yugoslavia and the answer was the Communist partisans under Tito, then Churchill adjusted British support for Yugoslav communist partisans, at the expense of their rivals. After the German invasion of the Soviet Union in June 1941, Churchill courted Stalin and won the support of the Soviet Union for the war against Germany. As early as July 1940, the world saw Churchill's determination to root any descent against the Allies, when the Royal Navy destroyed the French Fleet at Oran, once the future of the French Navy was unclear and it was feared that the Germans might seize control of modern French ships. 1,300 French sailors perished in the British attack but the world saw that the British under Churchill meant business and the Germans were denied vessels that might have been useful in an invasion of the UK.[6] These events came out of Norway in 1940.

Despite my criticism of the democracies, preparations or lack of them for war, the British CIGS, General Edmund Ironside as the world, as he saw it, seemed to crash and burn around his ears confided to his diary that it was near on impossible for the democracies to prepare for war against Nazi Germany.[7] At the time of writing, Ironside was well aware of the fact that the democracies were fighting for their lives and the fear was that if France collapsed, the Nazis would triumph. However if one looks at the published diaries of General Brooke, soon to be Ironside's successor, it would seem that even though there are persistent rumours during April 1940 concerning an impending attack on both Belgium and Holland, Brooke considered that this was unlikely in the immediate future, as the Germans had only just invaded Scandinavia on 9 April and that fighting in Norway was keeping the Luftwaffe occupied.[8] Equally the Belgians were being extremely awkward about allowing the French and British to come to their assistance. The military on the whole seem quite quiet about events in Norway and elsewhere, at least on official papers, but certainly in the private diaries of Cadogan, more meat is put onto events concerning operations there. Without doubt those fighting had little time to get their thoughts down until they had reached a place of relative safety and the inquiries began of how disaster begat disaster, even if often they were portrayed as success. Dunkirk being an example to the exasperation of Churchill; who no doubt was pleased to see Allied troops being retrieved from Continental Europe but was acutely aware of the fact that these troops had been literally driven in to the sea at Dunkirk and elsewhere. The success or miracle as some have it was that so many troops were able to be recovered from France with 75% of them, as Ironside noted, bringing their rifles if nothing else.

The debate in the House of Commons, 7–8 May 1940, leading to Churchill being awarded the office of Prime Minister, is according to Roy Jenkins, one of Churchill's more influential biographers, was one of the most important of twentieth century British politics and, as already noted, of great consequence. It was a debate of first rank speakers and over the following five years altered the course of history, as anticipated in May 1940, many had expected the Germans to successfully invade and occupy the UK and so cast Europe back into a new dark age. Overall though Jenkins does dispute how Churchill came to be Prime Minister, as Churchill rather modestly suggested that he stayed quiet and allowed the inevitable to happen but Jenkins observes that the rather immodest Churchill manoeuvred Halifax out of the way and contention, while Cadogan had reservations about Churchill becoming Prime Minister. The bottom line is that it does not matter how, why

6 Ibid. pp. 622-5.
7 Ironside, p.316, 17 May 1940.
8 Alanbrooke, op. cit. pp.51-2, 12 April 1940.

and by whom Churchill became PM, as despite his difficult personality, he ensured that the UK was not invaded in 1940 and continued to lead the country until victory in Europe in 1945. Those others were indeed the problem and their leadership qualities verging on nil. Jenkins observes that if anything, the House of Commons was still uncertain about Churchill becoming PM, while a popular and well known cartoon in *The Evening Standard* printed in London illustrated, without mockery or irony, that at least his Cabinet, which crossed party lines, supported him, as did the British people. It was the failed politicians who were wary of lending Churchill support, at least in the short term. However as Jenkins noted, Churchill was more European than either Chamberlain or Halifax and so the Continent, as Churchill no doubt would have termed it, was important to him, indeed some consider to have been 'Eurocentric.'[9] Quite a reversal to the contemporary view of Churchill. While once more a further observation should be made of Churchill and his thinking during May–June 1940. The first was that he did not consider Dunkirk to have been a victory and said so to the House of Commons on 4 June 1940.[10] It was this rhetoric that made Churchill the obvious wartime leader of the UK, as it would seem that neither he nor the British people were willing to shirk the tasks and trials which lay ahead of them, as they faced a German invasion. Politicians and even senior officers, even if they were not craven about an impending invasion, were certainly extremely concerned and worried about what might happen, if only because they had information at their fingers tips from which genuine information flowed, rather than half-baked and unconsidered opinions manifesting from a miasma of ignorance. At times ignorance can be bliss but this would have been to ignore what was happening in Europe itself. If one is to return to the accepted origin of the Second World War, the invasion of Poland by Germany on 1 September 1939, one will discover that that country had plenty to take from Germany, as from the first days the Germans had behaved with great violence and the Poles serving in Norway would have been aware of this, but perhaps happy to see Churchill occupy 10 Downing Street rather than the failed pacifist Chamberlain. At least Churchill knew how to fight.

Churchill's supporters also came from within the establishment, as Lord Cranbourne in a letter supporting Churchill, as the newly appointed Prime Minister, made so good as to observe that even though Churchill had just been handed a most difficult task '...but at any rate the very fact that you (Churchill) are in charge will carry, both to our friends and our enemies abroad, a conviction of British resolution, in a way nothing else could do.'[11] This was a positively ringing endorsement and a prophecy of what was to come under Churchill's premiership. Another letter of support from the many which Churchill received on 11 May, came from Admiral of the Fleet, Sir Charles Forbes and was another ringing endorsement of Churchill being elevated to the office of Prime Minister. Furthermore, Forbes supported Churchill over Norway and considered that the Norwegian Campaign would end in victory and that the Germans would regret ever going there.[12] Even so, there were detractors even if they confined their thoughts to their diaries as John Colville, who served as Assistant Secretary to Chamberlain, Churchill and to Attlee, who succeeded Churchill in 1945, wrote that there were some in Whitehall who considered that Churchill will fail and that Chamberlain would return.[13] The influential broadcasting figure, Sir John Reith; later in 1940, Lord Reith, and part of Churchill's administration as Minister of Works having been

9 Jenkins, op.cit. p. 600.

10 Ibid., p. 597.

11 *The Churchill War Papers. Volume II Never Surrender: May 1940-December 1940*, Martin Gilbert (ed.) London, Heinemann, 1994, p.1. (Hereafter *Churchill 2*) (Churchill Papers, 2/393) Lord Cranbourne to Winston S. Churchill, 11 May 1940.

12 Admiral of the Fleet Sir Charles Forbes to Winston S. Churchill, 11 May 1940 (Churchill Papers, 2/405) *Churchill 2*, p. 6.

13 John Colville: diary, 11 May 1940 (Colville Papers) *Churchill 2*, p. 12.

Minister of Information between 1939 and 1940, was quite gloomy when it was announced that Churchill was not only to be Prime Minister but also Defence Minister. As Reith wrote 'Heaven help us.' He also noted that the three service departments were to be overseen by ministers who, in Reith's opinion, Churchill could ignore and thus be able to deal directly with the Chiefs of Staff, Reith commented 'Awful'.[14] This was probably a fair comment, as Churchill and his service chiefs endured a very difficult relationship with both parties being equally frustrated with each other: Churchill was usually impatient with the lack of pace of campaigns and perhaps a touch petulant in his behaviour; his chiefs especially Field Marshal Alan Brook were totally exasperated with Churchill, with Brook often snapping pencils in the face of Churchill as they sat in meetings.[15] This was not really the behaviour of adults, let alone men trying and indeed winning a war. Even so, Churchill was not too sure what he might be able to give to the British people, as General Ismay recalled. Ismay in his memoirs wrote that a few days after Churchill became Prime Minister, he and Ismay were walking from Downing Street to the Admiralty. People wished Churchill well, crying 'Good luck Winnie. God bless you.' Churchill (as ever) was reduced to tears once he and Ismay entered the Admiralty building and said 'poor people. They trust me, and I can give them nothing but disaster for quite a long time.'[16] Churchill was perhaps being hard on himself but he was nothing but realistic in May 1940, but the overall impression was that he always thought that the British Empire and her allies would eventually defeat Germany but how and when and from where was not clear at that perilous time.

As the UK stood prepared for the fall of France and the possibility of a German invasion of the British Isles, the British government under Churchill carried on, indeed cracked on, with the tasks which lay before them. So long as the British Army was not defeated, there was no need to carry on as if it already had been. Fighting continued in France albeit a fighting retreat, while operations in Northern Norway were very much alive.

An interesting departure was that Churchill agreed with Alfred Duff Cooper, the new Minister of Information, that the British general public should be put into the picture regarding how badly the war was going. At that point most were in complete ignorance of the true facts and were relying on propaganda. In the same Cabinet meeting, Narvik was also discussed and it was decided that a telegram should be sent to Lord Cork that he must deal with the situation in Norway as best he could, but could expect no more in the way of equipment or men but his views would be welcome. At this point it was considered that operations in Northern Norway remained successful, as Germans were still being captured and British casualties were light; Narvik might fall to the Allies at any moment.[17] However, it is from Churchill's wayward son, Randolph, that we find the true Churchill grit, as he related a domestic incident of mid-May 1940. Winston Churchill was shaving with an old razor and making quite a hash of it, when suddenly the Prime Minister turned to his son and said 'I think that I can see my way through' and then resumed shaving. Churchill junior was a little at a loss to understand exactly what his father meant and so asked for details. Randolph asked if Churchill meant that the British could avoid defeat or to actually defeat the Germans, except his language was slightly more colourful. The Prime Minister turned to his son and said that he meant that the British would be able to defeat Germany by bringing the USA into the war.[18] Unlike Chamberlain, Churchill did have a plan but he was not forced to drag the USA into the

14 Sir John Reith: diary, 11 May 1940 (*The Reith Diaries*) 11 May 1940, *Churchill 2*, 13.

15 Andrew Roberts, *Masters and Commanders: How Roosevelt, Churchill, Marshall and Alanbrooke Won the War in the West*, London, Allen Lane, 2008, p. 58.

16 General Ismay: recollection, 13 May 1940 (*The Memoirs of General the Lord Ismay*, p. 116) *Churchill 2*, p. 19.

17 War Cabinet: minutes (Cabinet papers, 65/7) 17 May 1940, *Churchill 2*, pp.65-6.

18 Randolph S. Churchill: recollection (Randolph Churchill papers) 18 May 1940, *Churchill 2*, pp. 70-1.

war, as he had described his plan to Churchill junior, as Hitler did this for him when Germany, following the Japanese attack on the US naval base at Pearl Harbor, declared war on the USA. An incredibly rash act by the Germans.

It was not long before Churchill turned his attention once more to the events in Norway and he was not slow in expressing his disappointment with the campaign, as can be seen in a private paper sent by him to Lord Cork. Churchill writing at a distance told Cork of his increasing disappointment at the stagnation in operations in Norway, especially the inability of the Allies to take Narvik. Churchill observed that the Germans had few troops in the town itself and only 1,500 troops in the surrounding countryside but held up three to four times that number of Allied troops. Churchill was critical that the Allies had dug in around Narvik and its environs and kept the Germans under constant fire but failed to advance into the town. Churchill was especially vexed as the Norway expedition ate into valuable resources, which could be used elsewhere namely France and if necessary defence of the UK and he was particularly anxious to have British Destroyers released from Norwegian waters. Churchill was also angry that the slow pace of repairing the airfield at Bardu, meant that the British aircraft carrier HMS *Glorious* had to return to its base at Scapa, in order to refuel and then perhaps set out once more for Norway. In Churchill's opinion the lack of action was costing more in men and ships than 'vigorous action'. Churchill demanded an explanation from Cork, as to why there had been very little action in Norway.[19] Of course Churchill, as with so many of those in Whitehall, had little idea of local conditions in Norway, where snow was still on the ground and that blizzards were still liable to blow up from nowhere; something that was very unlikely to happen in the third week of May in the UK. Despite Churchill not really understanding the situation in Norway, he still galvanised the situation there even if it was to terminate hostilities, in order to release men and equipment for France and the UK. Churchill was not a man to allow a situation to lie fallow if he considered that something had to be done and Narvik was one of those situations. Churchill, in a Cabinet meeting on the same day, raised the same issues that he had set out in his message to Lord Cork. The Defence Committee decided to stay its hand until a reply had been received from Cork.[20]

Cork replied the next day and put the local situation to Churchill and clearly the two men had different agendas. Cork expressed that he regretted Churchill's disappointment but was quite blunt in telling him that this was inevitable and then told Churchill what was actually going on in Norway, rather than what Churchill thought should be happening. The main difference was that while Churchill considered that the entire operation hinged on the capture of Narvik, Cork stated that the operation was about whether the Allies could establish themselves in Norway or not. The main problem, and one that was the priority for overcoming, was that of German air superiority and how the Allies could overcome this and so rejected the charge of stagnation, as operations at Bodo were designed to try to remove the airpower of the Germans.

Cork moved on to Churchill's charge that the Allies shrank from engaging the Germans at close quarters. Lord Cork pointed to the French campaign against the enemy, which had caused the Germans to retreat before the French advance, which he admits had been slow owing to German aerial attacks to which the Allies had little in the way to reply. The French were waiting to make a direct attack on the Germans but required tanks and landing craft to transport them. The problem with landing craft was that they were being used to land stores and guns in order to complete airfields, which Cork had designated as a priority. There was to be another three to four days before this work would be complete.

19 Winston S. Churchill to Lord Cork (Admiralty papers, 199/1929) 20 May 1940, *Churchill 2*, p. 98.
20 Defence Committee: minutes (Cabinet papers, 69/1) 20 May 1940, *Churchill 2*, pp. 99-100.

Cork agreed with Churchill regarding the unfortunate situation where HMS *Glorious* had to return to refuel but he informed Churchill that establishing an airfield in Norway was not very easy. The first thing to be done was to remove three to four feet of snow before any work could begin. Cork told Churchill that the lack of air cover was a serious hindrance to Allied plans, as only the previous day Harstad, which the British were using as a landing post, had been attacked by enemy aircraft using incendiary bombs. As a result, oil tanks had been set ablaze, two ships had been burnt out, several casualties were suffered and many houses burnt or ruined. Cork was quite incensed that he was not to receive any bombers, as this meant that the Allies could not delay the enemy advance by road to the north and it was quite clear to the Allies, and to the enemy, that the Allies had no way of effectively striking back at the enemy from the air.[21] Clearly Lord Cork was not going to be bullied by Churchill and was able to take the opportunity to put the Whitehall based politicians right, regarding the situation faced by the Allies in Norway. There was nothing that could be done about the deep snow still found in late May, while as ever London-centric politicians forget that there is such a thing, but the lack of aerial support was something that could have been dealt with but for the danger posed to both France and the UK by this time.

However, by 23 May the discussion within the British War Cabinet was to capture Narvik and then to abandon it and Norway; hardly the Churchillian spirit. Churchill was against such thinking, as for one thing it meant that troops would be killed and wounded to take the town and then to abandon it, it would have been callous and clearly for nought. Therefore Churchill sought to make sense of the situation and provide for some joined up thinking and requested that regarding the evacuation of Norway, the service chiefs in London and Lord Cork off the Norwegian coast, should work out a plan that was rational and address the local problems of Norway and return troops and arms to the UK ready to face invasion. Churchill was reluctant to agree a withdrawal from Norway but if it was to come about, it should be orderly and not for several weeks later. Basically Churchill wanted to see a solid result from the Allied efforts in northern Norway and suggested the maximum mining of the approaches to Lulea. A major consideration was that any talk of evacuation was to be a secret until the last possible moment when King Haakon VII and his government could be offered evacuation and sanctuary in the UK. It was decided that plans for the evacuation of Norway should be drawn up.[22] The following day Churchill wrote to General Ismay regarding Norway. Churchill, as ever when discussing Norway, was insistent that Norwegian waters be mined and Lulea remained Churchill's target. He also discussed the impending evacuation of Norway and how it should be carried out. By now Churchill was well aware of the necessity of air cover given the bleak nature of the Norwegian terrain, which afforded no cover, whilst its rocky geology gave little or no chance for infantry to dig in. However, it can be seen that the aircraft to be provided were outmoded, as Churchill spoke of Gladiators based at Bardufoss and Skua dive-bombers operating from aircraft carriers. He also wrote of his regret that HMS *Illustrious*, an aircraft carrier owing to it being deployed off Norway would therefore be absent from operations at Dakar in West Africa.[23]

The mention of Dakar is interesting as it is an example of how thinly the Allies were to spread themselves in 1940, as they tried to reduce the serious consequences of being ejected from the European mainland and find bases elsewhere. Once France had fallen, General Charles de Gaulle, a renegade officer, as far as defeated French officials were concerned, bought French forces to the UK and offered an alternative vision of France to that of the collaborative Petain government operating in unoccupied France, the so-called Vichy regime. De Gaulle saw that the French Empire, especially in Africa, would be crucial in the defeat of Germany, as well as maintaining French influence in

21 Lord Cork to Winston S. Churchill (Admiralty papers, 199/1929) 21 May 1940, *Churchill 2*, p. 107.
22 War Cabinet: Confidential Annex (Cabinet 65/13) 23 May 1940, *Churchill 2*, p. 120.
23 Winston S. Churchill to General Ismay (Churchill papers, 20/17) 24 May 1940, *Churchill 2*, pp.128-9.

the war. He was partially right as French North Africa was used to fight and defeat German and Italian armies in North Africa, before the Allies invaded and conquered Italy. De Gaulle wanted his influence felt in French Africa and it was decided that Dakar should be forcibly brought under de Gaulle's control and not maintain its pro-Vichy stance. The operation was a fiasco, as the entire operation had been compromised by slack security, starting with de Gaulle himself before its ships had even sailed from the River Mersey in Liverpool. The attempts at trying too many things at once in 1940, should be noted, and helps to explain events later, when to the fury of Stalin and the Soviet government, a second fighting front to be launched in the West to relieve Soviet forces fighting the bulk of the German was put off until the summer of 1944, when the British and Americans felt able to land in France. 1940 had been a learning curve for the Allies and had taught Churchill to be more cautious than perhaps he was happy with. Meanwhile Churchill urged all possible action regarding the mining of the waters at Lulea (Operation 'Paul'), which should at least deprive the Germans some of the iron ore, which they hoped to receive during the summer. Churchill wished the operation to begin just before the completion of the evacuation from Norway.[24] At times it would seem that Churchill was willing to make some incredible sacrifices in evacuating Norway, as in a War Cabinet meeting after speaking to the First Sea Lord, Churchill learnt that HMS *Glorious* had left Scapa for Narvik on the afternoon 24 May carrying 16 Hurricanes. It had been deemed by the Defence Committee acting on advice of the Chief of the Air Staff that these aircraft were essential for the successful and rapid evacuation of troops at Narvik. It had already been accepted that this aircraft might well be lost once the Allies left Norway but it was hoped that the pilots might be got away.[25] This was quite an incredible attitude to take given that much depended on the UK defeating the Luftwaffe to prevent a German invasion. Of course this had to be balanced with the fact that to repel a German invasion, troops on the ground would be needed and there were thousands of such men in Norway. In an ideal world they would also get away with much of their equipment, especially anti-tank and anti-aircraft artillery. So much depended on the successful evacuation of Norway, to provide the necessary forces to throw the Germans back into the English Channel, if they were to try to land on the English southern coast.

Even though the operations in Norway were based on a withdrawal from that country, Churchill was sought to maintain an Allied presence there. He was yet to throw in the towel, yet Churchill had to balance what could be left in Norway but decide how best to defend the UK. France by early June was more or less lost to the invading Germans. On 1 June 1940, the evacuation of the BEF was underway at Dunkirk, while the French had accepted British proposals for the future of Norway. Even so the French government continued to request further assistance from the British, even though by this point most British troops had been evacuated from the Dunkirk beaches. The British War Cabinet was still willing to entertain French requests but thought more along the lines of aerial attacks against Italian industry but the overall tone of the War Cabinet was not encouraging, as it was known that France could not hold out for much longer.[26] In a further address to his War Cabinet, Churchill still asked that perhaps a garrison might be maintained at Narvik but was able to see that this was quite impossible. Evacuations were to begin on the evening of 3 June 1940, having been delayed by 24 hours, to allow Norwegian troops in northern Norway to regroup.[27]

The problem, which was presented to Churchill, was that events in Europe moved faster than had been anticipated, indeed Churchill in correspondence to Ismay made the point that if a week

24 Defence Committee: minutes (Cabinet, 69/1) 24 May 1940, *Churchill 2*, p. 139.
25 War Cabinet: Confidential Annexe (Cabinet papers: 65/13) 25 May 1940, *Churchill 2*, p. 145.
26 War Cabinet: minutes (Cabinet papers, 65/7) 1 June 1940, *Churchill 2*, pp. 222-4.
27 War Cabinet: Confidential Annex (Cabinet papers, 65/13) 2 June 1940, *Churchill 2*, pp. 229-31.

earlier events at Dunkirk could have been anticipated, then operations in Norway could have been presented in a different light. Churchill was still considering maintaining a garrison there, despite the stark evidence that France was about to be overwhelmed by German aggression.[28]

Even though much of the narrative for Narvik is given, over to the victory at Narvik and the Allied evacuation, which had already been planned before the victory had been gained, there was another side to the campaign. It should be known that another part of the Norwegian campaign was the attempt to round up straying German units heading towards the Swedish frontier. The pursuit of the withdrawing Germans was conducted from three sides and the Allies determined to destroy totally the enemy, who were definitely heading towards the Swedish frontier. The fear within the allied command was that even though the German government may have respected Swedish neutrality, the presence of German troops, no matter how they got there, might give the Germans the necessary levers to control Sweden. The Allies were not willing to run such a risk.

On 30 May 1940 at about midnight, Major Kobyliński's company left the Kvanta Pass and moving cross country through the hill, moved towards the direction of Sildvik. However owing to a blizzard the company became disorientated and got lost in the terrain. FFL chased the Germans along the Narvik-Sildvik railway line from the Beisfjord side. However, the enemy put up such strong opposition that they were even able to counterattack. In relation to the situation during the morning 31 May, Colonel de Magrin asked General Bohusz-Szyszko if it was possible that the Poles might be able to attack to the rear of the German positions and, in doing so, might be able to relieve the leading FFL battalions, who were fighting in the area of the railway station at Stromsnes.

This was agreed to and Kobyliński's battalion moved across country, once more towards Sildvik. This time, the second time of moving within 24 hours, the battalion were supported by the 'battalion artillery,' which actually were two 81mm Stokes-Brandt mortars, carried by the Polish troops on their backs, while the mortar ammunition came in heavy ammunition cases. Mules were used to carry the ammunition but it was all very heavy going and very demanding. It was not only that the snowy hills made travel difficult but the mules lived up to their stubborn nature and often had to be helped if not pushed, in order to get them going once they decided on a halt.

3rd Company were already in position on Hill 844 waiting for orders. The description of what lay before was interesting – there was nothing there except wilderness. Even so the Polish troops searched around for a way to be useful. As the Poles moved out as a 'caravan,' as travellers in the Middle East, the whine of a mortar came down, firing from above them. Then there was a break; the Polish troops initially stunned by the mortar fire snapped to after a nervous break and their legs began to move and the Poles began to react, as they had been trained to do and returned fire using their rifles. The initial fire was somewhat poor with mistakes, as a result of tired and red eyes. The Poles were exhausted and it was quite possible that the Germans had been watching their approach.

The German mortar position was murderous to any further Polish advance in the area but it also served little purpose overall to the German operation in Norway. It was there more or less out of sheer cussedness, but all the same the Poles had to deal with it and destroy it. It had already caused a two hour halt. The Polish company commander surveyed the area around the Polish position and noticed a series of broken rocks near the lakes. The rocks were to be the Polish shield but to build with them was to be slow and hard work, as they yielded to neither shovels nor explosive charges such as the Polish troops had with them.

The sun burnt off the fog and lit up the icy surroundings. Then once more renewed fighting and mortar fire was heard. The sound of an explosion from 1st Platoon's position was heard and then a report came through regarding casualties: one dead and two wounded. To post (take up

28 Winston S. Churchill to General Ismay (Churchill Papers, 20/13) 2 June 1940, *Churchill 2*, pp. 226-8.

positions) ordered the Cadet Officer, commanding the Polish mortars, gave firing orders for three mortar bombs to be fired against the Germans. This drew accurate German mortar fire in retaliation with two German mortar bombs exploding near the Polish Cadet Officer commanding the Polish mortars, who was lightly wounded in the face. The Poles, undaunted, returned fire and shelled the Germans, landing ten mortar bombs amongst the enemy, which caused them to begin to move from their present location. The Polish Cadet Officer using binoculars checked on the Germans and their activities and once more, sent a salvo of mortar fire against them. This time under the cover of smoke, the Germans withdrew.

By the evening, two companies of 1st Battalion had got to the area around the railway line and by 1 June had linked up with units from the French Foreign Legion in the Klubnes region. In this formation the Poles and French patrolled together in the foreground and attracted the unwanted attentions of the enemy. This continued until 8 June, when the Allied evacuation of Norway was completed. There was a small episode of humour in this week, when a patrol commanded by Second Lieutenant Jackiewicz mistook their way while crossing over the vastness of the Norwegian countryside and reappeared in front of a FFL position but emerging from the direction of the enemy. French officers expressed admiration of the Poles not only for their ability to return from such a hazardous position; no doubt the Germans had not detected them.

The problem with the evacuation from northern Norway, was how did it leave the Poles? They had been part of a victory but it had been for nothing; the Allies were not quite in disarray but the French civilian politicians certainly seemed to be. The Podhalians were to be evacuated and sent back to France to help defend that country. As we have seen, the decision to evacuate Allied Forces had been arrived at following conversations between Lord Cork and General Bethouart, but this was an extremely secret decision and up to a point few Polish officers other than Szyszko-Bohusz knew of it. There were many factors for arriving at this hard and sad decision, the most obvious being the state of the war in Europe, with the Low Countries falling to the Germans, while France was threatened with being overrun. Furthermore, Italy was showing every indication of invading France in the south, which meant that Allied ships were also required in the Mediterranean Sea area, as well as French troops being sent to southern France. Even though the Podhalians had fought in a successful campaign in Norway, the problem was that their deployment had substantially reduced the Polish land force remaining in France and about to face the German onslaught. Dec only learnt of the evacuation from Norway on 2 June. At first Dec thought that he and his comrades were being sent to central Norway to aid the British in their operations there.

The Polish evacuation was to be covered by the 1st French Light Infantry Division, predominately 13th Demi-Brigade FFL and Major Kobyliński's Battalion, who were still fighting the enemy, as well as 4th Battalion Podhalians, under the command of Major Jaśkowski, in the inhabited area of Beisfjord. First in line to be placed onto the vessels were gun crews, especially anti-tank guns and their equipment and guns but weight had to be carefully managed, so prioritising had to be undergone to ensure the maximum efficiency of the withdrawal. These measures meant that much of the heavy equipment was destroyed or thrown into the sea. Dec and his men moved to the evacuation point in Skjomnes via Haakvik-Skole. In the woods to the left of the highroad, a roll call was made and the Poles fell in, as if on parade. The Poles were about to take leave of their fallen comrades, who were now interned in Norwegian soil. It was difficult and so final but orders were orders and afterwards the survivors of this brief campaign had to return to their duties and hope and pray that one day they may well return to Poland.

The Polish units made it to the beach, where waiting cutters stood by to convey them across the waters of the Ofotfjord to the warships ready to take them away from Norway. To get to the decks of the Destroyer, the troops had to climb lowered storm-ladders, in an attempt to aid the troops to get on board. Obviously the embarking troops had brought their personal arms, haversacks with blankets, unexpired food rations, as well as ammunition for their weapons. Quite a lot to carry up the side of a huge heaving and pitching ship and no doubt the first time that many of the Poles had had to do this, but this was the only way that the Poles could be transferred from the small cutters onto the larger warships.

During the night 4–5 June, the British Destroyer in effect gave the Poles a lift to the Polish vessel *Sobieski,* which was anchored in the deep gulf off Tromso. Getting aboard a Polish ship was symbolic to the Polish troops, who mentioned that it was good to be standing in Polish territory again. It was also heartening to see the Red and White national flag of Poland flying from the ship. All of the Polish troops asked where they were sailing for and discovered that they were to return to France. It was no secret anymore.

As the Polish troops sailed away from Norway contemplating what may lie ahead of them, the entire infrastructure at the port in Narvik and the railway station was being destroyed by the Allies. This of course was designed to deny the Germans not only port facilities at Narvik; the waters there were already choked by German warships sunk by the Royal Navy in April, but also denied the enemy use of the railway line there. Basically the electric rail line, which ran to and from the very far reaches of north Norway and Sweden was disrupted by the Allied action. Overall the Germans would not be able to easily receive the rich Swedish iron ore imported into Norway, as easily as they had been prior to the outbreak of war and so steel mills in Westphalia and elsewhere in Germany would be denied ore, in the short term at least. However, as Dec reflected this particular phase of the war had finished and another was beginning.

Even though the advantage in Norway was to the Germans, the task of capturing the entire country was enormous. The Germans may have decided on well thought out plans for the invasion and occupation of Norway, but it was still a shock to be confronted with the topography of northern Norway with its sharp and extremely lofty hills and mountains, with routes that were almost vertical in all directions. However the fjords of northern Norway were to prove an asset to the German Navy, even if its surface fleet was crippled at Narvik; German submarines were able to use Norwegian bases to attack British convoys later in the war, as the British tried to supply the Soviet Union with essential war materials via the Arctic towards Murmansk and Archangel.

At the time of writing his memoirs, Dec recalled the horrors of the war and the part that Norwegian territory had played, the ability of German U-boats to attack Allied shipping; lost owing to German torpedoes but of course the huge cost in human lives also had to be considered. Another aspect of the war and Norway, was that from the Loften Island, off the coast of Norway, the Germans tried to isolate what was termed 'Heavy Water,' which would have been essential for the production of nuclear weapons. However, as Dec wrote, that is another story but does illustrate the importance of Norway to the Germans, especially the use of its fragmented coastline as a base for German U-boats. As we have seen, this was realised even before the war by senior officials of the German Navy.

Regarding the Norwegian Campaign, Dec was clearly proud of his men (1st Battalion) and how they had campaigned against the Germans in Norway. 1st Battalion, until the dying moments of the fighting in Norway, had been out patrolling and had taken the war to the enemy. It would seem that the Poles were the most daring in their action against the Germans and would be the most remembered. Even if the Allies were seen by the world as having been ejected from Norway, the reality was that it was other events which had caused this and were beyond the control of the Poles. Dietl might have claimed victory but the Poles were still able to remember 'Narvik' as the single word that would sum up the Norwegian Campaign and it was a word to be remembered with pride.

11

The End of the Podhalians?

Even though the Poles were leaving Narvik on the pre-war luxury passenger cruiser *Sobieski,* which must have been quite a surreal experience after the battles and discomfort of the Norwegian Campaign, the Poles were actually heading off to another war: the defence of France. Even so, Dec with Neuman managed to get a luxury twin cabin with an en suite bathroom for the voyage back to France. Close by was also a bar and a hairdresser. After a few minutes taking in what lay in front of them, Dec refocused and remembered why he was there and considered that the route back to Poland was going to be long and a nightmare.

In the morning of 6 June, *Sobieski* weighed anchor and set sail. The night fog was melting away as the sun rose and the day got warmer. It seemed that it was going to be a lovely day and one could appreciate the fresh green colours of the bay. This was to be the Poles' farewell from Norway, as they headed out to the open seas. The routine on the *Sobieski* was relatively military, even if Dec and others could take their main meal and supper at the Captain's Table; the rest of the time even aboard a luxury cruiser was taken up with military matters. It could not be forgotten that despite their surroundings the ship was actually under military orders and was sailing from one scene of war to another. The Polish troops in the morning had to keep their fitness up by exercising out on the decks, as well as help with navigation and taking part in lookout duties. There seemed to be a lot of staring at the smoke of other vessels sailing alongside the *Sobieski,* as well as watching the escorting Destroyers, which shepherded their charges as the convoy steadily made its way to its final destination. Dec considered that the Destroyers acted as wise shepherds trying to escort some erratic sheep to safety. At all time the topic of conversation was where were the Germans. Even before Dec's convoy had set sail, two German aircraft complete with swastika emblems appeared over the convoy. Despite every AAA gun in the gulf opening fire on the enemy aircraft, the Germans pressed home their attack and bombed the Allied position. Luckily the bombs failed to explode. Transporters, taking war materials, sailed later in another convoy, did not enjoy such luck. They were unlucky, as along with the aircraft carrier HMS *Glorious*, two Destroyers and a single tanker, as well as a vessel carrying the baggage of the Podhalians, was all lost right down to the life rafts; Dec was always aware of the cost of lives lost in operations but he could not help mourning the loss of his photographs. No doubt for any exile, the loss of personal mementoes pertaining to a happy time is more important and a greater loss than those of us who thus far have led settled and sheltered lives.

Dec described that once they had passed out of the Arctic Circle, they were once more in an area where the sun 'worked normally'. For the first time, in a while, there was now day and night. The following night actually was dark and stars could be seen twinkling above the masts of the ships. For the Poles, it felt like they were returning to their family homes owing to the familiar sights, which had been denied them from the first day they had landed in Norway.

Radio communications were continuously bleak. It was obvious from news received that the campaign in France was not going well and that soon France would fall. On 10 June, it was learnt that the Italians had attacked France in the rear but had really crossed from Italy into France; attacking and capturing the French southern coast. Finally on 11 June, Dec and his men reached the Clyde Gulf and dropped anchor near Greenock. Motorboats conveyed the Poles to the Mole and once more they were ashore. In the town itself there were few signs of war, it was only once back later in Brittany that the war was more apparent. Dec left information that General Bohusz-Szyszko, with Major Iliński speaking with Colonel Żołtek-Mitkiewicz, that General Sikorski might present to the Allied High Command in London. Regrettably nothing came of this and no orders or instructions were issued. Instead Colonel Mitkiewicz restricted his conversations to the Commander of the Podhalians. It went nowhere else. There appeared to have been a struggle of wills and that Mitkiewicz was doing his level best to get his own way but how should the Podhalians be deployed after Norway, as it was quite clear that France was about to fall and perhaps, to send them to France would be a waste of resources, as well as the possibility of losing them if they were to go into battle to try to defend a lost cause. Risk had to be measured and assessed. Dec had an idea that now that the Podhalians now found themselves in Scotland, perhaps it might be a good idea to suggest that they might be the nucleus of a Polish Army to be formed on British territory. It was a good and logical idea, but unfortunately Colonel Mitkiewicz was not available and General Sikorski was away in France conducting a visit to the 1st Grenadier Division, still on the Maginot Line. Therefore it was with no real sense of commitment that Bohusz-Szyszko reported to the Chief of the Polish General Staff in Libourne, regarding the Norwegian evacuation and how to proceed to France. The Podhalians arrived back in France, landing at Brest on 14 June 1940. There were still no orders or telephone communications or anything regarding what the Podhalians were to do next. Some officers set off in cars looking for Sikorski, trying to divine the best place where they might catch their Supreme Commander. Nobody could be sure of Sikorski's movements, as chaos reigned supreme in France. It should be noted that Sikorski had, after the September Campaign, charged senior officers with dereliction of duty, as he considered that some Polish commanders had left Poland earlier than was decent and now in June 1940, Sikorski knew that France was lost but he wanted to be seen at the head of Polish forces, rather than trying to establish yet another Polish exiled government in London.

Dec recalled that on 13 June, *Sobieski* moved towards the French coast in preparation for landing the Podhalians, who only had a vague notion of the task before them, was to help rescue France but it was obvious to most that France was beyond help. The following day as Dec and his compatriots were finalizing disembarking from *Sobieski*, its Captain urged Dec to think about what he was actually doing and bluntly told Dec that it was not a good idea to land in France but it might be better to return with the ship to the UK. The second in command of *Sobieski* told Dec that Paris had just fallen to the Germans. It seemed that all was lost.

No doubt Dec agreed with the commanders of *Sobieski* but he was acting under orders and he had received orders by radio from General Bohusz-Szyszko that he and the rest of the Podhalians were to land in France and undertake such orders that the French military should issue. Dec, naturally enough, was willing to obey his orders being a good soldier but he could not help reflecting that his battalion had no equipment after the sinking of their transport ship. As *Sobieski* was mooring, a French naval band struck the French National Anthem followed by that of Poland. It was all the same as when the Podhalians had set out on their adventure back in April. Dec's battalion took their leave of *Sobieski* receiving from the ship's company the most heartfelt best wishes and good luck for the future and what may lie ahead of them. Upon disembarking Dec reported for duty and of course immediately reported that his battalion had no equipment, as it had all been lost at sea. Dec was assured by a Colonel Molle that the Poles would be fully re-equipped before being sent to the

Front. Szyszko-Bohusz told Dec that they were still trying to locate Sikorski, in order to assert what was to be done with the Podhalians.

Dec next related how he and his men were taken by military transport to a hanger at the destroyed airfield at Guipavas near Brest. Large groups of soldiers, both British and French, flowed from the Front and were heading towards Brest. British troops were scheduled to be evacuated back to the UK but French troops had no such provision scheduled. There were countless crowds of people, both refugees and deserters, who were steadily heading towards Brest, which was already full. The chaos and masses of people moving away from the fighting and towards, what seemed to be safety, reminded Dec of the Polish September Campaign. There were many refugees coming from Holland, Belgium and from northern France, notably Lille. It was clear to Dec that so many of the fleeing crowds had seen too much, in too short a space of time. Western Europe is normally peaceful and these people had seen bombing, shooting, their homes set alight and had been forced to flee, travelling either on foot or, if they were lucky enough, by some mode of transport carrying what they could of their former lives. Dec could see that these poor people had fled the horrors of invasion and attack and that death was still hunting them down. There seemed to be no relief to their appalling situation.

During this period, Sikorski was still at the fighting front conducting Polish troops, therefore it seemed that the Podhalians should continue with undertaking orders from Bethouart, as they had done in Norway. There had been, to date, no orders countermanding those already standing, regarding the Bethouart authority over the Podhalians, announced Bohusz-Szyszko in an evening briefing in Brest. Lieutenant-Colonel Kamionko admitted that the return of the Podhalians had been a shock to Sikorski's Staff. Dec reminded Kamionko that the Podhalians still lacked equipment and that they should not be sent to the Front, whilst lacking equipment to fight with. However Bohusz-Szyszko urged Dec not to be so worried, as the Poles were to be completely reequipped using French equipment from French stores.

During the afternoon 15 June, the Poles were taken by train (there was even a Polish carriage) to Dol still in Brittany. It remained quite clear that even though the Front was not that far away, the Poles were still underequipped at least and could not serve yet on it, however it was asserted that in the military stores at Rennes were wide ranging equipment and that the Podhalians would be completely reequipped from there and would have everything that they needed to fight on the Front. However General Bohusz-Szyszko was not one to risk unnecessarily his men and after having a personal conversation with the illusive Sikorski, decided on the best course of action for the Podhalians, as it would seem that the French could not be trusted.

Dec is quite clear in what, in many ways, was his contempt for the French and its military policy, as he wrote, the French had made a fetish of the Maginot Line, that series of concrete fortresses along the French frontier until it reached the Belgian frontier where it halted, in order not to offend the Belgians. The French thought that they could sit out any German attack against the Maginot Line but the Germans merely went around, by invading Belgium and moving into France. For the Poles, the Brittany Redoubt was born.

In the Staff of the Command of Operation 'Rennes' was General Altmayer, another French General, who generated another fetish of war, along with the regional war fetish, which was of course the Brittany Redoubt. Overall the French military strategy was based on defence and had no depth to it. It would seem that until Churchill took over in the UK, there were far too much defensive measures amongst the Allies, having had their collective bluffs called by the Germans.

Countless French commanders wanted to use the idea of a redoubt but the problem appeared to be bureaucracy. Even the normally level headed and sensible Colonel Molle lost his head in the mess and got into wrangles with gendarmerie and every mayor from every quarter, while trying to organise defensive measures. It was so trying and the French seemed to have no comprehension of what was really going on and the Poles were left with little weaponry, especially anti-tank guns. As Dec commented the French wanted the Brittany Redoubt defended but did not provide ammunition, anti-tank weapons, vehicles, and not even field kitchens to feed troops. It was a complete shambles and the French only seemed interested in protecting themselves. As Dec observes, orders may have been given to do this and that and to engage the enemy and hold ground – but with what? The Poles had no arms to speak of, no artillery support and no flank support; it was impossible to operate under such conditions.

The Germans meanwhile were pressing home their war plans and were rolling straight towards the Brittany Redoubt, in a rapidly moving column of armour. Before the advancing Germans lay three weak divisions of the 10th French Army, who were fighting to the fore of the Redoubt but had no chance in stopping the German armour, as it moved towards them. At this time, 16 June, the Podhalians took stock of their situation and began to move their battalions in positions. 4th Battalion moved to La Vivier to the north of Dol; 3rd Battalion went to Baguer Pican; 1st Battalion to the town of Dol and 2nd Battalion was kept in reserve in the forest, about four kilometres west of Dol.

Because Colonel Chłusewicz was yet to establish contact with the Polish formation, the command of the 1st Demi-Brigade fell to Dec. On 17 June, the new concept of a 'free town' or 'open town' was established in France. In apprehension and fear of German bombardment, as well as the fear of German retribution later everywhere from small and large places, civilians demanded that the armed forces leave and stop fighting the Germans.

As Dec wrote; the concept of the Brittany Redoubt was clever. Within the Brittany Redoubt, every Mayor declared his town, village settlement to be a 'free town,' which made the defence of the redoubt almost impossible without endangering civilian lives. This was extremely frustrating for the Polish troops and some of the Polish officers were all for ignoring French wishes and taking anti-tank weapons but it was pointed out that this was illegal and that other measures had to be taken. Colonel Molle considered that their greatest enemy, at the time, was the complaining mayors. Dec recalled that everything was so unseemly: Hitler, the war, the chaos and mess and most of all the French.

From the Front came the entire transport of the French Army and it was in disarray and already lacking arms. Drunken French soldiers were shouting that the 'War is finished' and 'Let's go home.' It was also said that there was to be an armistice and that the fighting in France was to be suspended. This information had come from a German radio station pretending to be *Radiodiffusion Française.* Dec's French assistant, Captain Baron, dismissed the information as rubbish. Dec sent Captain Krupop to seek clarification of the situation from Bohusz-Szyszko and whether the German message was true or not. Krupop returned and said that the Germans had given this message and that he had orders for 1st Battalion. The order was simple, during the night 17–18 June, they were to march to Combourg and wait there for further orders. The night march was difficult and was conducted in part by road and part cross country, arriving at Meillac where they stayed until morning. The road ahead remained hazardous as the Germans were largely in possession of it, while if the Poles wished to press ahead they would need to explain that they were not the 'Bosch' or Germans but actually are their Polish allies.

Second Lieutenant Lityński reported to Dec, that Bohusz-Szyszko had ordered the destruction of all vehicles that had to be left behind; this was at 0700 hours, 18 June. It was all too reminiscent of the September Campaign, when the Polish Army was ordered to destroy all mechanized vehicles, in order to prevent their use by the enemy. So in September in Poland this had happened, recalled

Dec, and now once more within a year it was happening again but in Brittany. It was sad but it had to be done, reflected Dec. From the right approach came some several Staff Officers from 2nd Demi-Brigade. Orders had been delivered from Bohusz-Szyszko, who had studied the Polish position and had decided that units should press forward for several kilometres and then to the far south towards the River Loire.

Dec and his men now had orders of how to proceed and to where, but the final decision of how to execute the orders still lay with the men in the field. Dec wondered how Bohusz-Szyszko knew that the Germans were still several kilometres away from Dec's position; he also noted that that night was moonlight. A quite heated discussion began of how best it would be to move to the Loire, as they knew that the enemy could be anywhere and might appear from any direction, given how the German offensive in the West had been conducted. It seemed that the Germans were quite unpredictable in their moves but then so is war. Dec was against going as a group towards the Loire, but his arguments did not suit the Brigade Commanders.

However there was some information to go on, which had been gleaned the previous evening from the French and confirmed by Captain Śledziak from 3rd Battalion Podhalians, who was moving with his company towards Pontorson. In vain Dec tried to explain the information received was probably outdated, or was indeed outdated because French post offices in small villages and hamlets are closed from six o'clock in the evening until eight o'clock the following morning, and so, as a result, any information that might have been received during those hours was suspect and could not be confirmed and so endangered the Poles, as they were still deciding what to do. Basically Bohusz-Szyszko's last observations of the enemy's whereabouts might by now be totally wrong.

Dec remained unconvinced by the General's observation and left the meeting. As he was departing, Major Majorkiewicz and Captain Tonn stopped him and began to discuss the overall situation of the Polish position, as they knew it, such as it was, and debated what equipment they actually have to hand? Perhaps they might be able to fight their way out if needs be but there was little in the way of weapons and ammunition for a sustained fight. Dec also observed the limitations that the Poles were operating under. They were not allowed to cut the highways, one was not allowed to bring down telegraph poles and it was not allowed to make defensive stands from farm buildings. As Dec pointed out, what were they allowed to do in order to get away or to wage war and who benefited from the slaughter of the Poles: the French or the Poles?

In the meanwhile, Dec received information from Bohusz-Szyszko that in conversation with Sikorski on 16 June, it was ordered that he expected Polish soldiers to remember their duty until the end and were expected to make every effort to get away from France and make their way to the UK and report for further duty from there. However, the first part of the orders contradicted the second part, as it at first dealt with the honour of the Polish soldier and fighting to the end, but the second part dealt with leaving the field and getting to the UK. It was Bohusz-Szyszko who observed that the honour of a Polish soldier had nothing to do with failure. Clearly he was thinking that Polish troops could still win the war, even if they had lost individual campaigns but still it must have been galling for the Podhalians to have lost three campaigns on the trot.

It was quite clear to Dec that the French had no wish to fight for France, while the Poles were expected to risk all to the very end. It didn't seem right and Dec made sure that Polish troops understood that by breaking off contact with the enemy and leaving France, hopefully for the UK, there was no dishonour; if the French did not want to fight for their own country, why should the Poles risk their own necks. Major Majorkiewicz and Captain Tonn supported Dec but Bohusz-Szyszko and Lieutenant-Colonel Kamion did not, therefore three against two. The atmosphere was tense, as the officers argued to the point that Tonn in tears begged Bohusz-Szyszko to ensure the rescue of the Brigade, while Dec was quite prepared to return to his battalion. Even so, taking the Brigade might have its problems, as what might they do there. Would they like the conditions of exile and why they had to go further away from Poland? They were all difficult questions to be faced at a later date.

There was no answer at the time, however General Bohusz-Szyszko asserted that commanders demanded to the Brigade in order to allow them to march from the River Loire. While eating, Dec surveyed the empty railway yard and thought that the Brigade had been game enough to try for success once more, or quite simply it had been right to give it a chance once again but unfortunately without any result. Regarding a final chance to rescue the Brigade; General Bohusz-Szyszko remained silent. Finally Dec and his battalion, with a company from the Staff, moved out towards the La Chapelle region.

It was 0900 hours when they set off. Before Dec was the Brigade's vehicles moving to Meillac, everything went well for a half hour. Dec tried to recommend the march or breakout. The Company Commanders reported to Dec the mood of the ranks. There was a division: those soldiers who had homes in France, owing to pre-war emigration wanted to remain in France, whilst those who had come from Poland were quite willing to make their way elsewhere, in order to continue the fight against the enemies of Poland. At the same time German aircraft did their level best to retard the preparations for the Polish march.

At around 1130 General Bohusz-Szyszko arrived at Meillac with the Brigade Staff. He recommended to Dec that the march might be sped up if it did not move to La Chapelle but straight to the Loire. There were heated exchanges about who was to go further on the march, as it was clear that the emigrant soldiers had no interest in fighting further, as Dec had already learnt. Bohusz-Szyszko ordered that only the infantry should go on, as reason was beginning to prevail on him and that perhaps Dec was right all along.

Dec asked about details for the route of the march and was told to go via Tinténiac – Romille – St. Gille – Mordelles to the Loire. Most importantly Dec was given a free hand and was told that he could make operational decisions according to the needs and conditions that he met en route. At the end of the march, Dec was to wait in the forest 25 kilometres to the south-west of Combourg. Dec confirmed that he understood his orders. Bohusz-Szyszko cautioned Dec against hurrying, as it might well attract attention from the enemy and with this gave Dec his hand before driving away in a southerly direction.

On the march, there were various incidents. Moving with the vanguard of the march at 1230 hours, Dec got to St Domine, where two motorcyclists from 13 Demi-Brigade FFL barred their way. Dec asked what they were doing and learnt that they could not proceed any further, as the Germans were already in Rennes. Dec was placed in a predicament – he had orders but wondered about the new information, as he knew that the situation in France was fluid and that the Germans moved very quickly. After a few minutes Second Lieutenant Rydel from 4th Battalion reported to Dec that Major Kobyliński's battalion, who had remained in Combourg, had all been taken prisoner by the Germans.

Dec had to think quickly as he analysed the new situation, as it unfolded before him. It was impossible to go to Mordelles, as the Germans already occupied it and the enemy was already breathing down his neck, as the sounds of shooting could be heard. The Loire was only 200 metres away. The only way to get there was on foot but Dec was also all too aware that before and behind him and no doubt towards the east were enemy columns of armour. Basically, Dec and his men were surrounded and about three quarters of his men did not want to fight anymore. They were all in.

There was no time for lengthy discussion, instant, yet sane, decisions had to be made there and then, as the enemy was upon them. It would not be right to order a senseless fight, in which the Polish troops had no chance or heart, as at best they would all be taken prisoner so another cause of action had to be taken, also there was a need to preserve the battalion's honour. It was already 1250 and time was pressing.

There was the sound of footsteps on the right of the road where the men stood waiting for a decision and then it was made. Those who wanted to remain in France were to stand on the left hand side of the road. Cadet Officer Deniszewski went straight to the Company Staff car and retrieved the colours. Second Lieutenant Kurzeja, with two section leaders acting as escort to the standard, took two lorries, in which the Staff officers of the Demi-Brigade sat, as well as those troops from the company charged with their defence. In a third truck were officers from the Brigade staff. The communication and pioneer platoons, as well as the reconnaissance group commanded by Lieutenant Iwańczyk, took to requisitioned vehicles. The entire group was commanded by Major Krizar and was to move via Vannes to the UK. Krizar asked for permission to go to Brest, in order to get to the UK. This was agreed.

Three vehicles were placed at the disposition of 2nd Battalion. As there was not enough room for everybody, small groups of five were arranged under the command of Captain Stańczyk. Other officers joined this group, including Zamoyski, Staszko, Dr Boniarczyk, Lieutenant Manczarczyk, Second Lieutenant Serwas and several others. Krupop divided the remaining rations between the groups, while Mostowiec disposed of machineguns and mortars in a nearby pond. The group, which had elected to remain in France, had to disperse, destroy their weapons and dress as civilians and go into hiding. And that was it. There was no dawdling as the Germans might arrive at any minute. Time was of the essence. Everything had been decided and agreed upon and now it was finished. Fates had been decided and dies cast. The Podhalians were evacuating for the third time in a year.

Dec went and sat with Stańczyk. They wondered how their group was going to manage the near future, as they sat in the last available vehicle. It had been decided that they were to travel to Vannes or to Nantes but it was discovered en route that the Germans were already heading in that direction. Therefore they turned towards Brest and using a forest road, at about 2200 hours, reached the port where chaos reigned. Despite this, Dec found other Polish officers who were determined to get out of France and to the UK, in order to rejoin the Polish Army from there and one day return to Poland, as part of a victorious Polish Army. Dec's luck held, as he managed to make contact with an officer of the French Merchant Navy, who in turn placed Dec and his comrades with a Captain of the collier *Moncousu,* which bought Dec and the other officers to the UK.

As Dec relates not all of his comrades had such luck, as many of the Podhalians were fated to remain in France. Major Kobyliński's battalions ceased to exist, as they were surrounded by the Germans at Combourg on 18 June at 1130 that morning. During the same afternoon, Colonel Mackowski battalion, as a single commanded entity, also ceased to exist but they were able to disperse through the terrain and so evade capture by the enemy. Only Major Jaśkowski's battalion avoided extinction as a complete military unit, even if by the evening 18 June they had dispersed; small groups form this battalion after long and difficult journeys into unoccupied France finally arrived in the UK ready to fight once more.

General Bohusz-Szyszko and his entourage from the Brigade Staff came across a reconnaissance platoon in lorries and together reached the forest laying about 25 kilometres south-west of Combourg. At 1500 hours, it was decided that they could not wait any longer for the arrival of 2nd Battalion and so Bohusz-Szyszko's group, after destroying their transport, began to march towards the south. The infantry marched swiftly at about four to five kilometres an hour. 2nd Battalion got to the forest at 1700 hours.

Stańczyk's group eventually became a larger group than the original five members when they had first set out to evade the Germans, as they met with other straggling groups, some from other battalions and Polish formations. Eventually, in dribs and drabs, these men planned and did escape from France via the Pyrenees and eventually to the British colony of Gibraltar and eventually to the UK and back to the Polish Army. Not all of the Podhalians managed to get back to the UK and some endured Spanish captivity once they arrived there, while others suffered hardship in France with many Poles becoming quite active in the French resistance movement.[29]

Once the Podhalians and other Polish troops arrived in the UK with a determination to fight the Germans, they felt a sense of frustration as for the next four years politics was to dominate the relationships between the allies. Polish concerns were totally ignored and after 1941, when the Soviet Union was invaded by Germany, by default became an ally of the British; Poland as an ally certainly became an irrelevance, as it was frequently sidelined in order to appease the demands of the Soviet government. This was quite obvious from the very outset of the British-Soviet relationship, when in July 1941, Sikorski and his government were more or less forced to accept an alliance with the Soviet Union. It is true that this did include the release of hundreds of thousands of Poles, who had been kidnapped from eastern Poland to be used as slave labour in the Soviet Union. How the Soviet release was half-hearted and somewhat in bad faith, especially when Sikorski and General Anders, who had been charged with forming a Polish Army on Soviet territory, began to ask questions about the whereabouts of thousands of Polish officers who could not be located. Stalin, when questioned, was extremely evasive in his answers and so he might well have been, as he knew that his internal security forces the notorious NKVD had murdered thousands of Polish officers in April 1940 at Katyń and other such places. By the time that the murders at Katyń were revealed in 1943 by the Germans, Polish-Soviet relations were dire. The Soviet government claimed that the Germans had actually committed the murders and when the Polish government-in-Exile demanded an International Red Cross investigation into the entire affair, the Soviet government broke off diplomatic relations with the exiled Polish government. At the same time the British and American governments, despite the fact that they knew that the Soviets had committed the atrocity, did little to help the Poles. The problem was that by 1943, the Soviets were fighting most of the German armed forces and their allies and the Allies feared that the Soviets might make a unilateral peace treaty with the Germans, as Trotsky had done in 1917 following the Bolshevik coup in the late autumn of that year in Russia. A further matter was that by 1943, the Red Army was on the offensive and was driving the German Army back to Berlin, following the German defeat at Stalingrad in January 1943. The Soviets needed no allies and were about to communise half of Europe; a mission completed by 1949. The Poles were small beer by this stage of the war, especially in the West once the Americans entered the war in December 1941.

The Podhalians had fought well in Norway and France and were clear symbols of a fighting Poland but that was the Polish problem; it was all symbolism. They lacked the men and resources and by 1943 were extremely unpopular with their hosts; the British people. However, the Podhalians did return to Europe in 1944, as did Dec, as part of the First Polish Armoured Division and distinguished themselves in the fighting in Normandy during August 1944. But few of them returned to Poland as young men, as their country may have been liberated from the Germans by the Red Army but it was also annexed by the Soviet Union and a Communist Poland established there. This was the fate of many Poles who fought in the West for the British and Americans; they

29 Dec, op.cit. pp. 126-142.

were not betrayed as Polish mythology has it but were simply unimportant and had the most impossible geography. That is the fate of Poland and it remains so until Europeans can learn to live with each other.

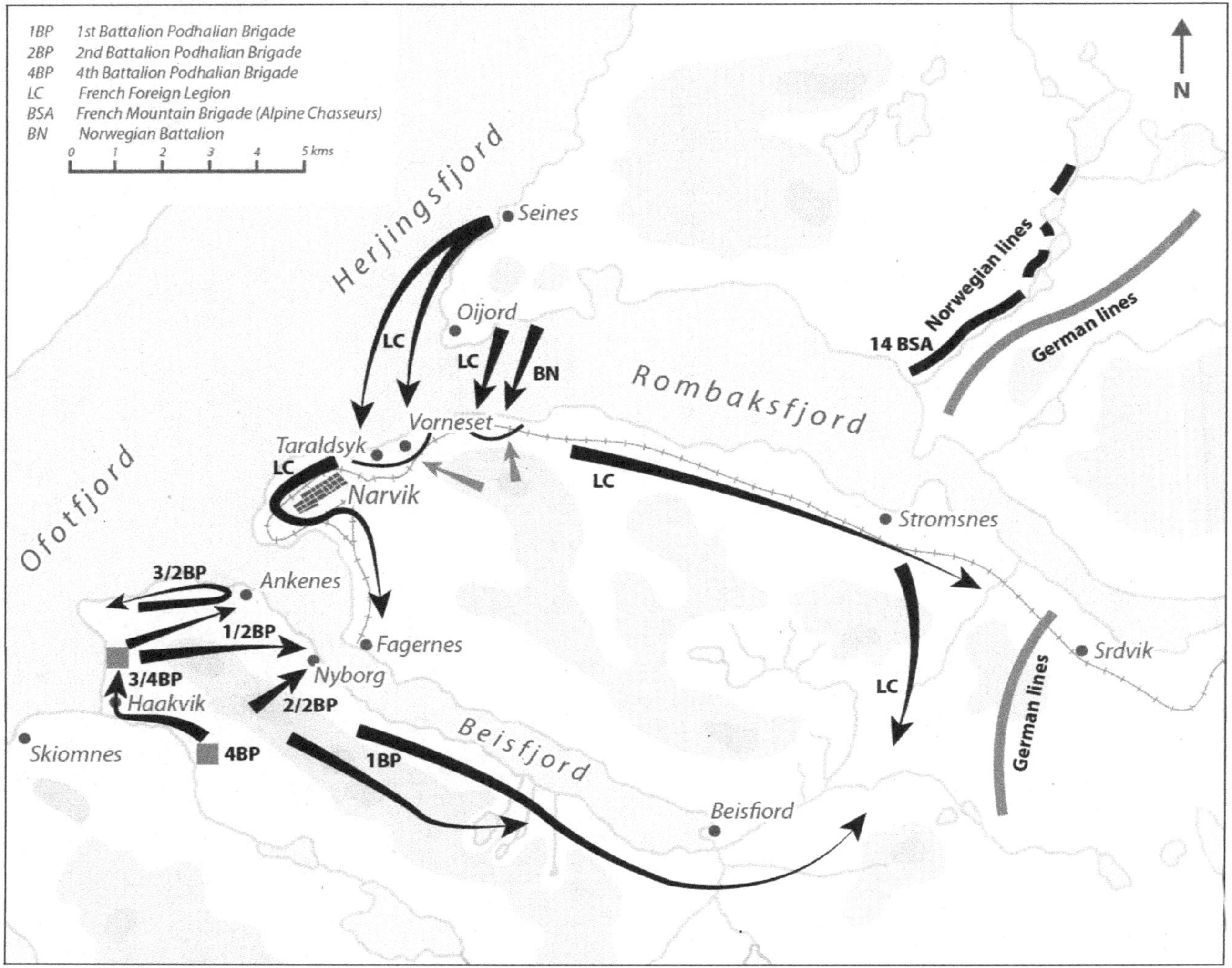

Map of Narvik

Bibliography

Archival Sources

Brotherton Library, University of Leeds:

Special Collections, Liddle Collection, 1939-45, Army, Barthorpe, Sydney, Liddle/WW2/Army/007.

The John Rylands Library, University of Manchester:

John Rylands, Special Collection, GB133 AUC, The Papers of Field Marshal Auchinleck. Also cited as MUL.

Polish Institute and Sikorski Institute (PISM) London:

A.IV.11, The Independent Podhalian Rifle Brigade.

B.1.86/A, General Sosnkowski, Memoirs of September 1939.

C.671, History of the Communication Units, Podhalian Rifle Brigade, 1940.

KGA, The General Anders Collection.

PRM, Papers of the Polish Prime Minister in Exile.

The National Archives (TNA), London:

CAB 65, War Cabinet Minutes.

CAB 66, War Cabinet Memoranda.

CAB 79, Chiefs of Staff Minutes.

CAB 80, Chiefs of Staff Memoranda.

CAB 83/3, Evacuation of Allied Forces from Central Norway.

CAB 106, The Polish Brigade in Norway.

FO 371, Foreign Office General Correspondence.

FO 800/309, Papers of Lord Halifax.

FO 800/317, Germany, Conversations, 1939.

PREM 1 & 3, Prime Ministers' Office.

Printed Primary Sources

Alanbrooke, Field Marshal Lord, *War Diaries, 1939-1945*. (London: Weidenfeld & Nicolson, 2001).

Black, Jeremy (ed.), *The Ironside Diaries*, Colonel Roderick Macleod, Denis Kelly (eds.) (London: Constable, 1962).

Burdick, Charles & Jacobsen, Hans-Adolf (eds.), *The Halder War Diary 1939-1942* (London: Greenhill Books, 1988).

Cannistraro, Phillip V. & Wynot, Edward D. & Kovaleff, Jr. P. (eds.), *Poland and the Coming of the Second World War. The Diplomatic Papers of A.J. Drexel Biddle Jr. United States Ambassador to Poland, 1937-1939* (Columbia: Ohio State University, 1976).

Craig, Gordon A. & Lowenheim, Francis L. (eds.), *The Diplomats, 1939-1979* (Princeton: Princeton University Press, 1994).

Danchev, Alex & Todman, Daniel (eds.), *The Second World War: Volume 1. The German War, 1939-1943* (Aldershot: Ashgate, 2007).

Dilks, David (ed.), *The Diaries of Sir Alexander Cadogan, 1938-1945* (London, Cassell, 1971).

Domarus, Max, *Hitler: Speeches and Proclamations,. 1932-1945. The Chronicle of a Dictatorship, Volume III, 1939-1940* (Wauconda, IL. USA: Bolchazy-Carducci, 1997).

Gilbert, Martin (ed.), *The Churchill War Papers. Volume 1 At the Admiralty, September 1939–May 1940* (London: Heinemann, 1993).

Gilbert, Martin (ed.), *The Churchill War Papers. Volume 2 Never Surrender, May 1940–December 1940* (London: Heinemann, 1991).

Great Britain. Foreign Office Weekly Intelligence Summaries, Volume 1, October 1939–June 1940. Nos. 1-38 (London: Kraus, 1983).

Hansard (1940).

Maier, Klaus A. et al *Germany and the Second World War, Volume 2. Germany's Initial Conquests in Europe* (Oxford: Clarendon Press, 1991).

Miscellaneous Notes No.9 (1939) Documents Concerning German-Polish Relations and the Outbreak of Hostilities between Great Britain and Germany on September 3, 1939 (London, HMSO, 1939), Cmd. 6106.

Rommetveit, Karl, *Narvik 1940. Five Nations in the High North* (Oslo: Institutt for Forsvarsstudier (IFS), 1991).

Turnbull, Elizabeth & Suchcitz, Andrzej (eds.), *The Diary of a Military Attaché in Warsaw, 1938-1939* (London: Polish Cultural Foundation, 2001). (Roland Sword was the original diarist).

Wacław, Jędrzejewicz, *Papers and Memoirs of Józef Lipski, Ambassador of Poland. Diplomat in Berlin* (New York: Columbia Press, 1968).

Woodward, E.L. & Butler, Rohan (eds.), *Documents on British Foreign Policy, Third Series, Volume 3, IV, 1939* (London: HMSO, 1951).

Woodward, E.L. & Butler, Rohan (eds.), *Documents on British Foreign Policy, Third Series, Volume 7* (London: HMSO, 1954).

Woodward, Sir Llewellyn (ed.), *British Foreign Policy in the Second World War, Volume I*, (London: HMSO, 1970).

Printed Secondary Sources

Aspinall-Oglander, Cecil, *Roger Keyes* (London: The Hogarth Press, 1951).

Beck, Joseph, *Dernier Rapport: Politique Polonaise, 1926-1939* (Brussels: Histoire et Société D'Aujourd'Hui, N.D).

Beevor, Antony, *The Second World War* (London: Weidenfeld & Nicholson, 2012).

Bloch, Michael, *Ribbentrop* (London: Bantam Press, 1994).

Borzęcki, Jerzy, *Pokój Ryski Roku 1921 i Kształtowanie Się Międzywojennej Europy Wschodniej* (Warsaw, Polski Instytut Spraw Międrzynarodwych, 2012).

Brookes, Ewart, *Prologue to a War. The Navy's Part in the Narvik Campaign* (London: White Lion, 1977).

Carter, Humphrey, *W.H. Auden. A Biography* (London: George Allen & Unwin, 1981).

Carton de Wiatr, Adrian, *Happy Odyssey* (London: Jonathan Cape, 1950).

'Cato' (Frank Owen, Michael Foot and P.D. Howard) *Guilty Men* (Victor Gollancz, 1940).

Churchill, Winston. S, *The Second World War. Volume 1, The Gathering Storm* (London: Cassell, 1948).

Debicki, Roman, *Foreign Policy of Poland, 1919-1939. From the Rebirth of the Polish Republic to World War II* (London: Pall Mall, 1963).

Dec, Władysław, *Narwik i Falaise* (Warsaw: MON, 1972).

Deszczyńki, Marek Piotr, *Ostatnio Egzamin Wojsko Polskie Wobec Czechosłowiego 1938-1939* (Warsaw: Neriton, 2003).

Greenwood, Alexander, *Field Marshal Auchinleck* (Witton le Wear, UK: The Pentland Press, 1992).

Holland, James, *The Battle of Britain. Five Months that Changed History, May-October 1940* (London: Corgi Books, 2011).

Jenkins, Roy, *Churchill* (London: Macmillan, 2001).

Kershaw, Ian, *Fateful Choices. The Decisions that Changed the World, 1940-1941* (London: Allen Lane, 2007).

Kershaw, Ian, *Hitler, 1936-1945. Nemesis* (London: Penguin, 2001).

Lehmkuhl, Herman K, *Hitler Attacks Norway* (London: The Royal Norwegian Government Information Service, 1943).

McCauley, Martin, *The Soviet Union, 1917-1991* (London: Longmans, 1994, Second edition).

McGilvray, Evan, *Hamilton & Gallipoli. British Command in an Age of Military Transformation* (Barnsley, UK: Pen & Sword, 2015).

McGilvray, Evan, *Man of Steel and Honour. General Stanisław Maczek. Soldier of Poland, Commander of 1st Polish Armoured Division in North-West Europe, 1944-45* (Solihull: Helion & Company, 2012).

McGilvray, Evan, *A Military Government in Exile. The Polish Government-in-Exile, 1939-1945, a study of discontent* (Solihull: Helion & Company, 2010).

Moorehead, Alan, *The Desert War. The Classical Trilogy of the North Africa Campaign, 1940-43* (London: Aurum Press, 2009, originally published Hamish Hamilton, 1944).

Olson, Lynne, Cloud, Stanley, *For Your Freedom and Ours. The Kościusko Squadron. Forgotten Heroes of World War II* (London: Arrow, 2004).

Prażmowska, Anita. J, *Britain and Poland, 1939-1943: The Betrayed Ally* (Cambridge: Cambridge University Press, 1995).

Roberts, Andrew, *Masters and Commanders: How Roosevelt, Churchill, Marshall and Alanbrooke Won the War in the West* (London: Allen Lane, 2008).

Roberts, Andrew, *'The Holy Fox'. The Life of Lord Halifax* (London: Phoenix Giant, 1997).

Roos, Hans, *A History of Modern Poland. From the Formation of the State in the First World War to the Present Day* (London: Eyre & Spottiswoode, 1966).

Seton-Watson, Hugh, *Eastern Europe between the Wars, 1918-1941* (New York: Harper & Row, 1967, 3rd edition).

Strabolgi (Lord) Kenworthy, J.M. *Narvik and After. A Study of the Scandinavian Campaign* (London: Hutchinson, 1940).

Newspapers

The Manchester Guardian, September 1939–June 1940.

The Times, September 1939–June 1940.

Papers

Nick Hewitt (Imperial War Museum) 'Norway 1940: How Churchill and the Navy Saved Britain'. BCMH 2010, Spring Conference, Oxford, *Britain and Scandinavia in the Second World War.*

Internet

http://www.youtube.com/watch?V=6aks1mcfQNA 1 March 2014, accessed 1 March 2016.

Jozef Beck's Speech: www.youtube.com/watch?V=12ps7xSHwcy accessed 11 September 2014.

Index

Index of People

Index of Places

Index of Military Formations & Units